Computer Programming for Absolute Beginners

Learn essential computer science concepts and coding techniques to kick-start your programming career

Joakim Wassberg

BIRMINGHAM—MUMBAI

Computer Programming for Absolute Beginners

Commissioning Editor: Richa Tripathi
Acquisition Editor: Karan Gupta
Senior Editor: Nitee Shetty
Content Development Editor: Tiksha Lad
Technical Editor: Gaurav Gala
Copy Editor: Safis Editing
Project Coordinator: Deeksha Thakkar
Proofreader: Safis Editing
Indexer: Pratik Shirodkar
Production Designer: Nilesh Mohite

First published: July 2020
Production reference: 1300720

Published by Packt Publishing Ltd.
Livery Place
35 Livery Street
Birmingham
B3 2PB, UK.

ISBN 978-1-83921-686-2

www.packt.com

To my mother, Anna-Lena, and to the memory of my father, Björn, who gave me the chance to grow into the curious person I am today.

- Joakim Wassberg

Packt.com

Subscribe to our online digital library for full access to over 7,000 books and videos, as well as industry leading tools to help you plan your personal development and advance your career. For more information, please visit our website.

Why subscribe?

- Spend less time learning and more time coding with practical eBooks and Videos from over 4,000 industry professionals

- Improve your learning with Skill Plans built especially for you

- Get a free eBook or video every month

- Fully searchable for easy access to vital information

- Copy and paste, print, and bookmark content

Did you know that Packt offers eBook versions of every book published, with PDF and ePub files available? You can upgrade to the eBook version at packt.com and as a print book customer, you are entitled to a discount on the eBook copy. Get in touch with us at customercare@packtpub.com for more details.

At www.packt.com, you can also read a collection of free technical articles, sign up for a range of free newsletters, and receive exclusive discounts and offers on Packt books and eBooks.

Contributors

About the author

Joakim Wassberg is a software developer who for the past 30 years has worked in a variety of areas, such as security in financial systems, secure payment systems, and as a specialist and architect of development methods.

Throughout his career, he has always worked with education in programming, from introducing children in a playful way to take their first steps, to teaching senior developers a new technology or development methodology, and from company training to university courses. Since 2014, together with his wife, he has run the company Arthead, which works exclusively in education and educational development.

I would also like to thank my wife, Susanne. Her input, suggestions, and ideas have been brilliant, and without her support, writing this book would have been much harder. She did not know anything about programming before I started writing this book, but now she knows quite a lot. If she can learn it, so can you.

About the reviewer

Dr. Jie Liu received his Ph.D. from Oregon State University in 1993. He is now a full professor at Western Oregon University and has been working there for 31 years. Dr. Liu has taught a wide range of classes, such as Computer Organizations, Theory of Computation, Databases, Operating Systems, Introduction to Blockchain, and graduate-level Data Mining, just to name a few.

Beside teaching and research, Dr. Liu enjoys working as a consultant for the industry on big data and database-related projects. His recent projects involve DBMSes such as Amazon's Redshift, Google's BigQuery, and Snowflake.

Dr. Liu's research interests are in blockchain, big data and data mining, distributed systems, parallel processing, and software architecture.

Packt is searching for authors like you

If you're interested in becoming an author for Packt, please visit `authors.packtpub.com` and apply today. We have worked with thousands of developers and tech professionals, just like you, to help them share their insight with the global tech community. You can make a general application, apply for a specific hot topic that we are recruiting an author for, or submit your own idea.

Table of Contents

3

Types of Applications

4

Software Projects and How We Organize Our Code

Section 2:
Constructs of a Programming Language

5

Sequence – The Basic Building Block of a Computer Program

6

Working with Data – Variables

7

Program Control Structures

8

Understanding Functions

9

When Things Go Wrong – Bugs and Exceptions

10

Programming Paradigms

11

Programming Tools and Methodologies

Section 3:
Best Practices for Writing High-Quality Code

12

Code Quality

Appendix A
How to Translate the Pseudocode into Real Code

Appendix B
Dictionary

Other Books You May Enjoy

Preface

Welcome to the beautiful world of programming. Programming is an art form in which you will use your imagination and creativity to create things. If you know how to program, your possibilities will be endless.

You can use it to create a fun game. Or maybe you want to automate things in your life. Maybe you want to become a professional programmer, and then you will use your skills to work in teams with others to create solutions that will be used by many people for a long time.

Having programming skills is also something that is needed in more and more professions. Your job title will not be that of a software developer. Instead, programming will be a tool that you can use.

I have been teaching programming for over 30 years. I have been teaching people of all ages, from beginners to senior professional developers. During this time, I have seen patterns, especially among beginners.

It took some time before I realized what made so many of my beginner students struggle with grasping programming. The problem was that they had to learn two things at once. First, they needed to understand the very concepts of programming. There are so many concepts and words, both new ones and some that they already know, but that have a slightly different meaning. Secondly, they will also need to learn a programming language. Taking in all this at the same time will become overwhelming for many people. For some, it will be so much that they give up programming for good.

The idea of this book is to focus on one of the two things you need to learn. This book will not focus on any language, but instead, teach you the concepts you need to know and understand to become a programmer. After you have read this book, you can learn any programming language you want, and when you do, you can focus on just learning the language, as the rest you will already know.

With this book, I also want to put things into context, so there will be a bit of history, and some parts will be rather technical. I believe that if you are going to learn something, you cannot just scratch the surface. You need to dive into it and see how things work.

And yes, I was that kid who disassembled my RC car to see how it worked.

Good luck with your endeavors to learn this fantastic art.

This book was written to the music of Talking Heads, and I suggest you listen to it as you read it.

Who this book is for?

This book is written for everyone who is either just curious about computer programming and wants to know more about the topic, or is about to learn their first programming language and wants a solid introduction to the topic. It doesn't matter whether your goal is to create small hobby applications or whether you want to be well prepared for your university programming courses.

What this book covers?

Chapter 1, Introduction to Computer Programs, will give you an understanding of how computer programs work and how they interact with the computer hardware.

Chapter 2, Introduction to Programming Languages, will teach you the evolution of programming languages, how they are related, introduce different types of languages, and give you a basic understanding of some fundamental programming concepts.

Chapter 3, Types of Applications, explores how software comes in many forms and is created to solve a wide variety of problems. This chapter will introduce you to some of the essential application types and give you an understanding of how they work.

Chapter 4, Software Projects and How We Organize Our Code, covers how, when writing programs that are beyond the most trivial level, we will need to organize our code into several code files. In this chapter, we look at how this can be done efficiently. We will also see how we can incorporate code written by others into our software projects.

Chapter 5, Sequence – The Basic Building Block of a Computer Program, outlines how a computer program is, at the most fundamental level, built by putting statements in the correct sequence. We will see how this is done and how the computer will execute these statement sequences when our programs run.

Chapter 6, Working with Data – Variables, explores how all computer programs will perform operations on data and modify it in some way. In this chapter, we will get to know the types of data we will work with when programming and what types of operations we can perform on them.

Chapter 7, Program Control Structures, discusses how, when writing programs, we need to control the path that the execution takes through our code. To help us, we have different types of control structures that we can use to accomplish this.

Chapter 8, Understanding Functions, explores functions as a fundamental concept in programming that let us package code into a reusable unit. In this chapter, we will see what functions are and how they can be used.

Chapter 9, When Things Go Wrong – Bugs and Exceptions, reminds us that things will not always go according to plan. The code we have written might contain errors, or we might get data that we can't work with. In this chapter, we will see how we can deal with both situations.

Chapter 10, Programming Paradigms, explores several ideas for how we should write and structure our code to be able to write programs as efficiently as possible. These are called paradigms, and we will look at the most prominent ones in this chapter.

Chapter 11, Programming Tools and Methodologies, examines how programmers use different tools when developing software. We will look at some of them in this chapter, and also consider how teams of programmers can collaborate efficiently.

Chapter 12, Code Quality, explores the many aspects of code quality. How can we write programs that run fast, or efficiently use the computer's resources? How can we write code that can easily be read and understood by other programmers that will need to modify our code? These are some of the things we will cover in this chapter.

Appendix A – How to Translate the Pseudocode into Real Code, covers how to translate pseudo code into different programming languages.

Appendix B - Dictionary has all the words which are unique or have a technical meaning and are used in the book.

To get the most out of this book

If you are using the digital version of this book, we advise you to type the code yourself. Doing so will help you avoid any potential errors related to copying/pasting of code.

Download the example code files

You can download the example code files for this book from your account at www.packt.com. If you purchased this book elsewhere, you can visit www.packtpub.com/support and register to have the files emailed directly to you.

You can download the code files by following these steps:

1. Log in or register at www.packt.com.
2. Select the **Support** tab.
3. Click on **Code Downloads**.
4. Enter the name of the book in the **Search** box and follow the onscreen instructions.

Once the file is downloaded, please make sure that you unzip or extract the folder using the latest version of:

- WinRAR/7-Zip for Windows
- Zipeg/iZip/UnRarX for Mac
- 7-Zip/PeaZip for Linux

We also have other code bundles from our rich catalog of books and videos available at https://github.com/PacktPublishing/. Check them out!

Download the color images

We also provide a PDF file that has color images of the screenshots/diagrams used in this book. You can download it here: https://static.packt-cdn.com/downloads/9781839216862_ColorImages.pdf.

Conventions used

There are a number of text conventions used throughout this book.

`Code in text`: Indicates code words in text, database table names, folder names, filenames, file extensions, pathnames, dummy URLs, user input, and Twitter handles. Here is an example: "We know that as this function divides two values, we might get an exception if y is given a value of 0."

A block of code is set as follows:

```
if current_time > sunset_time {
    turn_on_light()
}
```

Any command-line input or output is written as follows:

```
SyntaxError: invalid syntax in line 1 column 2
1:2 syntax error: unexpected apple at end of statement
Compilation error (line 1, col 2): Identifier expected
error: unknown: Identifier directly after number (1:2)
```

> **Tips or important notes**
> Appear like this.

Get in touch

Feedback from our readers is always welcome.

General feedback: If you have questions about any aspect of this book, mention the book title in the subject of your message and email us at customercare@packtpub.com.

Errata: Although we have taken every care to ensure the accuracy of our content, mistakes do happen. If you have found a mistake in this book, we would be grateful if you would report this to us. Please visit www.packtpub.com/support/errata, selecting your book, clicking on the Errata Submission Form link, and entering the details.

Piracy: If you come across any illegal copies of our works in any form on the Internet, we would be grateful if you would provide us with the location address or website name. Please contact us at copyright@packt.com with a link to the material.

If you are interested in becoming an author: If there is a topic that you have expertise in and you are interested in either writing or contributing to a book, please visit authors.packtpub.com.

Reviews

Please leave a review. Once you have read and used this book, why not leave a review on the site that you purchased it from? Potential readers can then see and use your unbiased opinion to make purchase decisions, we at Packt can understand what you think about our products, and our authors can see your feedback on their book. Thank you!

For more information about Packt, please visit `packt.com`.

Section 1: Introduction to Computer Programs and Computer Programming

This section gives you an understanding of the relationship between computer programs and programming languages, as well as providing you with an understanding of how code is executed on a computer.

This section has the following chapters:

- *Chapter 1, Introduction to Computer Programs*
- *Chapter 2, Introduction to Programming Languages*
- *Chapter 3, Types of Applications*
- *Chapter 4, Software Projects and How We Organize Our Code*

1
Introduction to Computer Programs

Programming is the art and science of writing instructions that a computer can follow to accomplish a task. This task can be playing a game, performing a calculation, or browsing the web, for example. However, before we can learn how to write programs, we should understand what a program is and how a computer can understand and execute the instructions we give it. In this chapter, we will study this in more detail, along with the basics of what a computer is, how it works, and its history.

Even a basic level of understanding of these topics will help us later on when we discuss the different aspects of writing programs, as we can then relate to how the computer will treat the code we write.

In this chapter, we will cover the following topics:

- A perspective on the history and origins of the computer
- Background knowledge of the original ideas behind programming
- Understanding what a computer program is
- Learning how a computer program works
- An understanding of what machine code is

A brief history of computing

Humans have always built tools and made innovations to make life more comfortable and to allow us to do more things faster and more efficiently. We need to go back in time a few hundred years in order to see the first attempts at building a tool that could resemble a computer. However, before we do that, we might want to define what a computer is. Wikipedia offers the following definition:

> *A computer is a machine that can be instructed to carry out sequences of arithmetic or logical operations automatically via computer programming.*

So, a computer is a programmable machine that performs arithmetic or logical operations. Let's review a few inventions from the past using this definition to ascertain which of them could be considered a computer.

To begin, we can rule out the Jacquard machine, which was the automated loom invented in the early years of the 19th century. These looms could be programmed using punch cards, but they produced woven silk, which, of course, is not the result of an arithmetic or logical operation. Programmability, using punch cards, was an idea that survived well into the computer age, but these looms were not computers.

If we go even further back in time, we find devices such as the abacus that helped us to get the results of arithmetic operations; however, they were not programmable.

In the 1770s, Pierre Jaquet-Droz, a Swiss watchmaker, created some mechanical dolls that he called automata. These dolls could read instructions and could thereby be considered programmable, but they did not perform arithmetic or logical operations. Instead, he created one doll that could play music, one that could make drawings, and one that could write letters (they are referred to as the musician, the draughtsman, and the writer):

Figure 1.1: The Jaquet-Droz automata (photograph by Rama, Wikimedia Commons; Cc-by-sa-2.0-fr)

In order to see something that resembles a computer, we will need to look at Charles Babbage's inventions. He originated the concept of a programmable computer with his ideas for a machine, called the Difference Engine, and later, a more advanced version called the Analytical Engine. Of the two, the Analytical Engine was particularly groundbreaking as it could be programmable, which meant it could be used to solve different problems. He presented his work in the first half of the 19th century, and even if the machines were never completed, we can agree that Babbage is a very important person behind the basic concept of the programmable computer.

During the first half of the 20th century, we witnessed some analog computers, but it was not until the second world war, and the years following, that we saw the birth of real digital computers. The difference between an analog and a digital computer is that the former is a mechanical machine that works with an analog input such as voltage, temperature, or pressure. In comparison, a digital computer works with input that can be represented by numbers.

Many people consider the **Electronic Numerical Integrator and Computer (ENIAC)**, constructed by J. Presper Eckert and John Mauchly between 1943 and 1946, as the first digital computer because it was the first one that was both completed and fully functional:

Figure 1.2: Betty Jean Jennings and Fran Bilas, both programmers, operate ENIAC's main control panel – U.S. Army Photo (Public Domain [PD])

Since then, we have seen tremendous development up until the point we are at today. However, even though our modern computers can do so much more and at a much faster rate than these earlier inventions, the basic principles of how they operate remain the same.

A brief history of programming

A programmable computer needs to be, well, programmed. So, of course, the history of programming goes hand in hand with the evolution of computers.

In 1833, Charles Babbage met Ada Lovelace, daughter of poet Lord Byron. She became very impressed and interested in Babbage's plans for his programmable machines, and their collaboration began. Among other things, she wrote some notes outlining her ideas for how the Babbage Analytical Engine could be programmed. We can call her the inventor of programming, even if we had to wait over 100 years until we had the machine that could make her ideas come true. Her status today is summarized in a *History Extra* article, from 2017, by James Essinger:

> *Today, Ada is quite rightly seen as an icon of feminist scientific*
> *achievement, a heroine of the mind, and one of the earliest visionaries in*
> *the early history of the computer.*

In her notes, Lovelace did a couple of remarkable things. The first was that she wrote an algorithm for how Bernoulli numbers, a sequence of rational numbers often used in number theory, could be calculated by the Analytical Engine. This algorithm is considered by many to be the first computer program. Second, she outlined the future of what these machines could do, and, in her vision, she saw that they could be used to draw pictures and compose music. The fact is that when we finally could build a computer, the way they were programmed was heavily influenced by her ideas:

Figure 1.3: Ada Lovelace, aged 17 (portrait by Joan Baum; PD-Art)

The first digital computers were programmed using machine code – the only thing a computer understands. Later in this chapter, we will talk more about machine code and explore what it is. And, as you will discover, it is just a sequence of numbers.

In 1949, John Mauchly proposed something called Brief Code, which was later renamed to Short Code. Short Code can be considered to be one of the first higher-level programming languages. A higher-level programming language is a way for us to write instructions to the computer in a way that is more understandable to humans, which is better than a machine code. The Short Code program is then translated into machine code, and it is that code that the computer executes.

In 1954, the language Fortran was invented at IBM, by John Backus, and this can be considered to be the first widely used high-level, general-purpose programming language. Fortran is, in fact, still in use.

The 1950s saw the birth of some other languages that have also survived, such as Lisp and COBOL. Since then, we have had over 2,300 new programming languages. In the next chapter, we will look at how programming languages have evolved and how they are related, but also why people keep inventing new ones.

What is a program?

A computer is dumb in the sense that, without programs, it can't do anything. A computer program is a set of instructions that the computer can execute, and it is our job, as programmers, to write these programs using one or more programming languages.

Most applications that we run, such as a web browser, word processor, or mail client, can't communicate with the computer hardware directly. They require a layer in between that takes care of this. This layer is called the **operating system**. Windows and Linux are two examples of well-known operating systems. The main purpose of an operating system is to take care of the direct communication between the applications that we use and the hardware, such as the processor, memory, hard drives, keyboards, and printers. To be able to perform this communication, the operating system requires special programs that are designed to communicate with a particular device. These programs are called **device drivers**. A somewhat simplified diagram of how this works is shown here:

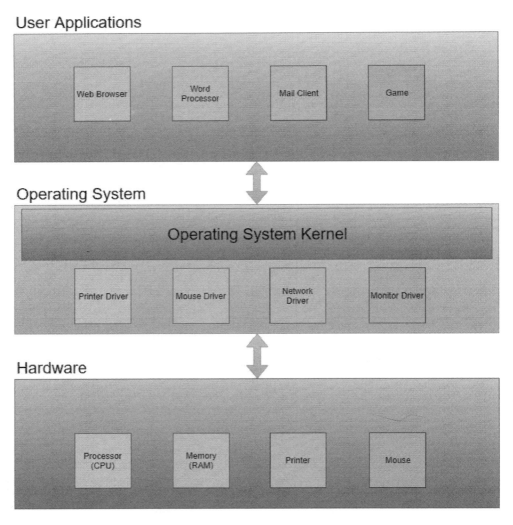

Figure 1.4: The system architecture

Programmers will write the user applications, the operating system, and the device drivers, but the user applications category is by far the most common. The programs we write will communicate with the system kernel, which is the core of the operating system. The operating system will take care of the direct communication with the underlying hardware. The good thing about this structure is that we only need to talk to the operating system, so we don't need to think about what kind of mouse the user has or how to send a line of text to a particular printer model. The operating system will talk to the device drivers for the mouse and the printer, and the driver will know precisely how to communicate with that device.

If we write a program and that program wants to print the text **Hi there computer!** to the screen, then this request will be sent to the operating system. The operating system will pass this on to the device driver for the monitor, and this driver will know how to send this to the monitor connected to this computer:

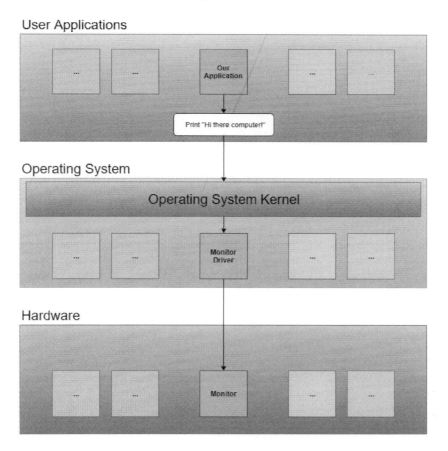

The text entered will not magically appear on the screen, though. It will pass through several layers inside the computer. In 1945, the Hungarian-American mathematician and physicist John Von Neumann, and others, created a document titled *First Draft of a Report to the EDVAC*. In this 101-page document, the first logical design of a computer using the concept of a stored program was presented. Additionally, the design of an electronic digital computer was described. This design is today known as the Von Neumann Architecture, and it defines four different components that can be used to construct a computer. These components are as follows:

- A processing unit that has an arithmetic logic unit and registers for the processing unit to use.

- A control unit that contains an instruction register and a program counter. These are used to execute programs.

- Memory that stores data and instructions. This memory is volatile, meaning that its content will be erased when the power is turned off or the computer is restarted.

- External mass storage. This is long-time storage for programs and data that can also be preserved after a computer restarts.

- Input and output mechanisms. Today, this is typically a keyboard, a mouse, and a monitor.

All of these components, except external mass storage, come into play when text is entered on the keyboard and displayed on the screen.

As mentioned in the previous section, the computer can only understand one thing, and that is machine code. The machine code is a set of numerical values that the computer interprets as different instructions. The computer only works with numbers in the binary form, also known as base 2, and that is why we often hear that a computer only understands zeros and ones.

To understand the different bases, let's consider how many digits they have. In our daily life, we use the decimal system, called base 10, because we have 10 digits, from 0 to 9 (we assume the reason for this is that we started counting on our fingers). In the base 2 binary system, we only have two digits, 0 and 1. In base 16, the hexadecimal system, we have 16 digits. As we only have digits for 0 to 9, we must use some letters in the hexadecimal system to represent the values between 10 and 15. Those letters are A to F. We do this because we must understand the difference between digits and numbers: a digit is a single symbol representing a value, whereas a number is a sequence of one or more digits. So, for example, we can talk about the digit 7, but not the digit 12 (as it is a number made up of 2 digits). In the hexadecimal system, we need to represent 16 values; therefore, we need 16 digits. Since we only have 10 digits in our decimal system, we need to use something else. In this case, it is the letters A to F.

Refer to the following table for a comparison between decimal, binary, and hexadecimal numbers:

Decimal	Binary	Hexa-decimal
0	0	0
1	1	1
2	10	2
3	11	3
4	100	4
5	101	5
6	110	6
7	111	7
8	1000	8
9	1001	9
10	1010	A
11	1011	B
12	1100	C
13	1101	D
14	1110	E
15	1111	F

Table 1.1: The numbers 1-15 in the decimal, binary, and hexadecimal format

How does a computer program work?

All the tools that we, as humans, have created have helped us with physical labor. Finally, we reached a point where we could invent a tool that would help us with mental labor: the computer.

When planning the design of such a machine, the inventors discovered that it must perform four different tasks. The computer would need to take data as input, store that data, process the data, and then output the result.

These four tasks are common to all the computers we have ever built. Let's take a closer look at these tasks:

1. We can provide input to the computer in many ways, such as with a keyboard, a mouse, voice commands, and touch screens.
2. The input data is sent to the computer's storage: the internal memory.
3. The **CPU** (which is the **central processing unit**) retrieves the data from storage and performs operations on it.
4. The result of these operations is then sent back to be stored in memory again before it is sent out as output.

Just as different devices can be used to send input to the computer, so too can the output be in different forms, and we can use various appliances to present the result, such as text to a printer, music through the speakers, or video to a screen. The output from one computer can even be inputted to another computer:

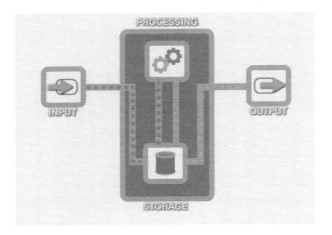

Figure 1.6: The four tasks of a computer

All four steps – input, storage, process, and output – handle data. Let's explore what this data is and what form it takes.

Understanding the binary system

Why is it that computers only work with zeros and ones? Why can't they work directly with text or images, for example? The answer is that it is rather easy to build circuits that can represent two states. If you have an electrical wire, you can either run electricity through it or not. The flow or no flow of electricity could represent several things, such as on or off, true or false, or zero or one. Let's think of these two states as zero and one for now, with zero representing no electricity flowing and one symbolizing that we do have flow. If we can serve these two states, we could add more wires and, by doing that, have more zeros and ones.

But what could we possibly do with all of these zeros and ones? Well, the answer is that we can do almost anything. For example, with only zeros and ones, we can represent any integer by using the binary numeral system. Let's demonstrate how that works.

To understand binary numbers, we must start by looking at the decimal numeral system. In the decimal system, we work with 10 digits, from 0 to 9. When we count, we go through these digits until we reach 9. Now we have run out of digits, so we start over from zero and add a one in front of it, forming the number 10. Then, we continue until we reach 19, then we do the same thing again; start over from zero and increase the value in front of the zero by one, so we get 20.

Another way to think about different numeral systems is to think about the value a position represents. Let's consider an example. The number 212 has the digit 2 in two places, but their position gives them two different values. If we start from the right and move to the left, we can say that we take the first digit, 2, and multiply it by 1. Then, we take the second digit, 1, and multiply it by 10. Finally, we take the last digit, 2, and multiply it by 100. If we move from right to left, each step is worth 10 times as much as the previous step. Take a look at this calculation represented in the following table:

100	10	1	
2	1	2	
2x100=200	1x10=10	2x1=2	200+10+2=212

Table 1.2. The positional values of a decimal number

When using the binary system, we do the same thing, but only using the digits 0 and 1. We start our counting with 0, followed by 1. At this point, we run out of digits, so we start over from 0, adding a 1 in front of it.

Counting in binary looks like this:

0, 1, 10, 11, 100, 101, 110, 111, 1000, 1001, 1010, 1011, 1100, 1101, 1110, 1111, and so on

When it comes to the values each position has for binary numbers, it works just as it does with decimal numbers. However, the value for each position is not multiplied by 10 but instead by 2. We multiply the first digit by 1, the second digit by 2, the third digit by 4, and so on. To make things simpler, we could say that a one in a particular position means that the number representing that position shall be a part of the final value, and zero means it shall not. Take a look at this table for binary number 11010100:

128	64	32	16	8	4	2	1	
1	1	0	1	0	1	0	0	
1x128=128	1x64=64	0x32=0	1x16=16	0x8=0	1x4=4	0x2=0	0x1=0	128+64+16+4=212

Table 1.3: Interpreting binary number 11010100

Here, we have ones at the positions represented by 128, 64, 16, and 4, so now we can add them together (we can ignore the positions with zeros as adding zero to something will not make any difference) to get what the binary number of 11010100 is in decimal form, which is 212.

If we want to convert a decimal number, say 27, into binary, we start by thinking how far we can go through the sequence of positional values: 1, 2, 4, 8, 16, and so on. Which is the largest of these that we can find that is smaller than or equal to 27? The answer is 16, so the first 1 in this binary number will be at this position. On all positions before 16, we can insert 0:

27							
128	64	32	16	8	4	2	1
0	0	0	1				

Figure 1.7: Finding the first position that is less than or equal to 27

We then subtract 16 from 27 and get 11 and repeat the process with this value. The largest value that is less than or equal to 11 is 8:

27-16=11							
128	64	32	16	8	4	2	1
0	0	0	1	1			

Figure 1.8: Finding the first position that is less than or equal to 8

We subtract 8 from 11 and get 3. The next value, 4, is larger than 3, so we insert a 0 at this position:

11-8=3							
128	64	32	16	8	4	2	1
0	0	0	1	1	0		

Figure 1.9: We encounter a position that is greater than 3 so we insert a 0

As we have not inserted a 1 yet, we keep the value of 3 and try to find a value that works for it. The next one, 2, is less than or equal to 3, so we insert a 1 here and then subtract 2 from 3 and get 1:

11-8=3

128	64	32	16	8	4	2	1
0	0	0	1	1	0	1	

Figure 1.10: 2 is less than 3, so we insert a 1 at this position

We repeat this until we reach 0:

3-2=1

128	64	32	16	8	4	2	1
0	0	0	1	1	0	1	1

Figure 1.11: When we have reached the end, we have arrived at the complete binary number

We now know that 27 will be 11011 in binary. We can ignore the leading zeros.

When we have one single binary digit, we call it a **bit**, and if we place them in groups of 8 bits, we call them a **byte**. One byte can hold values between 0 and 255. This is because a 1 in all positions (11111111) will be 128 + 64 + 32 + 16 + 8 + 4 + 2 + 1= 255.

By using lots of zeros and ones, the computer can represent any number in binary form, and if it can represent numbers, it can serve other things too, such as text.

Understanding ASCII and Unicode

If you give each letter of the English alphabet a numerical value, you could represent text with numbers. We could, for example, say that A=1, B=2, and so on. The computer does not use these values for the letters, but instead, it can either use something that is called the ASCII table (pronounced *as-key*) or another representation that is called Unicode. It is not important to understand exactly how they work; the only thing we need to understand is that a number can represent every character. This number can then be looked up using either the ASCII table or Unicode.

The ASCII table uses one byte to represent different characters. The table starts with characters that are non-printable. Eventually, it reaches the characters in the English alphabet. So, A, for example, is 65, B is 66, and so on. 255 characters will not take us far as we have lots of different alphabets around the world, and we also want to represent other symbols. That is why we also have Unicode. Its mapping to individual characters is not as direct as it is in the ASCII table, but all we need to know right now is that with it, we can use numbers to represent characters.

> **Note**
> Non-printable characters are symbols that are not used for visual representation; for example, when we need a way to indicate a tab or a new line, or if printing text to a printer, we want the printer to continue to the next page.

Representing other forms of data

We've learned how to represent text in binary, but what about things other than text and numbers? What about images? And video? And sound?

Images are made up of pixels, and three values, RGB, represent each pixel. These values tell the computer how much red, green, and blue a pixel has:

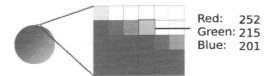

Figure 1.12: Three values represent a single pixel, indicating how much red, green, and blue it has

A video is nothing more than a composite of many images, so every frame is an image; therefore, it can be represented the same way.

A waveform can represent sound. Each peak and valley can be a number:

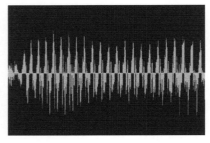

Figure 1.13: Audio depicted as a waveform

Now that we know how the computer can represent data, we have to find out how it processes it. To understand that, we must first dive into a corner of mathematics that is called Boolean algebra.

Boolean algebra

George Boole, who lived between 1815 and 1864, was a self-taught English mathematician and the inventor of Boolean logic, which is the basis of how all our computers work.

Boolean logic, sometimes referred to as Boolean algebra, is a form of mathematics that works with only two values: **true** and **false**. It also defines three operations that we can perform on these two values: **AND, OR**, and **NOT**.

NOT is the simplest of these operations as all it does is just switch the value, so not true is false, and not false is true. For example, if I say, "It is raining today," this statement can be true or false. It is true if it rains and false if it is not. If I instead say, "It is **NOT** raining today," then the statement will be true if it doesn't rain and false if it does.

AND takes two statements that can be either true or false and evaluates them into a single value. The outcome will be true if both incoming values are true and false in all other situations. If I say, "It is raining today, **AND** I have a blue umbrella," the statement will only be true if both parts are true, that is, if it is actually raining and my umbrella is actually blue. However, if it is raining but my umbrella is pink, what I say will be false, even though half of it was true.

OR works on two parts, just like **AND**, but now only one of the two must be true to make the statement true. If I say, "Today I will go to the beach **OR** I will go to town," then the statement will be true whether I either go to the beach or to town, and also if I manage to do both.

We can illustrate how these three operations work in something called a truth table. A truth table is a way to describe how an input of the **true** and **false** values is transformed by an operation. The input is often referred to as **P** if we only have one input value, or **P** and **Q** if we have two. The result is shown in the last column.

If **P** is the input value, the truth table for **NOT** will look like this:

P	NOT P
True	False
False	True

Table 1.4: The truth table for NOT

For **AND**, the truth table looks like this if **P** and **Q** are the input:

P	Q	P AND Q
True	True	True
True	False	False
False	True	False
False	False	False

Table 1.5: The truth table for AND

For **OR**, the truth table looks like this:

P	Q	P OR Q
True	True	True
True	False	True
False	True	True
False	False	False

Table 1.6: The truth table for OR

As you can see, the only way an **AND** operation can be **true** is if both parts are true, and the only time **OR** can be false is if both parts are **false**.

When Claude Shannon, an American mathematician and electrical engineer, published his master's degree thesis in 1937, *A Symbolic Analysis of Relay and Switching Circuits*, he based his work on the ideas of Boole. From Shannon's ideas, Boolean logic made its way into our modern computers because, with the help of the simple operations that Boole defined, we could transform any value that can be in one of two states: true or false, on or off, or, in the case of binary numbers, one or zero.

We can accomplish these operations with the help of transistors. There is no need for us to go into the details of how a transistor works – just knowing that it can be used to represent true/false, on/off, or 0/1 is enough. We can then connect several transistors into different configurations to accomplish operations such as **AND, OR**, and **NOT**. These combinations are called **gates**, so we will have a group of transistors called an **AND gate**, one that is called an **OR gate**, and one that is called a **NOT gate**. These gates can then be connected further to construct circuits that can add, subtract, multiply, and divide. We have now built a machine that can represent both numbers and these basic operations. We have done this using only numbers, and all these numbers will be in binary, so we have a machine that only works with zeros and ones: the computer.

Machine code – the native language of the computer

Now that we have circuits that can perform some basic operations on numbers, and we have data in the form of numbers, we can start to write programs that will perform operations on the data. We can do that with the only thing the computer understands: machine code. As numbers can represent everything, the instructions we give to the computer will be – yes, that's right – just numbers.

Each processor type has a specific set of instructions. That is why a program written for a Mac can't run on a PC running Windows, for example. So, the instructions can be machine code. Machine code has several operations, called **opcodes**. The operations can be things such as **AND, OR, ADD**, and so on. Each opcode has a unique number. For example, **AND** could have an opcode value of 1, and **OR** could have an opcode value of 9.

The processor will also have several registers. A register is a small area, sometimes referred to as a data holding place, where the processor can store data it is currently working with. Before executing an operation, we will need to move the data we want as input to the operation, from memory, into some of these registers. The result of the operation, the output, is also stored in a register. In reality, things are a bit more complicated than this, but we do not need to go into all the details here.

We can now recall the image of the four operations that were common for all computers: input, storage, process, and output. We first get some **input**, and it will go to the computer's memory for **storage**. The processor will then retrieve it from its registers and perform operations on it, which is the **process** part. When we have the result of the operations, it will go back into the memory so that it can later be sent to the **output**.

One way to write these instructions is to use something called an *assembly*. This is a way of writing a program where we use three-letter abbreviations for the opcodes and have names for the registers. By doing this, it will be easier to read and understand the instructions we give. We can then use a program that can translate the assembly code into machine code.

The assembly language is the first programming language we encounter. The assembly language can look like this:

```
mov     eax, 14
mov     ebx, 10
add     eax, ebx
```

Here, we are moving (mov) the value of 14 into one of the registers, called eax, and then we are moving the value of 10 into another register, called ebx. We are then performing the add operation on the contents of these two registers. The result will be written back into a register; perhaps eax will be reused for this.

If the **move** operation has an opcode of 136 and the **add** operation has an opcode of 1, we can use these values together with the numerical representations of the registers to have all of this in only numerical format. And, as we know, everything that is numerical can be represented in binary form, that is, with zeros and ones.

Now we have all that, we need to look at some machine code.

Example machine code

Remember that the instructions we give will be different depending on what processor and operating system we use. The following is an example of what machine code can look like for a program printing the text **Hello, World!** to the screen on a computer using the Linux operating system:

b8	21 0a 00 00
a3	0c 10 00 06
b8	6f 72 6c 64
a3	08 10 00 06
b8	6f 2c 20 57
a3	04 10 00 06
b8	48 65 6c 6c
a3	00 10 00 06
b9	00 10 00 06
ba	10 00 00 00
bb	01 00 00 00
b8	04 00 00 00
cd	80
b8	01 00 00 00
cd	80

When looking at this program, we can write the numbers in binary or decimal format if we want to. However, to make it easier to read, we often use hexadecimal numbers as we can then use fewer digits. For example, 15 in the decimal format (two digits) is 1111 (four digits) in binary, but only F (one digit) in hexadecimal. It is just more compact – that is the only reason we do this.

Don't worry if you don't understand anything about the machine code program. It is not supposed to be readable for humans; however, for the computer, this all makes sense.

Writing code in machine code is error-prone. A number in the wrong place can be the difference between success and disaster. The natural next step, therefore, has been to create something more comfortable for humans to read and write, which the computer can then translate into machine code. One such measure has been the creation of the assembly language that we talked about earlier.

Here is the same program, written in the assembly language:

```
section     .text
global      _start
_start:
    mov     edx,len
    mov     ecx,msg
    mov     ebx,1
    mov     eax,4
    int     0x80
    mov     eax,1
    int     0x80
section     .data

msg     db   'Hello, world!',0xa
len     equ $ - msg
```

As you can see, this is still not that easy to understand. In the next chapter, we will learn how to write the same program using languages that resemble human language to a much higher degree.

Summary

In this chapter, we have gone back in history and explored the development of computers. The history of computers is a vast topic, but we touched on some important events that have made computers the fantastic machines that we know today.

For a computer to be useful, it requires programs, and to be able to write programs, we need programming languages. We learned that the development of programming was closely related to the development of computers, even if Lady Ada Lovelace managed to write what was considered to be the first computer program about 100 years before the first computer was built.

With the history of computers covered, we then turned our attention to what a computer program is and how the computer can use the instructions given in the program to accomplish the intentions of the programmer. To do that, we examined the smallest parts of data a computer can handle, the bits, which are the zeros and ones of the binary representation of numbers. We learned that the ideas of George Boole and his Boolean logic are the core of how a computer can transform data. Boole's ideas will return in later chapters, as we will use them when writing programs as well.

Finally, we took a closer look at the language of computers, machine code. We saw how hard it is for us to read and understand, and because of that, we will appreciate the next chapter, where we will learn what we can do to avoid working with this difficult code directly.

2
Introduction to Programming Languages

To be able to write a computer program, we need a programming language. However, we don't have just one or two to pick from; there are thousands of different languages available at our disposal. In this chapter, we will talk about what a programming language is, why there are so many languages available, how all of these languages are related, and how a computer can understand the code that we write. Toward the end, we will talk about the grammar of a programming language, also known as its syntax.

By the end of this chapter, you will be able to do the following:

- Understand why we have programming languages
- Understand how programming languages evolved from one language to another
- Understand how programming languages are related
- Understand the difference between interpreted and compiled languages
- Understand the concepts of syntax, keywords, and reserved words in a programming language

Why do we have programming languages?

Machine code is very difficult. As we saw in the previous chapter, machine code is not made for us humans. It is perfect for computers, but we need something more comfortable to read, write, and understand.

The time it takes to write a program, find errors and bugs in code, and update a program to add new features costs money. If the language we use can help us reduce the chance of introducing errors in code, it will reduce the costs. If it helps us understand the code when we read it, it will let us add new features faster, and so reduce costs. One goal of a programming language is that it must help us be efficient when we write programs.

It is at this point that the higher-level programming languages enter the scene. They enable us to write our code in something that often, at least to some degree, resembles English. In *Chapter 1*, *Introduction to Computer Programs* we saw one attempt to do this: assembly language. The introduction to this language helped somewhat, but it was still not good enough. What we need is something closer to human language.

Look at the following code snippet:

```
.data
    msgEqual db "Equal","$"
    msgNotEqual  db "Not Equal","$"
.code
main proc

    mov bl,"Alice"
    mov bh,"Bob"
    cmp bh,bl
    jne NotEqual

    mov ax, seg msgEqual
    mov ds, ax
    mov ah, 09h
    lea dx, msgEqual
    int 21h

    mov ah, 4Ch
    int 21h
```

```
NotEqual:
    mov ax, seg msgNotEqual
    mov ds, ax
    mov ah, 09h
    lea dx, msgNotEqual
    int 21h

    mov ah, 4Ch
    int 21h

main endp
end main
```

Now, compare it to the following code:

```
IF "Alice" == "Bob" THEN
    print "Equal"
ELSE
    print "Not Equal"
ENDIF
```

Believe it or not, they both do the same thing. The first one is in assembly language and the second one is something that resembles a high-level language. Even if you have never seen code before, it is not hard to understand what this program is doing. It compares two text strings, Alice and Bob, and if they are equal, prints this result to the screen, and if not, prints **Not Equal**. Of course, they are not equal, so the output here is **Not Equal**.

What these two examples show is the leap that was taken to prove how easy code could be if we compare machine code and assembly code.

In *Chapter 1, Introduction to Computer Programs* we saw a program that was first written in machine code and then in assembly that printed the text **Hello, World** to the screen. What would that program look like in some of the high-level languages that we use today? Let's look at some examples.

In Python, it would look as follows:

```
print("Hello, World")
```

In C, it looks as follows:

```c
#include <stdio.h>
int main(void)
{
  printf("Hello, World");
  return 0;
}
```

In C++, we have the following:

```cpp
#include <iostream.h>
int main()
{
    std::cout << "Hello, World" << std::endl;
    return 0;
}
```

In Java, we would see the following:

```java
class HelloWorld {
  static public void main( String args[] ) {
    System.out.println("Hello, World");
  }
}
```

In C#, we have the following:

```csharp
class HelloWorld
{
    static void Main()
    {
        System.Console.WriteLine("Hello, World");
    }
}
```

Finally, in JavaScript, we would observe the following:

```javascript
console.log("Hello, World");
```

We can see that they all are different and that some have some extra stuff surrounding the part that prints the text, but this comparison makes clear that the step from machine code is huge.

This step clears the path for several different ways to organize and structure code, and since the advent of the first high-level programming languages in the 50s, we have seen tremendous development. Right up to today, a vast amount of languages have been developed.

How programming languages have evolved?

Between 1943 and 1945, Konrad Zuse, a German civil engineer, developed a programming language called Plankalkül. Even though this language was not implemented at the time, it held the foundations for what we now call high-level programming languages and was an inspiration for other languages that followed.

In late 1953, John W. Backus, an American computer scientist working at IBM, submitted a proposal to his superiors to develop an alternative to assembly. In 1954, Backus and his team published the first draft specification for this language, and in April 1957, the first version of the FORTRAN (the all caps naming standard later changed to Fortran) programming language was released. At first, this language was met with some skepticism as it could not produce programs that ran as fast as the ones written in Assembly. However, the fact that programs written in this new language had far fewer lines and were more comfortable to write and understand soon outweighed the fact that it ran a bit slower than the handwritten assembly programs.

Fortran became a success and is still used today, even if it is only used for some very specialized applications, such as how to measure the performance of supercomputers.

Fortran was soon followed by some other programming languages that have influenced how we write programs today.

In 1958, a programming language called Lisp was created by John McCarty, an American computer scientist working at MIT. Lisp originated many concepts that were later adopted by other programming languages. In *Chapter 10, Programming Paradigms*, we will talk about the different paradigms used in programming, and Lisp introduced one such paradigm called functional programming. Lisp lives today through several languages, often referred to as Lisp dialects. Among them, we find languages such as Clojure, Common Lisp, and Scheme.

In 1958, another important language was created that has influenced several of the most popular languages we use today. It is called ALGOL and was developed by a committee of American and European computer scientists at a meeting in Zurich. The most important legacy of ALGOL is how we structure code into separate blocks, a concept widely used today.

The 1950s finally saw one more language that is worth mentioning as it is still in use, and that is COBOL. The idea was to create a language that was English-like and oriented toward business applications. The name is an abbreviation for **Common Business-Oriented Language**. A group of representatives from academia, computer users, and manufacturers developed COBOL at the University of Pennsylvania in 1959. One member of this group was Grace Hopper. She had earlier invented an English-like data processing language called FLOW-MATIC, which became an essential source of inspiration for COBOL. For a long time, COBOL was the number one language for developing business applications and is still in use today in the financial sector.

The modern era of programming languages

These languages created the foundation and served as an inspiration for languages developed during the 60s and 70s. We will mention a few languages developed during this time as they have been essential in either introducing new concepts to programming or have served as an inspiration to others.

In the late 1960s, two Norwegian computer scientists, Ole-Johan Dahl and Kristen Nygaard, invented a language called Simula, which popularized another paradigm, object orientation. We will talk more about what object orientation is in *Chapter 10, Programming Paradigms*. It has inspired several modern languages that use this paradigm, such as C++, Java, and C# (pronounced C sharp).

Between 1969 and 1973, Dennis Ritchie and Ken Thomson at Bell Labs developed a programming language called C, which is still one of the most popular programming languages and the primary influencer for many of today's top languages. Among these, we find languages such as C++, Java, Go, JavaScript, Perl, PHP, Python, and C#. What is it that makes C so popular and influential? There are several answers to this. One reason is the way the code looks and the rules for how the code is structured. This style inspires many languages, and they reuse it with minor or no modifications. Another reason is that programs written in C run fast and for that reason, when an application requires high speed or in some other way needs high performance, C or some of its related languages are perfect for the job.

Why so many languages?

There are several reasons why someone will develop a new language. One can be that the person uses language but doesn't think the structure of the code is good enough, or they think that some things could be done more efficiently. It can also be that a language is developed to target a special kind of application. In *Chapter 3*, *Types of Applications* we will look at some different types of applications, and these might have some requirements that make one language better suited to meet them than other languages will.

A programming language can give a programmer direct access to computer hardware. This means that it will let the programmer have more control over how data will be represented and stored in the computer's memory. The benefit of this is that programs written in this sort of language have the potential of being more efficient or running faster. However, this comes at the cost of complexity. When more control is given to the programmer, we also give the programmer more chances to make errors.

Some languages give us less control but are easier to use. The disadvantage here is that programs written in these languages tend to run slower.

For example, if we want to write a high-end game where we want the best possible graphics, the best sound, advanced computer AI, and multiplayer capabilities, we will need to do our best to get as much performance as possible out of the computer hardware. We will then select a language that will give us as much control as possible as we want to fine-tune all aspects of our program to their optimum configurations.

If we instead write some administrative software, the speed of the application will not be our focus; rather, we want a programming language that will help us write high-quality software with as few errors as possible. Some programming languages also have a structure that makes writing programs easier, which in turn reduces the time spent by the programmer in writing the software.

Requirements like this can also be the motivation for creating a new programming language. A programming language is nothing more than a tool that we use to create programs, and as with all tools, we want it to be as functional for the task as possible.

The family tree of programming languages

Forming a family tree of how programming languages are related is not easy as we can argue for a while over how much they have influenced each other. It would also be impossible for us to draw a tree that includes all of the existing languages as there are so many that fitting them into even a page of this book would be impossible. What we can do, however, is draw a tree that includes languages that are either popular right now or that have influenced these languages in a significant way.

The selection of languages we will use here is based on their popularity—that is, they are the languages that you are most likely to use. To know what languages are the most popular ones today, we can turn to several sources. The question is how to measure how popular a language is, and different sources use different criteria to make this selection. If we browse through several top lists online, we will soon discover that there are some languages that make it into all of these lists. So, let's start with them and see how we can build a tree from there.

The languages I will include, in no particular order, are JavaScript, Java, Python, PHP, C, C++, C#, and Ruby.

If we start with one language—for example, C—and look at what languages it is influenced by, we will find assembly language, Fortran, and ALGOL (if we just focus on the ones we mentioned earlier). We can now start to draw this tree. If we then do the same for the other languages and see which ones have influenced them and which ones they have influenced, we will end up with a tree that looks something like this:

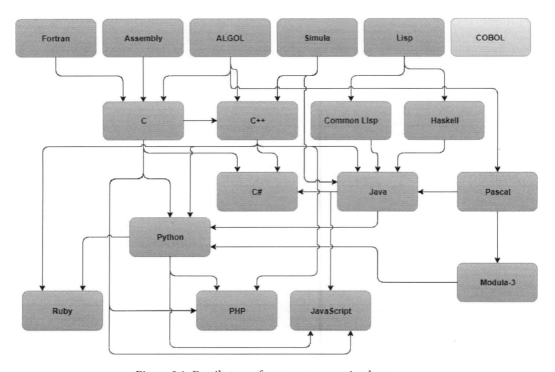

Figure 2.1: Family tree of some programming languages

We could have lengthy discussions on whether this is an accurate representation, but it gives us a general idea of how languages inspire each other. Of the languages we have talked about, only COBOL can't directly be linked to any of these languages. This does not mean that COBOL is not essential, but to the languages that made it into this tree, COBOL has not had any significant influence.

Another thing to note about this diagram is that languages that have ALGOL as their common ancestor are overrepresented. The reason for this is that among the most popular languages today, they all come from a group often referred to as the ALGOL family of languages. I have also taken the liberty to leave out some intermediate languages from some of these relationships to reduce the size of the tree. What we don't see in this family tree is a language that springs up that is totally unrelated to any existing language. What that means is that new languages are created as a reaction to an existing language. When creating a new language, we take the parts we like from one or more languages and change the parts we don't like.

The reason this tree can be interesting is that if I learn one programming language, then learning a related language is much easier then learning one that is further away in the tree.

Translating code into something that the computer understands

The code that a programmer writes is called source code. As we saw in *Chapter 1, Introduction to Computer Programs* this code must be translated into machine code so that the computer can understand it. There are two main principles of how this translation is done. We will first explore these two concepts and look at their pros and cons before we look at a combination of these two concepts.

Interpreting

One way to carry out this translation is by using an interpreter. An interpreter will look at a single line of source code, translate it into machine code, let the computer execute this line, and then move on to the next line of code. The way the interpreter works is a bit like how a simultaneous translator works with human languages. A simultaneous translator will, for example, work for the UN. In the UN, everyone is entitled to speak in their native language. A group of translators listens to the talk, and as they listen, they will translate it into another language. Delegates can then listen to the speech in real time in their native language through headphones, in this way:

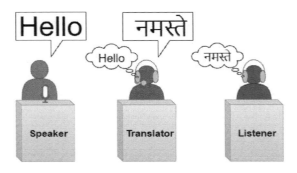

Figure 2.2: A simultaneous translator will translate everything in real time

Next, let's see how compiling works.

Compiling

Another way to carry out the translation is by using a technique called compiling. When we compile source code into machine code, we first translate every line of code, and it is not until the translation of all of the lines of code has been done that the program is executed. We can compare this to the concept of translating a book. First, an author writes the book in one language. A translator will then translate the whole book into another language. It is not until the translation of all of the text in the original book is done that it will be available to read:

Figure 2.3: When translating a book, a translator will translate all of the text before the book is published

After this, we will see how interpretation and compilation compare.

Comparing interpretation and compilation

Interpreting and compiling are two of the main techniques for translating source code. A programming language can use either one of these techniques, and a language is therefore often referred to as either an interpreted or compiled language.

Let's look more closely at these two techniques so that we can understand them better before we compare them.

When translating source code written by a programmer, a specialized program called an interpreter can do the job. The interpreter will read the source code line by line and translate each line immediately.

Let's see a diagram of this process:

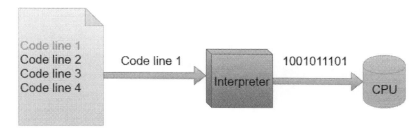

Figure 2.4: An interpreter translates one line of source code into machine code

First, the interpreter will read a line from the source code on the left. In this diagram, it reads the first line, called **Code line 1**. It will then translate this line into machine code and send it to the processor of the computer, the CPU, which will execute the instructions.

It will then go on to the next line, shown in the following diagram, and repeat the process for that line:

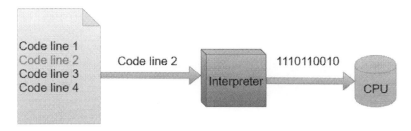

Figure 2.5: When one line has executed, the interpreter continues with the next line

The interpreter will repeat this process until there are no more lines to process in the source code.

A compiler will instead translate all the code in the source code document and store it in a file containing the machine code instructions. When we want to run the program, we can use this file to run it; it is at this point that the CPU will execute the machine code.

The following diagram illustrates this process:

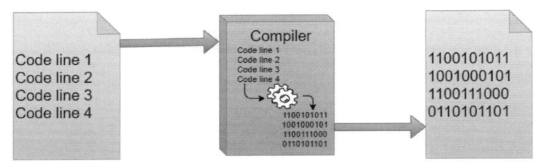

Figure 2.6: A compiler translates all of the source code and stores the resulting machine code in a file

What are the advantages and disadvantages of these two methods of translation? Let's start with interpretation and look at some of the benefits first:

- It has a smaller program size.
- If we have the code and an interpreter, we can run it on any platform (for example, Windows, Linux, macOS, and so on).
- Interpreted languages tend to be more flexible for programmers to use. One example of this is called dynamic typing, which is something we will talk more about in *Chapter 6, Working with Data – Variables*.

Some disadvantages of the interpreter approach are as follows:

- The program runs slower as it takes some time to do the translation.
- Anyone who wants to run the program must have an interpreter installed.
- The user of the program has access to the source code, so if it is a commercial application, all the code we have written will be accessible to anyone, including any potential business secrets.

For a compiled solution, the advantages and disadvantages are pretty much the opposite of those for an interpreter. The advantages are as follows:

- It runs faster as the translation is done all at once.

- No extra program is needed to run the application—that is, the application has all the information it needs to run, so the user does not need to have any other programs installed.

- Compiled programming languages tend to help the programmer with things such as type checking to a higher degree. Type checking is something we will discuss in *Chapter 6, Working with Data – Variables.*

The disadvantages are as follows:

- The programs tend to be larger as they need to come with instructions on how they will be executed.

- We need to make versions for all of the platforms that we intend the program to run on—that is, we need a Windows version, a macOS version, and a Linux version.

- The time it takes to complete the translation can be long, making it harder to try things out as we write the program.

As we can see, there are pros and cons to both techniques. A programming language is either interpreted or compiled, with some exceptions that we will look at soon.

> **Note:**
>
> Some examples of interpreted languages are PHP, Ruby, and JavaScript.
>
> Some examples of compiled languages are C, C++, COBOL, ALGOL, Fortran, and Lisp.

Languages that both compile and interpret

We also have a group of languages that both compile and interpret. When they compile the source code, they do not directly compile it into machine code. They follow an intermediate step where they compile the source code into byte code. This byte code is then interpreted as the program executes. The benefit of doing this is that we get some of the advantages of both techniques. For example, this byte code can be distributed to anyone who wants to run the program, and then an interpreter will interpret the byte code into machine code for the current system that the program is executed on.

Another advantage that compiled languages have—and this applies to the technique of mixing them, too—is that if there is an error in the source code, the compiler will detect this because the syntax (remember that the syntax is the grammar of a language) has to be correct and if it is not, the compiler can't proceed and will stop the translation. The programmer then needs to go back and correct the error before the program can compile again.

Mixed technique languages share a disadvantage with interpreted languages, which is that programs written with them will run slower than programs written in a compiled language.

> **Note:**
> Some examples of mixed technique languages are Python, Java, C#, and Perl.

Syntax and the building blocks of a programming language

Just as human languages have grammar to dictate the rules of the language, a programming language has syntax. The syntax is the rules for how we write a program using a language. There is one big difference between grammar and syntax and that is about forgiveness for errors. If you meet someone who speaks your native language but makes some errors here and there, you will still be able to understand what that person is trying to communicate to you. That is not the case for the syntax of a programming language. It does not forgive at all, and you will need to get it spot on:

Figure 2.7: Humans understand each other even if the grammar is wrong

As we discussed earlier, the code we write will be translated by either a compiler or an interpreter, and for that translation to work, the syntax must be flawless.

Each programming language has its own syntax rules, but as we saw in the family tree earlier, languages can be related. So, many languages share a syntax with only slight variations, where others have a more specialized syntax. When learning a new language, we must learn the syntax for that language. That is why moving between closely related languages is easier as they will most likely share a lot of their syntax.

If we have an error in the syntax, it will be discovered during the translation, and here is where a compiled and an interpreted language will differ. For a compiled language, all the translation will be done before we can execute the program. If we have an error in the syntax, the compilation will stop as soon as the compiler discovers the mistake. We must then find the fault and correct it, then let the compiler try to translate the code again. It is not until our code does not have any syntax errors that we have something we can run completely:

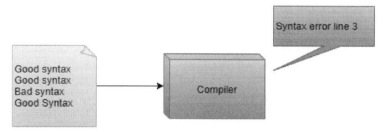

Figure 2.8: A compiler will not produce any output until there are no errors in the syntax

This is different for an interpreted language as it will translate line by line as we run the program. This means that a syntax error can be hidden in a corner of the program that is rarely executed and will not be discovered until we eventually want to run that line of code. When this happens, the program will crash with an error message letting us know what problem was there with our syntax:

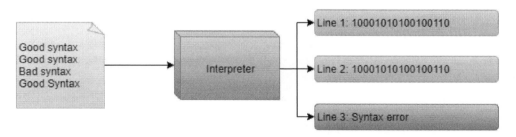

Figure 2.9: An interpreter will translate every line it encounters and
executes it until it finds a syntax error

This means that a source code document that we have written can either be syntactically correct or incorrect. The syntax is a set of rules defining how the source code will be written and structured. But that is not all. The syntax also defines other things, such as the words that make up the language. These are called **keywords**.

Keywords

When learning a new language, we must keep track of its keywords as these words are reserved by the language and so we can't use them to name things in our program. If we use a keyword by accident for something other than its intended use, we will get an error. Keywords are sometimes also referred to as reserved words.

A language will typically have between 30 and 50 keywords. Here is a list of some common keywords in many languages:

- `for`
- `if`
- `else`
- `break`
- `continue`
- `return`
- `while`

Most programming languages are case sensitive, so the use of uppercase and lowercase letters matters—for example, `if` is not the same thing as `If` or `IF`.

Apart from keywords, we also have something called operators, which we can use to represent the actions we want to perform on data.

Operators

A programming language will also have several operators, and these are what we use to accomplish things such as addition and multiplication, as well as to compare items. The symbols that can be used are also defined as part of the language syntax. Here is a list of some commonly used operators:

Operator	Description	Operator	Description
+	Addition	-	Subtraction
*	Multiplication	/	Division
==	Equal	!=	Not Equal
>	Greater than	<	Less than
>=	Greater than or equal to	<=	Less than or equal to
%	Modulo	=	Assignment

Table 2.1 – Commonly used operators in programming languages

Operators are so-called because they perform operations on data. As we can see in the preceding table, there are operators to perform arithmetic operations, such as addition and multiplication. Other operators are used for comparison—for example, to see whether two values are equal, whether one is greater than another, and so on. In *Chapter 6, Working with Data – Variables* we will see more about what operators are typically found in a programming language and how they can be used.

Having our code in one long sequence would make it difficult to read. It would be like having a book with no chapters or paragraphs. To add the concept of chapters and paragraphs to our code, we use something called **code blocks**.

Code blocks

It is common for a language to also allow us to define blocks of code. There are several reasons why you would want to do that, and we will talk more about them in later chapters. However, for now, we can think of a block of code like a paragraph in standard text. The language then defines how we mark the beginning and end of the block. A common technique that many languages employ is using parentheses, also called braces or curly brackets— { }. Everything within these parentheses is considered part of the block. Other languages might have different ways to do the same thing, so again, when switching between languages, we must learn what the syntax rules are for that language.

Now that we have covered some of the basic concepts that a programming language uses to define its syntax, we should make one clarification. Many concepts that come up in programming share names with concepts in mathematics. So, let's see how programming is related to mathematics.

Relations to mathematics

Programming is closely related to mathematics as programming has borrowed many concepts from it. One of these concepts is the use of variables. In *Chapter 6, Working with Data – Variables*, we will talk about what a variable is and how it works, but they are essentially the same as they are in mathematics in the sense that we can use a name to represent a variable (a value that can change). The rules for how we can name variables are also part of the language syntax.

Another concept borrowed from mathematics is functions. In mathematics, a function is something that takes an input value and transforms it in some way to produce an output. This is close to how we can describe functions in programming as well, but that is not all there is to functions in programming. We will talk about functions in *Chapter 8, Understanding Functions*, and then we will see that we need to think about programming functions in a different way than how we view their mathematical equivalent.

One thing we must remember when approaching programming is that if we understand how these concepts work in mathematics, that does not mean that we can apply this knowledge directly to programming, even if they happen to share the same name. They will be related, but how things are done in programming will differ from how things work in math.

Summary

In this chapter, we started by talking about why machine code is so difficult to understand and the motivation for creating programming languages that are easier to use for programmers. We then saw how programming languages have evolved over the years, and how most of them are similar as they have influenced each other as they evolved.

We also discussed some different techniques—interpreting and compiling—that are used to translate source code into machine code. We also saw how some languages use a mixed technique, employing both compiling and interpreting to complete translation.

At the end of this chapter, we learned about the grammar or syntax of a programming language and that each language has its own syntax rules. We also learned that there is a close relationship between mathematics and programming, and that programming has borrowed some ideas and concepts from mathematics but that even if they share the same name, they do not necessarily do the same thing.

All of this knowledge will give you a solid base to build on with what we will learn in the next chapter, where we will look at some of the main types of applications that we can develop. We will also learn about the ways in which they are related to each other.

3
Types of Applications

Computer programs, or applications as we sometimes call them, come in many types. Each type solves a special kind of problem. Some applications, such as a solitaire game or a word processor, just run on a local computer, and others need to communicate with other computers or networks to work, such as web browsers or email clients.

In this chapter, we will look at some special types of applications and discuss what considerations we need to take when creating them.

It would be impossible for us to cover all types of applications as there are way too many of them. Instead, we will look at some common types that we will encounter when writing our applications.

We create programs to solve problems, and in the process of designing our application and deciding what it needs to do, we will often look at solutions others have found for similar problems. The goal of this chapter is to familiarize you with some of these solutions so you can recognize the problem they solve when, in the future, you need to create your own solutions.

By the end of this chapter, you will be able to do the following:

- Understand what is typical for the different types of applications that the chapter covers
- Understand how the application type affects how we structure our applications
- Understand the importance of connected applications
- Understand the benefits of using cloud-based solutions
- Understand the problems the different kinds of applications we talk about can solve

Standalone applications

A standalone application is a program that can work offline, that is, it does not necessarily require a network connection. Therefore, when writing such an application, we will need to provide all the resources the program will require. These resources can be images, such as icons used in the application, files to store program configuration, and so on.

When learning to write applications, most of your programs will likely fall into this category. It is usually a rather straightforward affair to create these applications as we will not need to interact with other programs.

Examples of programs that fall into this category are text editors such as Notepad on Windows or TextEdit on Mac, simple games such as solitaire, and paint programs.

Client-server applications

Client-server is a model we can use to create distributed applications, which are applications that run on more than one machine.

The idea behind the client-server model is that we have at least two computers involved. One acts as the server, and all the others have the role of the client. Clients and servers need to communicate with each other. It is always the client who initiates the communication. Sometimes the server communicates with several clients at once; other times, the server only communicates with a single client at a time.

This means that we can use different computers to take care of different parts of an application's responsibility. We can let one computer deal with one aspect of a problem and another computer work on a different aspect of the same problem. These two computers then need to communicate their results, usually to a single computer, which can then assemble the different results into one solution.

We can also use this model when we have different roles for different parts of an application. For example, we have one role that is to display data to and get input from a user (user interaction) and another role that is to process and store this data. We can divide these roles so the processing and storing role is done by one computer and the user interaction role by another computer.

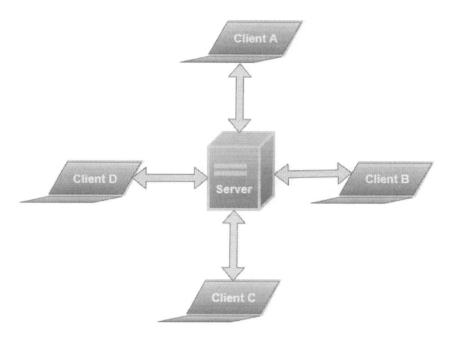

Figure 3.1 – A server connected to several clients

To illustrate this, let's take a couple of scenarios where we would use a client-server solution and see what the solutions would be.

Example of a chat application

Let's assume that you want to create an application where you and your friends can chat with each other. Everyone that will use this chat application will need the **client software**; this is the program we start when we want to chat.

When we start thinking about how to design this application, we will face our first problem. Imagine that you start your chat application because you want to chat with your friend Alice. Our application needs to connect to Alice's computer, running her version of our program. Both you and Alice will run identical programs, but how can they connect? How can our application find Alice's computer among all the computers connected to the internet? It would be like if you want to call Alice but don't have her phone number. Our chat application will be our phone, and Alice's client will be her phone. You can't just randomly enter a number in the hope of reaching Alice.

Figure 3.2 – How can you find Alice's computer when you want to chat?

An IP address (**IP** is an abbreviation for **Internet Protocol** and is part of a larger protocol stack, called TCP/IP, that describes how computers communicate over the internet) identifies all computers and other devices connected to the internet. We can think of this address as a phone number. This number can uniquely identify a telephone anywhere in the world. The same is true for an IP address; it can uniquely identify any device that is connected to the internet.

The problem is, how can we know what address Alice's computer has? And even if we knew what it was, we must understand that it is subject to change. If she is connected to her home Wi-Fi network, she will have one IP address, but if she takes her computer to a café downtown and connects to their Wi-Fi network, she will get another IP address. This is because when connecting to a Wi-Fi network, it is the network router that assigns an IP address to your computer.

A better solution would be if all clients connected to a computer that always has the same address. This would be our **server**. If both you and Alice connect to the same server, this server will know about both your addresses, and when you want to chat with Alice, you send a message to the server and the server will relay this message to Alice. When her chat client receives the message, it will make a sound so she knows a new message has arrived, and the problem is solved. To simplify things even more, we will use a domain name for the server instead of the IP address, as a domain name such as company.com is easier to remember than an IP address.

Figure 3.3 – Using a server to handle the communication between you and Alice

If more than two users are connected to the server, then the server will need to keep track of who is the recipient of the message. When you send your message to Alice, your client application will need to provide the identity of who should get the message so the server can make sure it is sent to the right client.

Example of an email client

Assume that you have been using several different applications to read and write emails, but you are not happy with how they work and you decide to write your own. What you will write is an email client.

Let's take our friend Alice again. What happens if she sends you an email? Your emails must be stored somewhere as you can't have your client application running all the time. The email Alice sends to you will end up on an **email server**. When you start the email client you wrote, it will connect to the server and ask for all new emails that have been received since the last time you connected. These will now be transferred to your client application.

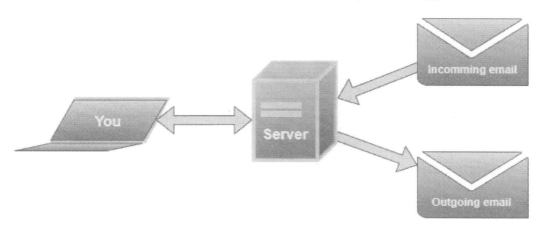

Figure 3.4 – An email server will handle incoming and outgoing emails,
and the client only connects to receive and transmit messages

Client-server, a two-part solution

In both these examples, we saw that the solution to a problem is divided into two parts. We need one part that will be the client, and the other will be the server. The characteristics of these two are that we have a server with its location known by its IP address, and we will have a client that will know about the server address and will be the part that initiates the communication. An IP address can also be in the form of a domain name, such as `http://some-server.com`. A domain name is a one-to-one mapping between an IP address and a name. In other words, a domain name is tied to one single IP address and is used because it is easier to remember a domain name than an IP address that is just four numbers in the form `123.123.123.123`.

This format is true for the version of IP addresses called **IPv4 (Internet Protocol version 4.)** A new version of the Internet Protocol is now starting to get widespread. The main reason for the upgrade is that we are running out of possible combinations to give all devices unique addresses. The new version is called **IPv6** (which is **Internet Protocol version 6**) and an address in IPv6 will look like `2001:db8:a0b:12f0::1`. These numbers are separated by colon instead of a period. In IPv4 the address was represented as a 32-bit value, and in IPv6 it is 128 bits. This means that we have many more addresses to distribute.

Sometimes these two roles are only distinct for how the two parts will connect; the client connects to the server, and when the connection is made, they can act as two identical parts. If we take the chat application as an example, if we knew Alice's address, we could connect directly to her application. Our application will initially be the client, and Alice's application would act as the server. But as soon as we have a connection, both parts will act in the same way, and the roles of who is the client and who is the server will be unimportant.

Next, we move to understanding web applications.

Web applications

A web application is a special form of client-server application where we have a client that interacts with a user in the form of a web page. The server is responsible for producing the results the user will see and to accept and process the input from the user.

This process works something like this:

1. Imagine that you visit a website and are prompted to log in. You enter your username and password. When you press the **Log in** button, the information you entered is sent to the server:

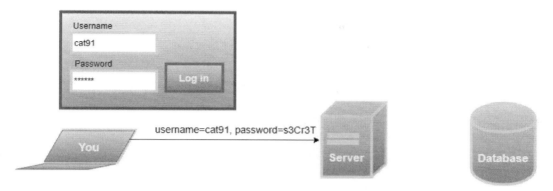

Figure 3.5 – When logging in to a web application, your credentials will be sent to the server

2. The server requests the information stored in a database about this user:

Figure 3.6 – The web server requests the user information stored in a database

3. The database returns the information it has for this user. Note that usually, the password will not be stored in plain text as illustrated here, but for clarity, we ignore that in this scenario:

Figure 3.7 – The database returns the information

4. The server application now verifies that the username and password are correct. If they are, it then produces a web page for this user and transmits it to the client's computer so that a web browser running on this computer can display this page:

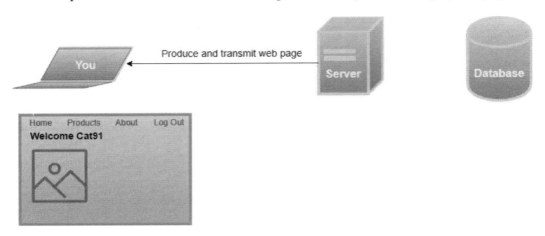

Figure 3.8 – The server produces a web page and transmits it to the client

Let's see what this means if we want to create our very own social network.

Example of a social network

You would need to create both the client and the server part of this application. First, the user needs to log in. To do this, the client will ask the user for their credentials. The client will then send the username and password to the server, and the server will verify if the information is correct. The result will be sent back to the client. If the login fails, the user will be asked to try again. If it is successful, the user will see the main window with all the posts from friends and relatives.

It might feel like there is some magic going on here, because how did we get the most recent post your uncle did 5 minutes ago on the other side of the world?

Your uncle uses his client to create his post. The information about this post is sent to the server, which stores it in a database. When you log in, the server asks the database for all users you are connected to, and among them, it finds your uncle. Then the server checks if your uncle has made any recent posts and then finds his post. This post is now part of the result, together with posts from other friends, that is sent to you:

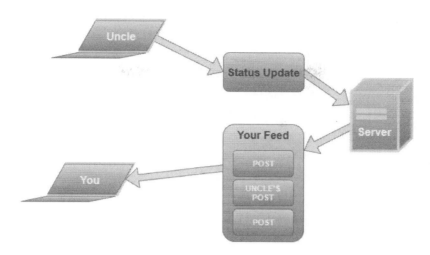

Figure 3.9 – Your uncle posts a new status update that gets included in your feed

Next, we will see how these apps are unique.

What makes web applications unique?

As we have seen, a web application is more-or-less just a client-server solution, but there is a twist that makes it not just a client-server application, and that is how the client interacts with the user.

If we think back to the client-server applications we talked about previously, the chat and email programs had been designed as *standalone applications*. This means that we have a program on our computer that we can start. That is not the case for our social network application. When users want to access it, they will start a web browser and navigate to the server's address. We can say that the web browser is a general-purpose client as it is not made to serve one solution but can be used to access any page on the web, our social network being one of them.

We will still need to design what this page will look like and what information will be displayed to the user, but the client usually has very little program logic built into it. The logic of our application is done on the server side, and it's the server that will produce the pages the user sees. They are transmitted to the client, which is the user's web browser, which then displays the result.

Next, we'll look at mobile applications.

Mobile applications

When we talk about a mobile application, we usually mean a program that is designed to run on a mobile device, such as a smartphone. These devices have some special characteristics that we need to consider when writing an application. First, their screen is smaller than a computer monitor. The screen can also be rotated in landscape or portrait orientation. We will also use the touchscreen of the device for input.

The mobile application might also use other features of the device, such as the GPS, sending text messages, or sensing the movement of the device using its accelerometer. These are things we usually can't do if an application runs on a normal computer.

A mobile application can be connected, but it does not have to be. Being connected means that it can communicate with another computer, maybe using the client-server techniques we discussed earlier.

When writing a mobile application, the platform the application will run on is very important. The reason is that the programs we write need to interact with the device more directly. This means is that it can dictate what programming language we will use to write these applications. The developers of the operating systems for mobile devices have some preferred programming languages. For iOS, Apple's operating system for mobile devices uses two languages, the old Objective-C and the new Swift. These are two languages you will hardly ever encounter if you are not creating applications for Apple devices. For the Android operating system, the preferred language used to be Java, but Google, which is the company behind Android, changed this in 2019 and now use a language called Kotlin as the preferred development language.

Having a preferred language for these systems does not mean that we can't use other languages. Still, Apple and Google recommend using these languages, so it is usually easier for us to use these languages when developing mobile applications. The reason is that the tools we use when writing our programs will be better suited to them than any other language.

Next, we look at distributed applications.

Distributed applications

A distributed application is an application that does not run on one single machine, but instead lets different parts of the program run on multiple computers that communicate with each other over a network. This might sound like the client-server solutions we talked about earlier, but here we don't have the distinct roles of a client and a server.

There could be several reasons to use this solution. One may be that what we are doing requires so much computing power that a single computer will not be enough. The idea is to use the computing power of many computers and distribute the calculations to all of them, letting each computer work on a small section of the problem and communicate the results to the other machines in the network. This will give us something of a *supercomputer* that will act as a very powerful single machine running a single application, when it is actually thousands of computers running small individual parts of the application.

Let's explore distributed applications in more detail.

SETI@home

An example of a project that uses this technique is **SETI** (short for **Search for Extraterrestrial Intelligence**), a scientific project trying to find extraterrestrial intelligence in outer space. To do this, they use radio telescopes to collect lots of data. The problem is that all this data needs to be analyzed in the search for a signal that can be of intelligent origin. The solution they use is to let people help them out either by installing a screensaver on their computer or a special program that will use the computing power of that computer when it is not used for any other task. By doing this, they will have the power of all these computers to do the analysis, and they will report back the result of the part of the data that was assigned to them.

You can try this out yourself by visiting `https://setiathome.berkeley.edu/` and installing the program:

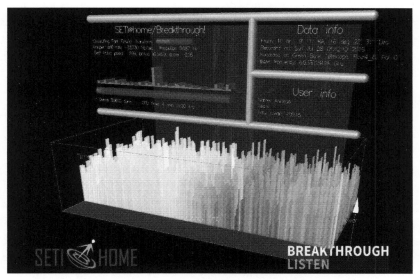

Figure 3.10 – SETI@home analyzing data. Copyright 2019 UC Regents. Used with permission

Peer-to-peer networks

A **peer-to-peer** network, also known as **P2P**, is a network of computers that are equal participants in the network. Each computer in the network is called a node, or a peer, and they make portions of their resources, such as processing power or disk storage, directly available to other participants in the network. This technique was popularized by file-sharing systems such as Napster in the late '90s. A peer in the network is both a supplier and a consumer of resources. This is what makes this solution different from a traditional client-server model in which the supply and consumption of resources are divided between the server and the client:

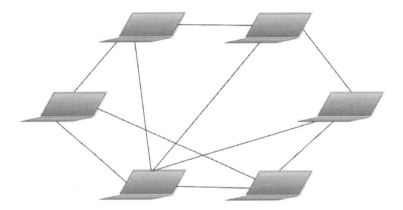

Figure 3.11 – A P2P network where computers, or peers, are connected without a server

Today, P2P networks are used by most cryptocurrencies making up a large portion of the blockchain industry (simply put, a blockchain is a database stored in separate copies on many nodes in a P2P network.). P2P is also used by web search engines, streaming platforms, and online marketplaces.

Next, we look at cloud-based applications.

Cloud-based applications

Cloud computing was first mentioned in 1996, but it was not until Amazon released its Elastic Compute Cloud in 2006 that it became widely popular. The idea behind cloud-based computing is to move away from the need to host your servers and other resources needed to run your project, and instead buy time from large data centers to use their computing power. There are many advantages to this. You don't have to make sure that your computers are up and running, that operating systems are updated, that you have implemented back-up solutions for your data, and so on. You can set up your server to be online, and then you can deploy your software on this server and run it from there.

The companies providing these services soon began to add other features that we can use as well. These are ready-made parts that we can use in our applications. What this means is that there will be parts of our application that we won't need to write ourselves. Instead, we can buy these ready-made parts from the provider and integrate them into our application that will run on a server, also provided by them.

There are many variations of this: we can buy a server, we might only buy storage, or we might buy one or more services that we will use, and these can then be combined in any way we want.

There are many reasons we would like to make our application using cloud-based resources. Let's look at some of them.

Advantages of adopting cloud-based applications

Here are a couple of reasons why using cloud-based applications is beneficial for us.

Reduced costs

By having our application on a cloud-based server, we will not need to buy a server computer, and we will not need to maintain this computer. We can pay for services so the cloud service provider will take care of ensuring that our server's operating system is updated and that security patches are installed as they are released.

If our application is storing data, we can let the provider take care of making backups, making sure we don't lose any data. We can also let these backups be stored at different locations in the world, so even if one of the data centers our provider is using gets destroyed or affected for some reason, our data will remain safe.

These are just two examples of how we can reduce our costs as the amount we pay to the cloud service provider will be drastically lower than if we had done all of this ourselves.

Scalability

Scalability is how we can adapt when the amount of work our application is doing changes. If we, for example, have a web application running and suddenly it gets very popular overnight, we might go from a couple of hundred users that are simultaneously connected to it to several thousand. If the hardware running our application is not capable of handling this growing popularity, our users will soon get tired of using it as they need to spend too much time waiting for a response from our application. If we manage the hardware ourselves, we will need to get more and better server computers, install our application on them, and make sure everything works. If the interest in our application then drops, we will now have invested in hardware we no longer need.

If we, on the other hand, are using a cloud-based solution, we could, with a few clicks, pay to get more power to our servers. And if the demand drops, we can downgrade again and only pay for what we use. This process can also be automated, so the server hardware adapts to the demand.

Cloud service models

Cloud computing providers offer different services according to three different models. These models define what parts the provider will handle and what is handled by us, the creators of the application. These different models can also be viewed as different layers, so when deciding what we need for our application, we can pick things from all three layers.

Let's look at these layers so that we understand what they can help us with.

Infrastructure as a Service (IaaS)

This is the layer that handles hardware resources such as servers, storage, firewalls, and so on. Investing in services on this layer means that you don't need to buy the hardware, you don't need to spend time on configuration, and space for data storage will be managed for you.

Some examples when IaaS is a good option for us are as follows:

- **Big data**: More and more applications need a huge amount of data. This can, for example, be data used when training **artificial intelligence** (**AI**) applications or applications that rely on a significant amount of what is known as unstructured data (that is, images, email, or social media content, for example). These applications will need to handle large workloads that can change over time. IaaS gives us tools to add storage and processing power with a click of a button; in fact, this can even be automated to suit our needs.

- **Disaster recovery**: The most valuable asset we have in software is data, and we should always ensure that we can recover from a disaster. If we store copies of our data in different geographical locations, we can rest assured that we can recover it even if the worst happens. IaaS makes it easy and affordable to do this.

- **Testing and development**: When developing applications, we often want to test them on different hardware configurations running different operating systems. Setting up different IaaS solutions is a cheap and easy way to do this.

Platform as a Service (PaaS)

In this layer, you will, among other things, find applications that will act as servers. Some examples are web servers that will handle web resources so users can access your website, and database servers that will manage storage and retrieval of data. This layer can also contain readily configured environments that are targeted to a programming language.

This level builds upon the IaaS level, so usually, you get the benefits of that layer plus the things that are included in this layer.

Here's some examples of some benefits of using PaaS:

- **Faster time to market**: Going from an idea to a product that we can start to earn money from is essential when developing software. Using PaaS will dramatically reduce the time for acquiring hardware and installing and configuring software. There are examples of start-up companies that had an idea on Friday and a product that could be used on the next Monday. This can be made possible with the help of PaaS.

- **Reduced costs**: Without the need to invest time and money acquiring hardware, configuring it, installing software, and ensuring all software is updated, our costs will be greatly reduced. The time we save can instead be used to develop our product.

Software as a Service (SaaS)

This layer will provide you with everything—the hardware, the server software, as well as applications—and the only thing you need to do is to configure it to work the way you want it to. A well-known example of SaaS is the array of Google apps. These are the applications provided by Google, such as Docs, Sheets, and Calendar.

Here's some examples of why you may want to use SaaS:

- **Less maintenance of office software**: When running a business, we need to provide email addresses to all our employees; we need to provide them with office applications such as word processors, spreadsheet applications, and presentation software. If we let someone else handle the installation, configuration, and updates, and reduce the time we spend on handling software licenses, we will free up resources and save money.

- **Sharing information**: Using services such as cloud storage will make it easier to share files and documents between co-workers and customers.

This completes our coverage of all the pertinent cloud service models.

As a software developer, you will most likely work on the PaaS layer as it is the one providing the tools we need to develop our applications:

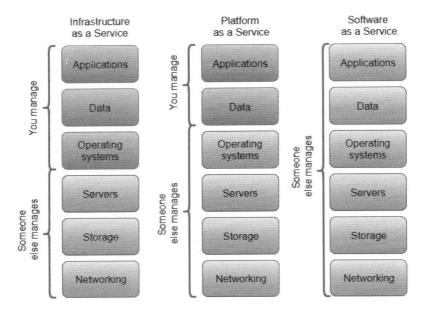

Figure 3.12 – What the different cloud system layers handle

Other advantages of cloud-based solutions

These are just some examples of the advantages we get from using cloud-based solutions. In a 2017 article, The *Business Journal* lists what they think are the five biggest benefits of cloud-based solutions. They are as follows:

- Boost cost efficiency
- Provide flexible pay options
- Promote collaboration
- Increase mobility
- Aid in disaster recovery

If you search the web for the benefits of moving to the cloud, you will find similar lists. Some will also add environmental advantages.

We should also consider that there are risks of using cloud-based solutions. The major one is the security and personal integrity issues that can be hard to handle when you don't have full control over where and how the data is stored.

Next, let's look at some other types of applications.

Other types of applications

Of course, we have several other categories that software can fall into. Let's look at some of them.

Systems software

The software in this category helps the user, applications, and computer hardware to interact and function together. These applications create an environment that other programs can work in. When a computer is powered on, the first thing that is loaded into the computer's memory is system software applications. They will mostly run in the background, even if some of them can have a visual user interface. Because these programs work directly with the computer's hardware, they are often referred to as **low-level software**.

The most well-known type of application we find in this category is operating systems. As we saw in *Chapter 1, Introduction to Computer Programs*, they let other software run and take care of the direct communication with the hardware.

The most well-known operating systems for desktop computers and laptops are as follows:

- Microsoft Windows
- macOS and macOS X (for Apple devices)
- Linux

For smartphones and tablets, we have the following operating systems:

- Android
- iOS (for Apple devices)
- Microsoft Windows Mobile

Programming software

In this category, we find the tools and applications used by programmers when they write and test software. First, we need the programs that are the actual language the programmers use. To be able to write a program in C++, Java, Python, or any other language, we must first install the software that will take care of the translation of the source code into machine code (see *Chapter 2, Introduction to Programming Languages*).

A programmer often uses specialized text editors that will assist them when writing code. Some programs are even more advanced and will provide not only an editor for writing the code but a range of other built-in tools that are useful to have access to when writing programs. These are called **Integrated Development Environments** (**IDEs**). An example of a built-in tool is a debugger, which is a program that will help the programmer to find errors in the code.

Serverless applications

A serverless application is a specialized variant of cloud-based applications. It can come in several different forms. Common to all these variants is that the cloud provider runs the servers needed, and dynamically manages all the resources the application needs. What this means is that we, for example, will not need to buy storage of a fixed size. The provider will add more storage as we need it, and we will pay for the storage we use. We can compare this to a scenario where if our hard disk is full, it just keeps increasing its storage capacity to meet our needs for more space.

This kind of software is interesting if you want to automate the maintenance of servers, storage, and other aspects of your infrastructure. These solutions are *intelligent*, so they can adapt to changes, for example, by giving us more storage when we need and reducing it again when the need drops.

Summary

In this chapter, we have talked about some typical types of applications and what makes them special.

We learned what a standalone application is and that this is the first type of application you will write when learning to program. After that, we looked at different types of applications that, in one way or the other, were divided to run parts of the program on different computers, and we saw that the parts communicate with each other.

We learned that a web application runs on a server but communicates with its users through web pages. We saw that mobile applications are special in that they can take advantage of the features of modern mobile devices including smartphones and tablets, such as the GPS and the camera.

Another category of applications is those that need lots of computing power and let many computers share the workload and perform parts of the computing. These are often referred to as distributed applications. Then we looked at a category that is growing fast, and that is cloud-based applications. The benefit of using these services is that it is usually much cheaper and more secure than if we manage everything ourselves.

Finally, we talked about a couple of other categories: system software, programming software, and serverless applications.

All software will need to be written by programmers and, in this chapter, we saw that applications can come in many forms. You have different resources available to suit your application development needs. As a developer, you can specialize in one or a couple of categories, or you can choose to jump between technologies. No matter what you choose, the challenges will be very different depending on what type of application you are currently developing.

In the next chapter, we will take a closer look at what a software project is and how we can structure our code as our projects get larger. We will also talk about some details that have to do with problems we might run into as our projects grow, and how we can resolve those issues.

4
Software Projects and How We Organize Our Code

When we write software and our program grows, we will need to organize our code so that it is easy to read when we need to maintain it. An application can be hundreds of thousands or millions of lines of code long, so having it all in a single file is impossible. We will need to divide the code into multiple files, but how will we do this? And even if we put the code into separate files, then we'll have lots of files, so we will need to organize them into folders. How can we do this so that the compiler or interpreter can find them? How will we know where to look when we need to edit a part of the application? In this chapter, we will discuss this and learn about some patterns that we can use.

The following topics will be covered in this chapter:

- Understanding code modules
- The concept of a code project
- Working with package managers to share code
- Delving into a namespace
- Using namespaces to avoid naming conflicts

Code modules

If programs are used, they are also updated, and if you are the developer of a program, this means that you will need to edit the source code in order to add features and fix errors. If your code is not well organized, it will be hard to read and maintain because you will need much more time to find where to insert your new code or where that nasty error might be.

One measure to make your code easier to handle is to distribute it into several logical blocks. But how do we decide what will go into such a block? There are no fixed rules for how this is done, but the language you use might give you some hints, depending on how it wants you to structure the code. In the end, it is up to you to make the final decision.

The code we write is logically connected, so to be able to do something, we often need to do a couple of other things first. It is as if you wake up in the morning and, while still in bed, you remember that there is nothing at home to make breakfast with, so first, you need to go shopping. But before you can do that, you need to do several other things, such as get out of bed and get dressed. These tasks are done to enable you to go shopping. In a way, you can say that these things are related and, by that logic, belong together. You could also see this differently and say that you want breakfast, but to be able to get it, you need to get out of bed, get dressed, go shopping, and finally prepare the breakfast.

In the same way, you will have sections of your code that logically belong together, where some things are done to enable you to do other things. We need to keep this in mind when deciding on how to split the code into some logical blocks.

There can be other reasons, other than readability, for having code separated from other parts of the program. You might have developed this smart thing that you want to reuse in other programs or even distribute it to others so they can also use it. To be able to do that, the code that defines this smart thing must be separate from the rest of the program. This means that it cannot be tightly entangled with other parts of the code. If it is, it will be hard to reuse this section of your program.

Let's look at an example. Imagine you are writing an application that goes online and gathers data from several different websites and then analyzes this data. This could be stock market values or temperature readings from several weather services. If we were to create this program, we would need to define the websites that our program will visit, go to each of them, download and store each page, and go through all the stored pages to extract the data we need.

Overall, we know what we need to do, and in what order we need to do things. We also know that the result will be that we have gathered the data we need so that we can start to analyze it. This is good, as we can think of these things as separate tasks that should be as independent of each other as possible. Why is it so important that they are independent? Let's explore the development process of this application further to understand this.

If we start with the first task, how do we define what websites to visit? Shall we ask the user of the application to provide us with the addresses by asking them to write them down in the user interface, or should we have them in a file that we can read from? Both work, but what we don't want to do is store the addresses in the actual code, even if it would be possible to do so. The reason for this is that we want to enable the users of our application to define what sites they visit. We can't ask them to change the code of the program, as we can't assume that all our users are programmers. However, we can give them a text file that they can edit and save, and we can then read this file to get their input. Another reason is that we want to be flexible. Today, reading the addresses might be the best option, but in the future, we might discover another way to get the addresses into our application. We don't want to hardwire a solution into our program, but instead make the program as independent as possible from the source that provides us with this data.

The next thing we will need to do is go to each of the sites that we defined in the previous step and download that page. Now, let's assume that we have written the code that can do this. We want to keep it independent of the previous step; that is, this part of the program should not care about how the addresses to the sites came into the application. It should be given an address that downloads that page and returns that page data. That is all. It does not know how the address to this page came and knows nothing about what happens to the page data when it completes its task. In that way, a part of the code can be reused in other projects, which might receive its addresses in other ways and do something completely different from the downloaded page.

For the remaining tasks, that is, storing the downloaded pages and processing the data within each page, we strive to do the same thing: construct them as independent parts of the code. The following diagram shows this concept:

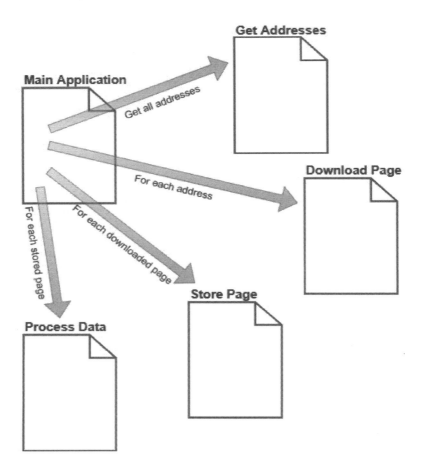

Figure 4.1 – An application that uses several independent blocks of code to fulfill its task

We can now say that we have independent code modules. The term *module* will have a slightly different meaning, depending on what language we are using. However, all of them will agree that it is a section of code that is independent, though how it is handled will differ. Some languages say that each module will go into a separate file, or multiple files if it is a large and more complex module. Others will have ways to define several modules within one single file. In some circumstances, the term module will hardly ever be used, even if the concept of independent sections of code exist.

One benefit of treating code as independent modules is, as we already stated, to be able to reuse the module in other applications. Another reason to do this is that it will be easier for us to change or replace a module. If our code sections are intertwined and depend heavily on each other, changing parts of the code will be harder as we need to make these changes at multiple locations throughout the code, and we need to make sure that we have found all occurrences where we need to make changes.

When we have broken up our code into these smaller modules, we need to put everything together into what will be our final application. To do this, we will need to store the modules in a project.

Working with software projects

The term *project* can be used in two different ways when talking about software development:

- A collaborative enterprise used to develop the actual program – in other words, as a group of people working together. For that, we need a project plan, a project leader, and so on.
- A container for all the files that make up the program we develop.

It is the latter meaning – a container for all the files that make up a program – that we will discuss here as the former is about project management and not software development.

When our code is broken up into well-defined modules – most likely in the form of several files – we need a way to let the compiler or interpreter find all the files so that they can be assembled into the executable machine code.

Creating the correct structure for the project is usually done by tools that programmers use to develop software. These tools come in many categories, but the most advanced form is called an **Integrated Development Environment** (**IDE**). The central part of an IDE is the editor that's used to write the code. It will also assist us with creating software projects. A programming language defines how a project shall be organized. This can, for example, be in a form where the different files shall be in relation to each other. Some languages will do this with the help of things called packages.

Working with packages to share code

In software developer culture, sharing code for free is very natural. This makes the industry unique as programmers share and use each other's code all the time. Using someone else's solutions to a problem is as natural as sharing my good ideas and code. It is usually wise to reuse the work of others as the code is often well developed, well tested, and well maintained. In software development, the term *open source* is well known. It means that someone has an idea for an application, writes the code for it, and then shares it online. Others are then encouraged to help with the development of this project. Several programmers will join in, and together they keep the project going. Everyone interested can then use this code free of charge.

The code that's developed in such a project is often in the form of one or several modules. If you want to use such a module, you must find it, and then you need to download it. The question is, how we can find it, download it, and make sure it is put in a location so that our application can find it?

Luckily, there is a solution to this: package managers.

Package managers

A package manager is a piece of software that will help us find, download, and install code. Most languages will have at least one package manager that can help us with this. It works by storing the code modules, now referred to as packages, in a central location. This central storage is called a repository, or just repo. This means that when you write a program, you can visit the package manager's website to search for any packages that might be useful in your project.

Here is a list of package managers for some popular languages:

Language	Package Manager	Repository
Java	Maven	`https://mvnrepository.com/`
Python	Pip	`https://pypi.org/`
Ruby	RubyGems	`https://rubygems.org/`
PHP	Composer	`https://packagist.org/`

Table 4.1

Let's look at the project example where we downloaded web pages. You decide that the coding part of downloading a page feels a bit too hard to write yourself, so instead, you search the package manager site for your language, find a package that does what you want, and then download a web page, when given an address.

You can now use the package manager application to download and install this package and then call the functionality in that package from your code.

Let's say we are using Python. Even if we know that we could go to the PyPI website, we might not be sure what to search for. Instead, we could do a Google search for something such as `Python download web page`, and we will find several suggestions for how to do it. We are likely to stumble upon several suggestions to use something called **requests**.

If we decide that we want to try the `requests` package and see if it is useful for us, we can go to the `pypi.org` website and search for requests. We will then see a page like this:

Figure 4.2 – The project page for requests at pypi.org

If we scroll down on this page, we will find installation instructions and even an example of how it can be used. There is also a link to the project website for this project where we can find documentation and more examples.

The installation instructions might look something like this:

```
pip install requests
```

Here, `pip` is the package manager. When installing the Python programming language, the package manager, `pip`, will also be installed. We can open a Command Prompt (if we are using Windows) or a Terminal window (if we are using Mac or Linux) and run this command.

The package manager will then go to its central repository online and download the package that was asked for, which is `requests` in our case. If this package is using other packages, we don't need to download them ourselves. The package manager will take care of this, and everything we need to be able to use this package will be downloaded and installed.

Now that we can download the package, we will soon be dealing with another problem. We must make sure that, when naming things in our code, all the names are unique. If not, the program will not run. This can be tricky, especially when using packages that others have written. How do we know that the names we're using are not already being used? The solution is in namespaces.

Avoiding conflicts using namespaces

When writing code, you will constantly name things. The problem is, what if you give something a name that is already being used? We now know that the code for an application can consist of thousands of lines of code divided into hundreds of files. How can you make sure that the names you give something are not already taken? We also learned that we can install packages with code that others have written. How can we make sure that they have not given their packages names that we have already used? Or how can we make sure that a package we install is not using names that another package we already installed is using?

As you can see, handling names can be tricky. Let's look at an example. In *Chapter 8, Understanding Functions*, we will discuss what a function is and how it works. For this example, all we need to know about functions is that they have a name and consist of several lines of code. We use the function name to call it, which will make the code inside it run.

In this example, we are constructing a calculator app. First, let's have a look at what the application might look like:

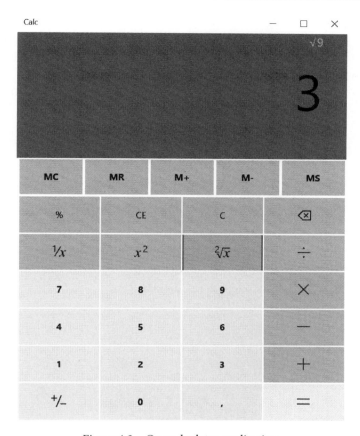

Figure 4.3 – Our calculator application

When the user clicks on the square root button, $(\sqrt[2]{x})$, we have to calculate the square root of the number currently in the display. This means that we need to connect some code with the event that occurs when this button is clicked. This code needs to perform the following steps:

1. It needs to get the value currently in the display.
2. Then, it needs to calculate the square root of that value.
3. Finally, it needs to put the result in the display of the calculator.

These instructions will be carried out when the square root button is pressed, and we stick them in a function. Now, this function needs a name. The name *squareroot* is rather long, so you might decide to shorten it to *sqrt*.

When you reach the point where you want to calculate the square root, you will most likely use a built-in function that will help us with this. Most languages will have such a function, and often, its name will be `sqrt`. This is a problem, as we gave our function the same name as a function that comes shipped with the language. We could, of course, rename our function to something else. Don't despair – namespaces will solve this problem for us.

Delving into namespaces

To understand what a namespace is, we can think of files and folders on our computer. Assume that you are going to have two parties soon: one summer party and a birthday party. You write two invitations to the parties and try to store them in a folder on your computer.

You have named both files `Party Invitation`, but you can't have two files with the same name in the same folder:

Figure 4.4 – Two files in the same folder can't have the same name

Instead of renaming one file, you can create two folders and store the files in one folder each. This way, the files can still have the name `Party Invitation`, and there is no longer a conflict between the names as they are in separate folders, as shown in the following diagram:

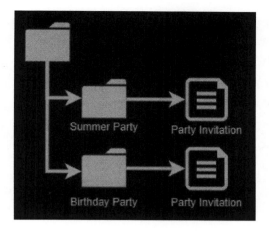

Figure 4.5 – Storing files in separate folders to avoid naming conflicts

To summarize this, on a computer, we can have multiple files with the same name, but within a folder, the filenames must be unique.

Many programming languages use a similar technique, called namespaces. Namespaces let us reuse the same name multiple times within an application, but in a namespace, all the names must be unique. The namespace acts like the folders on the computer, and the things we are naming are like the files.

How namespaces are implemented will differ between languages. Let's examine how some of the more popular languages have implemented them.

Namespaces in JavaScript

In JavaScript, when we define things such as functions, we can create a namespace by surrounding the part we want to belong to the namespace with curly brackets, { }.

If we represent our `sqrt` function in a namespace called `myCalc`, it will look something like this:

```
var myCalc = {
    sqrt: function() {
    }
}
```

On the first line, we define a namespace called `myCalc`. We use an open bracket to indicate the beginning of the namespace; the closing bracket on the last line marks the end of the namespace.

Within the brackets, we find a function named sqrt. The function also uses open and close brackets to indicate where it starts and ends. In this example, the function is empty, so there is nothing there.

We can now access both our own function and the built-in function, even if both are named sqrt. It could look something like this:

```
myCalc.sqrt();
Math.sqrt(9);
```

The first line calls the sqrt function within the myCalc namespace. The second line calls the built-in sqrt function. It is in a namespace called Math. That function will accept a value (the value we want to take the square root of), and here, we pass the value 9.

Namespaces in Python

In Python, namespaces are defined by individual modules. A module in Python is a file, so everything in a file (that is, a Python module) is in the same namespace.

We can now create a file called myCalc.py. The .py extension indicates that this file contains Python code. It is in this file where we add our sqrt function:

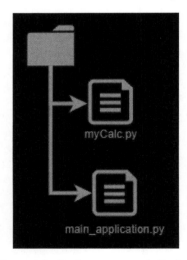

Figure 4.6 – Project structure in Python

Look at the preceding diagram. The `main_application.py` file is our main program that uses the code inside `myCalc.py`.

Inside the `main_application.py` file, we can now access both the built-in `sqrt` function and the `sqrt` function we created, as follows:

```
import math
import myCalc
myCalc.sqrt()
math.sqrt(9)
```

From the preceding code, we can see the following:

1. In the first line, we say that we want to be able to use things from the `math` module. Remember that Python uses the concept that a module is a namespace, so `math` is both a module and a namespace.

2. The second line does the same for our `myCalc` module, which contains our `sqrt` function.

3. On line three, we call the `sqrt` function in the `myCalc` module.

4. On the last line, we call the `sqrt` function in the `math` module and pass 9 to it.

Namespaces in C++

In C++, we have a keyword. A *keyword* is a word that is reserved by the language and has a special meaning. Refer to *Chapter 2, Introduction to Programming Languages*, for a more thorough explanation of keywords. Here, we have a keyword called `namespace` that we can use to define a namespace. It could look something like this:

```
namespace myCalc{
    void sqrt() {
    }
}
```

Here, we first create a namespace called `myCalc`, containing a function called `sqrt`. Note that just as in the JavaScript example, the function has an opening and a closing bracket, indicating the start and the end of the function, and just as in that example, the function is empty.

C++ then uses a special syntax to access something within a namespace. First, we state what namespace we want to use, followed by two colons, : :, and then what it is within this namespace we want to use. This can look like this:

```
myCalc::sqrt();
std::sqrt(9);
```

The first line calls the sqrt function in the namespace we defined previously.

The second line calls the sqrt function in the standard namespace, called std in C++, passing the value c to it.

Namespaces in other languages

These were just a few examples of how namespaces are used in some languages. Other languages have their own variants of this. For example, in Java, namespaces are closely connected to how packages are used. In C#, namespaces are implemented almost in the same way as they are in C++, but not accessed with a double colon. Instead, they are accessed with a dot, ..

Now that we know a little bit about namespaces, let's return to our calculator application.

Using namespaces in our calculator application

We are at the point where we want to name a sqrt function, and we have realized that the language we use also has a function called sqrt. This built-in sqrt function will calculate the square root for any number we pass to it. We don't want to rename our function; instead, we want to solve the naming conflict with the use of namespaces.

The first thing we need to do is understand how namespaces are used in the current language. As we saw previously, the way we define and use namespaces will differ between languages.

By adding our sqrt function inside its namespace, we don't need to worry about a naming conflict with the built-in sqrt function or any other function that we might get when importing packages using a package manager. Everything is defined within different namespaces and we will need to state in what namespace the function we want is located.

We already know what our sqrt function needs to do: get the value from the display, calculate the square root of that value, and then put the resulting value back into the display.

We will add our sqrt function to a namespace to avoid a naming conflict with the built-in version. We also want to use the built-in sqrt function from within our function. We can do that by specifying what namespace the built-in sqrt resides in.

Summary

In this chapter, the focus has been on organizing our code and how to name things so that we can avoid naming conflicts.

A book is divided into chapters to make it easier to read and navigate. In the same way, we want our code to be easy to read and understand. We don't have the concept of chapters in programming, but we do have modules. A module is a part of our application where the code is logically related; that is, one way or the other, it works with the code. A module is often defined as a separate code file.

In larger projects, we can end up with a large number of modules. Due to this, we need a way to organize them so that the compiler or interpreter can locate the correct file when all the pieces needs to be put together. We do this with the help of a project. We can see the project as a form of container for all our modules, but also for other resources that our application might use, such as images, configuration files, and so on.

Writing programs is about being efficient and focusing our time and attention on what is important to make the program do what it is intended to do. We will often face situations where we need to solve a problem that we know others have solved before us. It is therefore not considered a bad thing to reuse the work of others in our application. The software programming community/industry is very open and helpful, and programmers share and reuse code from others all the time. By doing this, we can focus our efforts on what makes our application unique and not spend time reinventing the wheel again and again.

One way we can make use of code that others have written is by using tools that often come shipped with the language, called package managers. These tools will store code that we can reuse in a central location online. They will also help us find what we need and download install, and configure it for us.

However, as our applications grow and we use code that's been written by others, we will need a way to avoid naming conflicts. If I use a name for something that has already been used elsewhere in my application, the language must have a way to distinguish between the two. This is done with something called namespaces. A name that we give something must only be unique within a namespace. If we divide our applications into several namespaces, we will reduce the risk of name clashes dramatically.

Now, we are finally ready to dig into the process of writing programs. In the next chapter, we will look at the most fundamental building blocks of any program in terms of sequences.

Section 2: Constructs of a Programming Language

In this section, we will look at all the key things that any mainstream programming language consists of, including coverage of how they work and when to use them.

This section has the following chapters:

- *Chapter 5, Sequence – The Basic Building Block of a Computer Program*
- *Chapter 6, Working with Data – Variables*
- *Chapter 7, Program Control Structures*
- *Chapter 8, Understanding Functions*
- *Chapter 9, When Things Go Wrong – Bugs and Exceptions*
- *Chapter 10, Programming Paradigms*
- *Chapter 11, Programming Tools and Methodologies*

5

Sequence – The Basic Building Block of a Computer Program

When it comes to programming, the most fundamental concept is the sequence. It indicates what we do and when we do it, one after another. However, when we take a closer look, we find that there is more to this, and, in this chapter, we will learn what it is.

We will also use the concept of a sequence to decide what steps a program will need to perform to accomplish its overall task. Since it can be tough to have both an overview of everything that needs to be done and, at the same time, look at all the details, we will require a concept that can assist us. Thinking of the sequence in which the program needs to do things in, for instance, could be such a tool.

When learning how to program, one problem many people face is how to transform an idea to go. Where should you start? In this chapter, we will learn that we can use the concept of sequential thinking to break down an idea into smaller tasks that we then can deal with. We will also see that we can apply the same concept to the code that we write to ensure that we do things in the right order.

In this chapter, you will look at the following topics:

- Understanding the importance of sequences
- What a statement is and how it is defined
- How different statements are separated
- How to format the code to make it more readable
- Different kinds of comments and ways to document our code

The importance of sequences

One day, when you come home, you start craving a pie, so you decide to make one. The reason you will bake a pie is not that you wish to cook, but to satisfy your desire for pie. However, to be able to get the pie, you need to perform several steps. First, you need a recipe, and then you need to get all of the ingredients. When you acquire them, you will follow each step in the recipe. Then, finally, after the pie has been in the oven and cooled down a bit, you can enjoy your well-deserved treat.

You just performed a few tasks in sequence. Some of them need to be completed in the right order, while others can be done in any order (or, at least, in a more relaxed order). You must turn on the oven before you can bake the pie, but it is not essential that you bring out the flour before the butter.

Programming is like baking a pie. We will have goals, such as we want pie, and to be able to achieve that goal, we will need to do several things: in some instances, the order is essential, while others are less dependent on the order.

Programming is all about problem-solving and the art of breaking things down into smaller steps. This will be done in iterations where you first have an overall solution and then break this solution down into smaller and smaller steps until you are on a level where you understand each step that needs to be taken.

This is one of the more difficult skills to master when you begin to learn programming. As with all new skills, it takes lots of practice before you will feel comfortable doing this. Some tricks can make it easier for you to acquire this skill. The essential ability you require is an overview of the full problem that you are trying to solve and, at the same time, a focus on details of one or more subproblems that need to be resolved. This means that you will need to zoom in and out on the details while keeping an overall view of the whole problem. You can practice this without doing any programming. Playing logical puzzle games such as Sudoku will train your brain to keep an eye on the overall game and, at the same time, focus on individual parts of the game such as what numbers can go into a certain cell.

Let's take a look at how we can go from a problem to a solution on a sequential level. First, we need to define the problem.

Defining the problem

You often arrive home after dark, and you always forget to turn on the outdoor lighting before you leave home. It is so dark that you are afraid of stumbling on your way to the door, and finding the keyhole is always a gamble.

On the other hand, you don't want the light to be on all day. You don't like the idea of those automatic lights that react to motion either, as it will be activated when the neighbor's cat passes by. There must be a better solution.

The solution to the problem

One solution would be if you could use your smartphone's GPS. If you had a program running on it that continually monitors your position, then when you come into a given radius from your home, it could somehow activate the lights. You soon realize that your solution will need to be a two-part application. One part runs on your phone, and the other part runs on a computer in your home. The program running on a computer in your house would get a signal from your mobile app that you now are close to home. It could then check with an online service to see what time the sun sets at your home's location during this time of year. If it is past sunset, the program can activate the lights.

What we have done so far is to start to define a solution. Now we must break down this solution further.

Solution breakdown

We now have an overview of what we want, and, at the same time, we have zoomed in on a couple of details. We have decided that we would like to use the phone's GPS. We don't know how this can be done yet, but that is not important at this stage. We know that other applications can use GPS. This means that we know it is possible to do it and even if we, at the moment, have no idea how this is done, we can learn it later on in the process. We have also decided that this will be a two-part application. The part on the phone will, aside from monitoring the GPS, also need a way to contact the other part of our solution, which is the application running on a computer in your home. Again, we don't know how this will be done, but we know it can be done, and that is good enough for now. We also understand that we need a way to detect that we are coming from outside the defined range and then entering it. It is only then that the lights should be turned on. If we don't do this, the lights would always be on when the phone is within a stipulated range and we don't want that.

The home application will need to wait for a signal from the mobile app and then contact a service that can tell us about the time the sun will set. On our to-do list, we add that we need to find such a service. Again, we don't need to bother about how this can be done. We will also find a way for our home application to control the lights. We will most likely require some hardware for this step, but that will be a problem that we can deal with later.

What we now have is a sequential list of steps that we need to take. That list looks something like this.

Here is a list of steps for the mobile application:

- Is the phone within the predefined range?

- If yes, was it previously outside the range, that is, have we just entered this range? Let us check:

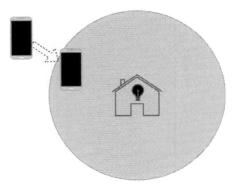

Figure 5.1: The phone enters the predefined region

- If yes, send a signal to the home application:

Figure 5.2: The phone application contacts the application running on the home computer

Here is a list of steps for the home application:

1. Wait for a signal from the mobile app.

2. When a signal is received, check the current time:

Figure 5.3: The application that is running on the home computer checks the local time

3. Check the online service for the local sunset time:

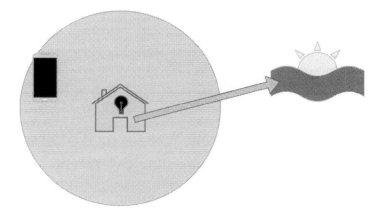

Figure 5.4: The application that is running on the home computer contacts
an online service to get the local sunset time

4.   If the time is after sunset, turn on lights:

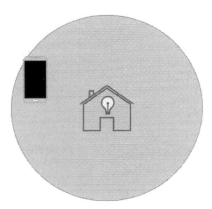

Figure 5.5: If the time is after sunset, the home application turns on the light

This is still a slightly rough breakdown of the sequential steps that we need to take. But now that we have them, we can zoom in on each of them and think about the things we need to do for each of the preceding steps.

A detailed breakdown for the phone application

Let's take each of the steps, one by one, and closely examine what we need to do for each of them.

So, how can we know whether the phone is within the predefined range? To understand this, we must first do some research. The first thing we need to understand is how the phone GPS knows where it is. Searching online will soon reveal that a GPS works with two coordinates: longitude and latitude. These two coordinates will pinpoint any location on the earth. This means that when we request the current location from the GPS, we will be given these coordinates.

When we have these coordinates, we need to check how far away we are from home. To do this, we will need to know where home is, so the application on the phone needs to store this location somehow, and it will also be in the form of a longitude and a latitude.

Calculating the distance between two geocoordinates is not a trivial task, but we don't need to worry as this is something that has been done many times before. In addition to this, no matter what language we are using, a simple Google search will give us many solutions for how this can be done. We might even be able to use the language package manager (refer to the *Package managers* section in *Chapter 4, Software Projects and How We Organize Our Code*, to learn what a packet manager is and how it works) to find a package that can do this calculation.

No matter what solution we use, we can assume that we will use the two coordinate pairs that we have, the phone's location, and our home location, and what we get back is a distance between them. We also need to decide how close to home we need to be for the lights to activate. This can be any distance.

Next, we have to check whether we have come from outside the predefined range. We need a way to tell whether we have entered the predefined range or whether we already were within the range. We could do this by keeping track of what the distance to home was before we check the current position. If we were outside the range and are now inside it, then we know that we are close enough to home to send the signal to turn on the lights.

So, now we need to send a signal to the home application. When we have entered the range, we need a way for the phone application to contact the home computer. This can be done in several ways, and there is no need for us to decide what technique to use at this point.

We can now summarize the sequence for the phone application.

Phone application sequence

Now we have the logic for the phone application in place. We also know what the sequence will need to look like. It will look something like this:

1. Get the current position.

2. Calculate the distance from home.

3. Is the distance within the range that defines when we are close enough to turn on the lights?

4. Was our previous distance, that is, the distance of the last time we checked our position, outside the given range?

5. If the answer to the questions in *step 3* and *step 4* are both yes, tell the home computer to turn on the light. If it is no, we can go back to *step 1*.

6. Store the distance from home as our old distance.

7. Start over from *step 1*.

These steps are illustrated here:

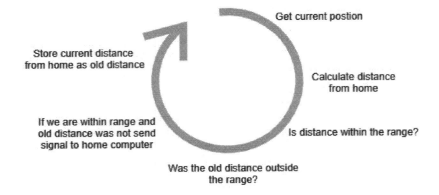

Figure 5.6: Sequence for the phone application

These seven steps will be repeated over and over. We will need to consider what will happen when we perform the first iteration as we will not have a value for the old distance. We can give this an initial default value that is well outside the range, for example, a negative number.

We now have a well-defined sequence of steps, and we have not written a line of code yet. This is good because it will help us when we start to write the code as we can zoom in and focus on each of these steps without losing track of the overview.

We can now turn our attention to the home application.

A detailed breakdown of the home application

At first, the home application will have absolutely nothing to do as it will just sit and wait for a signal from the phone app. However, when it gets that signal, it will wake up and start to do its work.

When the home application gets the message from the phone, the first thing it needs to do is one of two things. Either it can check the local time, or it can contact the sunset service to get the current sunset time. The order of these two operations is not essential as we need both, so we can compare them.

When we have the local time and the sunset time, we need to compare them to see whether it is after dark. If it is, all the conditions for turning on the light are met, and we get a signal that the phone is within range and that it is dark outside.

Now we need to turn on the outside light. We still need to figure out how this can be done. One way to do this is to use LED lamps that can be controlled wirelessly. These can often be interacted with from an application such as the one we are about to create. We should do some research before buying the lights since we need to select a brand that can be controlled by our application.

Home application sequence

The sequence for the home application is as follows:

1. Wait for a signal from the phone app.

2. When the signal is received, get the local time.

3. Contact the sunset service to get the local sunset time.

4. Compare the current time with the sunset time.

5. If it is after sunset, turn on the light.

6. Go back to step 1.

Step 2 and step 3 can be performed in any order. If the current time is before the sunset time, the application will skip turning on the light and go back to step 1. The sequence is depicted here:

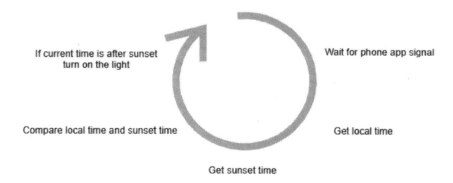

Figure 5.7: Sequence for the home application

We now have an excellent starting point regarding how to build this application. Even if several things are still unclear to us, such as how the phone application shall contact the home application, what service the home application will use to check the sunset time and how it will get in touch with it, and how the home application will turn on the light, the sequence that the different things must be performed in, is now clear to us.

At this point, we have a good idea of what our application needs to do, but we still have a number of things we need to do. First of all, we need to learn the necessary things to create this application. How can we get the position from the phone GPS? When learning things like this, it is usually a good idea to create a *toy project* where you can just try to get the coordinates and print them to the screen. When you have figured that out, you can then take this solution into your real project. Doing it in a separate project is smart because you can focus on learning one particular thing at a time. Another example is that we need to implement a way to calculate the distance between two geocoordinates. Apply the same principle of doing it in a separate application when testing different solutions. When you get a result, you should find an online service that does this calculation so that you can verify your results. In programming, you never stop learning new things and technologies. There are always things you have never done before. But don't let that stop you.

This is one aspect of sequencing in a computer program. Another point is what happens on a smaller level. In the code that we write, every step we perform needs to be broken down into something known as a *statement*, and those statements will be performed in sequence.

Understanding statements

In many programming languages, the sequence of code that we write is made up of what are called statements. A statement expresses some action to be carried out and is made up of several internal components. These are called expressions.

Expressions

Statements are made up of expressions, and expressions are made up of even smaller parts. Let's refer to an example:

```
5 + 4
```

This is an expression made up of three parts. Here, we are operating using the addition operator, +. On both sides of the operator, we have the operands in the form of two constant values, 5 and 4.

A statement can be made up of more than one expression. Take a look at the following code:

```
result = 5 + 4
```

Here, we have the same expression as we had earlier, 5 + 4, but now with a new expression to the left:

result = 5 + 4

Figure 5.8: A statement with two expressions, one addition and one assignment

Again, we have two operands, the result of the addition, 9, to the right, and to the left, we have something called a *variable*, named `result`. A variable is a way for us to store data in memory using a name we define:

result = 9

Figure 5.9: When the result of the addition is calculated the assignment expression can be performed

We will talk more about variables in *Chapter 6, Working with Data – Variables*. We also introduced a second operator, =. This operator is called the assignment operator. It takes what is on the right and stores it in what is on the left:

Figure 5.10: The variable called result can be visualized as a box;
the assignment stores a value in that box

To be able to complete this statement, the expressions must be dealt with in the correct order. This is called the order of operations.

Order of operations

To store the result of the addition in the variable called `result`, we must first perform the expression to the right; that is the addition, as follows:

```
result = 5 + 4
         9
```

When the expression to the right is completed, we can imagine that our statement will look like this:

```
result = 9
```

Now, this final expression can be executed. The value of 9 is assigned (it is stored) in the `result` variable.

A statement can be made up of more expressions. Consider the following:

```
result = 5 + 4 * 2
```

The first thing we must understand here is the order of operations, that is, in which order the addition and the multiplication is performed. If we do the addition first, we will do 5 + 4, which is 9, and then 9 times 2, which is 18.

If we instead do the multiplication first, we would get 4 times 2, which is 8, and then 5 + 8, which is 13. So, the order is important. Every programming language has a well-defined order of operations, which is in what different order the operations must be performed.

In this example, the order will be the same as in mathematics; multiplication will be performed before addition:

```
result = 5 + 4 * 2
                8
result = 5 + 8
            13
result = 13
```

If we want to override the built-in order of operations, we can use parentheses like this:

```
result = (5 + 4) * 2
```

Now the addition is performed first because it is within parentheses, so the variable result will now store the value of 18 (9 times 2).

Some statements are made up of more than one single line. These are often called compound statements. Let's explore what those are next.

Compound statements

A compound statement is a statement that spans several lines. These compound statements are made up of one or more *normal* one-line statements. They can also consist of other compound statements, as we will learn later on. For example, in our application that turns on the light, we have some conditions that must be met before we do something. One condition is that we only turn on the light if the current time is after sunset. The logic can be visualized in a flowchart:

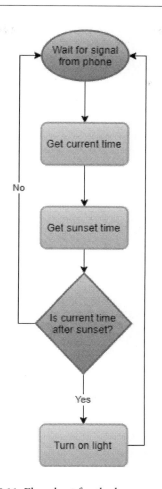

Figure 5.11. Flowchart for the home application

As you can see, the part where we turn on the light is only executed if it is after sunset. So, for that statement to be performed, we have a condition that must be met. That condition is a statement, but that statement includes the statement that turns on the light.

In code, it can look something like this:

```
wait_for_phone_signal()
current_time = get_current_time()
sunset_time = get_sunset_time()
if current_time > sunset_time then
    turn_on_light()
end_if
```

The first line of the preceding code contains one single statement. It is a function call. We will discuss functions in more detail in *Chapter 8, Understanding Functions*. We can see that it is a function because it ends with parentheses. For now, we can regard these parentheses as an indication that something is a function. Calling a function means that, somewhere, there are several lines of code that have been given a name. Calling the function means that we will jump to that location and execute those lines. In this example, the content of the function is not visible. This function will halt the program until a signal comes in from the phone.

The statement on the second line is made up of one operation, with one operator and two operands. We recognize the equals sign as the assignment operator. That means that whatever is to the right will be assigned (remember that we can see an assignment because the thing to the right will be stored in the item to the left) to what's on the left-hand side. To the left, we have a variable that can contain a value. It has the name `current_time`. What we have to the right is another function call. This function will grab the current time and return it. When this statement has been executed, the present time will be stored in the `current_time` variable.

Line 3 is like line 2. This statement is also made up of one operator and two operands. The operand on the right is again a function call. This is the function that will contact the sunset service online and return the sunset time for our location. To the left, we have a `sunset_time` variable and we assign the time we get back from the function to this variable. When this statement has been executed, we have the sunset time stored in the `sunset_time` variable.

Line 4 starts with an `if`. This is a special kind of statement, spanning over several lines. This one covers lines 4 to 6. It contains another statement, the one on line 5. Line 4 is a condition. It checks whether the value in the `current_time` variable is greater than the value in the `sunset_time` variable. This can either be true or false. If it is greater, that is, the statement is true, then the code inside this compound statement is executed. If it is false, the value in `current_time` is not greater than the value in `sunset_time`; the code inside the statement will not be executed. In this case, the end of the compound statement is the last line: `end_if`. It indicates that everything between the line starting with `if` and the `end_if` line is a part of that statement. It should be noted that there is a flaw in the logic as this condition will not work if the current time is after midnight, but let's ignore that for now.

The statement on line 5 that turns on the light is yet again a call to a function. Also, note that this line starts with some spaces. This is called an indentation and is something we will discuss in more detail later in this chapter.

We now know that statements are made up of expressions or other statements. To be able to figure out where a statement ends and another begins, a language will define how they are separated. How this is done will be a part of the language syntax. Let's explore how we can do that next.

Separating statements

A programming language will separate statements by defining where a statement ends. If the language can figure out where one statement ends, it also knows that what comes after it must be the beginning of another statement.

Languages have different ways to define this. If we compare how different languages terminate statements, we will see that we have three main ways for it to be done. Many languages will terminate a statement by inserting a new line. This means that, in general, every line is a single statement if it is not a compound statement, as it will need to be handled uniquely.

Another popular way to terminate statements is by using a semicolon, ; . For languages that use this technique, we can have several statements on a single line. The language knows that a statement ends as soon as it sees a semicolon.

A third variant is to use a period, . , instead of a semicolon. Apart from that, it works the same way as when a semicolon is used so that we can have more than one statement on a single line.

A few languages will use other techniques, such as using a colon instead of a semicolon.

Some languages that terminate statements with a new line include the following:

- BASIC
- Fortran
- Python
- Ruby
- Visual Basic

Some languages that end statements with a semicolon include the following:

- C
- C++
- C#
- Go (even if the compiler automatically inserts them)

- Java
- JavaScript
- Kotlin
- Pascal
- PHP
- Rust

Some languages that use other symbols to terminate statements include the following:

- ABAP (period)
- COBOL (whitespace, such as a space, tab, or newline; sometimes, a period)
- Erlang (period, comma, and semicolon)
- Lua (whitespace such as a space, tab, or newline)
- Prolog (comma, semicolon, and period)

For compound statements, we will need a way to define where they begin and where they end. As a compound statement is made up of one or more statements, many languages will use another method to terminate them.

Here, we will find three main techniques that languages use. One is to use curly brackets, { }, to indicate where a compound statement begins and ends. Everything that is placed between the brackets is considered to be part of the compound statement.

In such a language, the compound if statement that we saw in the preceding code should look like this:

```
if current_time > sunset_time {
    turn_on_light()
}
```

As you can see, there is an open bracket at the end of the first line and a closing bracket on the last line.

Examples of languages that use this technique include the following:

- C
- C++
- C#

- Go
- Java
- JavaScript
- PHP

Another way to do this is to use end statements. Different languages will have slight variations on this.

Here are some examples.

In the Ada programming language, an `if` statement looks like this:

```
if current_time > sunset_time then
    turn_on_light();
end if
```

The same statement in Modula-2 is just slightly different:

```
IF current_time > sunset_time THEN
    turn_on_light();
END;
```

Ruby has another variant that is along the same lines:

```
if current_time > sunset_time
    turn_on_light()
end
```

The last variant is the language that will use indentation to accomplish the same thing. Remember that indentation is when we use a space to push in the code.

If you look at all of the preceding examples, the line containing `turn_on_light` is always indented. In those languages, it is only because it makes the code easier to read for us as humans. However, some languages will use this to define where a compound statement begins and ends.

One such language is Python. The code example for Python should look something like this:

```
if current_time > sunset_time:
    turn_on_light()
```

Here, everything that is indented is part of the compound statement. To indicate that something that comes afterward is not part of the statement, it would be written on the same level as the `if` statement, like so:

```
if current_time > sunset_time:
    turn_on_light()
result = 4 + 5
```

Here, the last line is not part of the compound statement as it is written without any indentation.

As mentioned, an indentation can be used to make the code easier to read, while some languages will use it for compound statement termination. Let's go on to discuss why the readability of code is important and how we can use indentation and blank lines to improve it.

Making the code readable by indenting and using empty lines

Ever since we moved away from machine code, the motivation has been that we want code that is easier to read and write for humans. We shall keep this in mind when we are writing code, as code does not just consist of instructions to the computer, but also something that needs to be maintained by either us or others.

As we have learned, one tool that we can use to make the intentions of the code clearer to whoever reads it is indentation.

The indentation technique

Indentation is a technique that we use to show that certain code lines belong together in a block. This is typically done for compound statements. Since a compound statement can be constructed of other statements or other compound statements, indentation becomes essential to be able to see what code block a statement belongs to:

Figure 5.12: Indented code will be a visual aid that indicates how compound statements are constructed

Even if the lines in the preceding diagram are just lines, we could make out the individual components they represent. If we color them, as in *figure 5.13*, we can see that this page is made up of four statements. The first line is a single statement, but then we have the green lines: these are compound statements, starting at line 2. Again, the purple lines are compound statements and, in the end, we have a single line that makes up a one-line statement.

The dashed lines represent compound statements and are made up of single-line statements and a compound statement, as indicated by the indentation. It is the same thing with the dotted lines:

Figure 5.13: The dashed lines are a compound statement containing another compound statement; the same is true for the dotted lines

As you can see, the indentation will carry lots of information to the reader if we know how to interpret it. It is, therefore, crucial that we are careful to get the indentation right when writing our code. In most languages, this information is only interesting to human readers. The compiler or interpreter will ignore the indentation. But some languages, such as Python, use indentation as their tool to define compound statements, making the indentation mandatory and a part of the language's syntax.

Commonly, the text editor that a programmer uses to write the code will help with code indentation, either by automatically indenting code within a compound statement or by providing built-in commands that, when executed, will adequately format the code.

There is another formatting trick that we can use to make our code more readable to humans. One such trick is the use of blank lines.

Blank lines

Blank lines separate the paragraphs in this book. The reason is apparent. Without them, the text would be hard to read. These empty lines are not inserted at random. The text within a paragraph is logically connected. We can indicate that the text changes focus by creating a new paragraph, which is by inserting a blank line in the text.

The same thing applies to code. Blank lines are inserted for human readers. It is used to show the intent the programmer has. If three statements are somehow connected logically, we can indicate this by adding a blank line after the last statement.

The following is some Python code. It is not important to know what this code does, but look at the use of indentation and blank lines:

```python
for n in range(1000,3001):
    str_num = str(n)
    split_str = list(str_num)

    all_even = True
    for x in split_str:
        if int(x) % 2 != 0:
            all_even = False

    if all_even:
        print(n, ",", end = "")
```

Here, we can see that all the code is within one single compound statement as all lines, except the first, are indented. Further down, we can see other compound statements. Every time the indentation level increases, a new compound statement begins, and when it decreases, one ends.

There are also some blank lines. This indicates that there is a logical connection between the lines preceding the empty line.

Let's take a look at lines 2 and 3 and how they are connected. In line 2, we are preparing some data so that it will be in the right form for what we want to do on line 3. Here, we can see the importance of the sequence. Line 3 will require a number in a particular format. So, line 2 prepares the number so that it can be used on line 3.

When these two lines are completed, the program changes its focus slightly. Even if we don't understand anything about what the code does, the information carried by the indentation and the blank lines will give us clues that will make it easier to read the code.

Blanks lines are also something that compilers and interpreters will ignore, so they are there for us humans. Just as it is vital to use paragraphs in a line of text correctly, we must use blank lines in a way that makes sense and assist the reader of our code.

There is another tool that we also can use to make things easier to understand for a human reading our code, and that is comments.

Making the code understandable using comments

Indentation and blank lines are not always enough to make the intent of the code clear. In such cases, we can use comments. A comment is a line of normal text, inserted in the code, which is only for humans. We use them to explain lines of code that are not obviously understood at first glance.

As the compiler or interpreter ignores comments, we need a way to indicate that something is a comment. We have two variants of comments; one that runs to the end of the line, called a *line comment*, and one that spans multiple lines, often referred to as a *block comment*. Let's understand each in turn, in the following sections.

Line comments

A line comment has some symbols indicating the beginning of the comment, and it continues for the rest of that line. These can be inserted on a separate line or at the end of a line with code that will execute.

As a part of the language syntax, the symbol used to indicate the beginning of these comments is defined. Some are common, even if some languages will use more obscure variants.

The most common symbol used by many languages is a double slash, //, which is two slashes without any space between them. Even if this symbol is made up of two characters, it is treated as a single symbol.

The languages that use this method for line comments include the following:

- C
- C++
- C#
- Go
- Java
- JavaScript
- Kotlin
- PHP

Another common symbol used by a number of languages is the hash symbol, #. Despite being a different symbol, it is handled in the same way as the double slash.

The hash symbol is used for line comments by languages such as the following:

- Perl
- Python
- Ruby

Some languages have other ways to indicate a comment. In BASIC, the abbreviation **REM** (short for **Remark**) is used. Several BASIC versions have a variant as an option to REM and that is a single apostrophe, ' .

The **A Programming Language (APL)** language is known for its use of odd symbols, and it uses a symbol that looks like this: ⍝.

Ada and Lua are two languages that use double hyphens, - -, to indicate a line comment.

Haskell also uses this. Haskell also has another unique way to handle comments, called **Bird Style**. If used, all lines with code begin with a greater than character, >. All other lines are considered to be comments.

Pascal, and languages closely related to Pascal, such as Modula-2, use (* to indicate the beginning of a comment and *) to mark the end.

Languages that are related to Lisp, such as Common Lisp and Clojure, use a semicolon, ; , to indicate line comments.

Using line comments can look like this:

```
result = 4 + 5 //Adds 4 and 5 and stores the sum
```

The first part is the normal code that will be executed, but as soon as the compiler or interpreter sees the comment symbol, //, it will ignore the rest of this line.

The same code in a language that uses the hash symbol for comments will look like this:

```
result = 4 + 5 # Adds 4 and 5 and stores the sum
```

These comments can also be on a separate line like this:

```
// Adds 4 and 5 and stores the sum
result = 4 + 5
```

Alternatively, the comments can also appear like this:

```
# Adds 4 and 5 and stores the sum
result = 4 + 5
```

This separation will depend on the language.

Sometimes, we want a comment to span multiple lines. Instead of having a line comment symbol at the start of every line in the comment, we can use block comments.

Block comments

Block comments have one symbol that indicates the beginning of the comment and another symbol that marks the end.

Languages that use the double slash symbol for line comments will often use /* to indicate the beginning of a block comment and */ to indicate the end. Languages that use these symbols include the following, among others:

- C
- C++
- C#
- Go
- Java
- JavaScript
- PHP

Perl uses =begin to indicate the start of a block comment and =cut to mark the end.

Ruby has a similar concept, with =begin and =end marking the beginning and end, respectively.

Python does not have a block comment but, instead, something called a **docstring** can be used as a block comment. Docstrings both start and end with three single or three double quotes: ''' or """. They end with the same three characters that were used at the beginning. So, use three single quotes to end the comment if you used single quotes at the beginning; otherwise, use three double quotes.

In code, a block comment can look something like this if we use /* and */:

```
/* Program that receives a signal
   from a mobile phone, checks the local time,
   and sunset time and if it is after sunset
   turns on the outside light. */
wait_for_phone_signal()
current_time = get_time()
sunset_time = get_sunset_time()
if current_time > sunset_time then
   turn_on_light()
end_if
```

A programmer can also use several commonly used tags within comments to indicate certain things.

Tags

Sometimes, a programmer wants to mark a section in the code using a tag so that it is easy to find this location. These tags are informal, but some are commonly used:

- BUG: A known bug in the code that should be corrected.
- FIXME: Either a known bug or something else that must be corrected.
- HACK: Marking a section of code that is not structured or written optimally and should be rewritten.
- TODO: This marks a location where something will be inserted later.

These tags are written in comments and are mainly used so that they can be found with tools such as the Unix grep tool (a tool for searching in text files). Some programming editors will even highlight some of these tags.

Comments can also be used to remove code.

Commenting out code

Sometimes, a programmer needs to remove a couple of lines of code to try something out or to isolate a bug. Instead of deleting these lines, they can be commented out with either a line comment or block comments. It is then easy to remove the comment symbol to make the code active again.

This technique can also be used if we are rewriting a code section. In that case, it is a good idea to have the old code as a reference when we are constructing the new code, so we don't forget something we need to do. We can place the old code in a comment; however, when we are done, we should remove the old commented out code as it will distract us when reading the code.

The compiler or interpreter will ignore most comments, but not all. Some might have a special directive meaning.

Directive comments

There are some examples where a comment can have a meaning for the language compiler or interpreter.

Some languages, such as Python, can if we use it on a Unix system and use a symbol that looks like a comment on the first line in a code file. This symbol is called a *shebang* and is made up of the hash symbol followed by an exclamation mark, #!.

This is used as an instruction, not to other humans, but to the Python interpreter so that it knows what version of Python should be used to interpret this program.

Python also has something called a *magic comment*, which identifies the character encoding that the source code file is using. It begins with # -*- coding: and ends with -*-.

A Python program using both directives can start with two lines that look something like this:

```
#!/usr/bin/env python3
# -*- coding: UTF-8 -*-
```

As Python uses # as the symbol for line comments, it might look like these are two normal comments. This can be a bit confusing when reading the code, and we should be aware that these are instructions to the interpreter and not to humans.

As you can see, comments can be used in several different ways. Let's take a look at some typical uses in more detail.

Making use of comments

How to use comments in the best way is subject to dispute, and, often, you will get conflicting advice. Let's examine some typical uses before we discuss some of the opinions people have regarding comments.

Planning and reviewing

Comments can be used to plan the structure of the code before it is written. When writing an intricate part of an application, some people prefer to map out the logic with comments before focusing on the real code.

Code description

One everyday use of comments is to summarize what a section of code is doing and explain the programmer's intent. You should not use comments to rewrite what the code does in English. If you feel that you need to do that, the code is most likely too complicated and should be revised.

Algorithmic description

Sometimes, we implement complex algorithms that need an explanation with maybe both text and diagrams. This is usually the prerequisite knowledge required to be able to understand the code. This can, sometimes, be rather extensive explanations. Look at the following diagram as an example. This comment is taken from a part of the Python language itself. If we count the number of lines that are comments in that module, we will see that they are over 77%:

```
# Copyright 2009 Brian Quinlan. All Rights Reserved.
# Licensed to PSF under a Contributor Agreement.

"""Implements ProcessPoolExecutor.

The following diagram and text describe the data-flow through the system:

|======================= In-process =====================|== Out-of-process ==|

+----------+     +----------+       +--------+     +-----------+     +---------+
|          |     | Work Ids |       |        |     |  Call Q   |     | Process |
|          | => |          |       |        |     |           |     |  Pool   |
|          |     +----------+       |        |     +-----------+     |         |
|          |     | ...      |       |        |     | ...       |     +---------+
|          |     | 6        |  => |        |     | => | 5, call() | => |         |
|          |     | 7        |       |        |     | ...       |     |         |
| Process  |     | ...      |       | Local  |     +-----------+     | Process |
|  Pool    |     +----------+       | Worker |     |           |     |  #1..n  |
| Executor |     |          |       | Thread |     |           |     |         |
|          |     +---------- +      |        |     +-----------+     |         |
|          |     | Work Items | <=> |        |     | <= | Result Q  | <= |     |
|          | <=> |          |       |        |     +-----------+     |         |
|          |     +-----------+      |        |     | ...       |     |         |
|          |     | 6: call()  |     |        |     |           |     |         |
|          |     |    future  |     |        |     | 4, result |     |         |
|          |     | ...        |     |        |     | 3, except |     |         |
+----------+     +-----------+      +--------+     +-----------+     +---------+
```

Executor.submit() called:
- creates a uniquely numbered _WorkItem and adds it to the "Work Items" dict
- adds the id of the _WorkItem to the "Work Ids" queue

Local worker thread:
- reads work ids from the "Work Ids" queue and looks up the corresponding
  WorkItem from the "Work Items" dict: if the work item has been cancelled then
  it is simply removed from the dict, otherwise it is repackaged as a
  _CallItem and put in the "Call Q". New _CallItems are put in the "Call Q"
  until "Call Q" is full. NOTE: the size of the "Call Q" is kept small because
  calls placed in the "Call Q" can no longer be cancelled with Future.cancel().
- reads _ResultItems from "Result Q", updates the future stored in the
  "Work Items" dict and deletes the dict entry

Process #1..n:
- reads _CallItems from "Call Q", executes the calls, and puts the resulting
  _ResultItems in "Result Q"
"""

__author__ = 'Brian Quinlan (brian@sweetapp.com)'
```

Figure 5.14: Example of comment describing the process.py module in the
Python programming language
```

The Python language is open source, so anyone can look at or download the code for it. If you want to see what the code for a programming language looks like, you can view it at `https://github.com/python/cpython`.

Comments controversy

There is a never-ending debate regarding how and when comments should be used. Some people argue that code should be written using few comments, arguing that the source code should be written in a way so that it is self-explanatory or self-documenting. The motivation for this standpoint is that if you know a language, you should be able to understand the intent by just reading the code. If you can't, the code needs to be rewritten.

Others will argue that code should be extensively commented, as per the example in the preceding diagram.

In between these standpoints, you will find some that argue that comments, by themselves, are not beneficial nor harmful and should be used with care where they provide added value.

So, to sum it up, in this section, we learned that comments are a tool to explain the code. But they are also used for documentation. Additionally, tags can be used to make notes of things that need to be dealt with in the future.

Summary

In this chapter, we discussed the most fundamental concept that we have in programming: a sequence.

Sequential thinking can help us structure our ideas so that we can break them down into smaller pieces. As we have mentioned in this chapter, grasping everything a program needs to do can be hard, so we need a way to be able to focus on the details without losing the overview of what the program needs to do.

The concept of doing things in sequence is also at the very heart of any program, since the instructions we write are executed one after the other. This is important because we need to make sure that these instructions come in the right order.

The instructions we write are made up of statements, and we learned that some statements are short and simple, while others can span several lines and be made up of other statements. Some are smaller building blocks, called expressions. We are now on an abstraction level where we can deal with details such as adding two numbers together.

Breaking down the code into smaller and smaller chunks allows us to think about how to structure our solution. Sometimes, we will need to document our line of thought to help us or other readers of our code see what made us choose this solution. We learned that comments can be used for this.

Comments can also be used as a documentation of the code so that it is clear what it does and how it can be used. Additionally, we saw that comments can be directed to the language compiler or interpreter to give instructions to it.

As we know from previous chapters, a computer program takes data as its input, stores it in memory, processes this data, and produces new data as its output. Data is a key concept, so, in the next chapter, we will learn how to interact with it and why this type of data has such importance.

6
Working with Data – Variables

In previous chapters, we stated that a program is something that takes data as input and performs operations on it to produce new data. So, handling data is crucial in any application, regardless of whether it is used for accounting or whether it is a game.

When we work with data, it must be stored in the computer's memory, and this is done with **variables**. It is variables that let us store and retrieve data. In this chapter, we will get to know variables, see how they work, and, in the end, look at some operations that we can perform on them.

In this chapter, you will learn about the following:

- Declaring and initializing variables
- Understanding data types and applying them to variables
- Using composite types to handle multiple values
- Performing operations on variables using operators
- Operating on numbers and manipulating strings
- When programming, we need to work with data, and that data will be stored in the computer's memory. To be able to use this data, we need to have a way to reference where in the memory the data is. This is done by using a nice abstraction called variables. Variables hide the difficult stuff, such as working with memory addresses, and give us easy access to data by letting us assign a name to it. Let's see how this works.

Declaring and initializing variables

When writing programs, we continuously work with data. As we are using this data, we need a way to keep track of it. To do this, we use variables. Let's look at how this works in the following sections.

Understanding variables

To understand what a variable is, we can start with some code where we assign a value to a variable:

```
x = 13
```

Here, we have the value 13, which is a whole number. Usually, in programming, we refer to these as integers as they can be both positive and negative. Different programming languages treat integer values differently. Most languages will specify how much memory an integer will use. Let's assume that this size is 4 bytes, which is a common size used to store an integer value. Remember that one byte is 8 bits and that each bit can be either 0 or 1. With 4 bytes, we have 4 times 8 bits, which is 32 zeros or ones, at our disposal.

To store 13 in the computer's memory, the programming language will need to reserve enough space—4 bytes, in our case.

Each byte of computer memory has an address. A memory address works like a street address; it is used to help us navigate to the correct location:

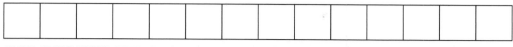

Figure 6.1 – Part of the computer's memory. Each square is a byte and has a unique address

In our example, 4 bytes that are not occupied by something else need to be located. These bytes need to be in continuous order.

The address of the first byte in this sequence is of interest to us. The programming language knows that we are storing an integer value at this location, and it knows how many bytes an integer occupies, so the first address is enough to locate this integer. The following diagram shows this:

Figure 6.2 – The programming language reserves enough space in memory for an integer value to be stored

When writing a program, we don't want to remember numeric memory addresses, so we give this memory address a name. It is up to us, as programmers, to come up with this name, and we should pick a name that describes the data that we are storing. We will talk more about what considerations we need to make when naming variables soon:

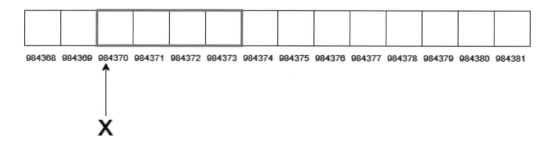

Figure 6.3 – The first address in the reserved sequence is given a name—in this case, x

Now that we have enough room for the reserved integer value and a name that can be used to refer to this memory address, the actual value can be stored at this memory location. This value will be stored in binary format. We talked about binary numbers in *Chapter 1, Introduction to Computer Programs*. In the preceding code snippet, we wanted to save the value 13, and 13 in binary is 1101. All of the bits preceding this value are filled with zeros. As you can see in the following diagram, one byte would have been enough, but as many languages have a fixed size for its integer type, all the bytes will be reserved, regardless of whether we need them:

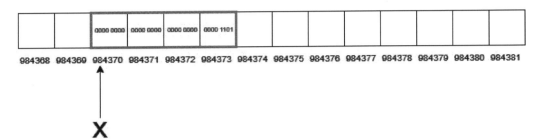

Figure 6.4 – The binary representation of the value we want to be stored is inserted at this memory location

Now, the value is stored in memory and we have a name that refers to this location. We can use this name to access this value.

We call x in our example a variable. A variable consists of several things. It has a name, which is x in our sample. It also has a type. The type defines how much memory the data needs. We wanted to store an integer and we assumed that the language we are using has decided to use 4 bytes for integers. This is the size of this variable. We also know that if an integer has a fixed size, there is a maximum value that it can store. Later in this chapter, we will talk about this limitation.

We also need to explore how we can name our variables and what types they can have. Let's start with the names.

Naming variables

The name we give a variable should reflect what data it represents, so if we use a variable to store an email address, a good name would be email, whereas b45 would be rather lousy.

The syntax of each language has rules for how we can name our variables. Some standard rules for naming variables are as follows:

- It must begin with a letter of the alphabet or an underscore (_).

- After the first character, the name can contain letters, underscores, and numbers.

- You cannot use names that are used as keywords in the language—that is, words that are reserved by the language, such as `for`, `if`, and `else`.

- Spaces or other special characters, such as +, -, and *, are not allowed to be part of the name.

Some examples of legal and illegal names are as follows:

Legal variable names	Illegal variable names
address1	1address
first_name	first-name
email_address	email address

Table 6.1

Many languages are also case sensitive when it comes to variable names. What that means is that the `name`, `Name`, and `nAmE` variables will be treated as three different variables.

Many languages will also have what is known as naming conventions when it comes to how we construct and format variable names. There are also conventions for how to create names that are made up of more than one word. We will study these conventions next.

Camel case

Camel case is where the words that make up a name are separated by an uppercase letter that starts each word. There are two sub-types—**upper camel case** (also known as **Pascal case**) and **lower camel case** (also known as **Dromedary case**). Some examples of variable names using upper camel case are as follows:

- `FirstName`
- `EmailAddress`
- `ZipCode`

The same names would look like this in lower camel case:

- `firstName`
- `emailAddress`
- `zipCode`

As we can see, the first variant capitalizes all of the first letters of the words that make up a name, whereas the second variant leaves the first word in lowercase and only uses uppercase with the second word's first letter.

Languages that recommend this naming convention are Java, C#, and Pascal.

Snake case

Separating words with an underscore is called snake case. When using this convention, we only use lowercase letters and separate words with an underscore character. Using this casing for the same variable names as the preceding examples would look like this:

- `first_name`
- `email_address`
- `zip_code`

Languages that use this convention for naming variables include Python, Ruby, C, and C++, in some circumstances.

What does it mean when we say a language has a convention for naming variables?

Naming conventions

Usually, a naming convention is a recommended way for naming things, such as variables. This means that we can break these rules and the program will still work. However, there are several good reasons for us to obey these recommendations. One could be that if many programmers are involved in writing some code, the style will be consistent and, therefore, more straightforward to interpret for human readers.

Some software companies have their own naming conventions. This is typically the case when the language itself has a weak or non-existing convention.

When coming across a new language, we should always learn its conventions. If you work on several projects that use different programming languages, it can be tricky to remember what convention to use.

Read more about naming conventions in *Chapter 12, Code Quality* in the *Using code conventions* section.

Now that we know how to name a variable, let's explore the different types that a variable can have.

Primitive data types

Every variable has both a name and a type. The type defines what kind of data can be stored in the variable. Typically, a language will have some built-in types, called primitive or basic types, to handle a single value.

Primitive types can be divided into two categories—Boolean and numeric—which we will look at next.

Boolean type

In *Chapter 1, Introduction to Computer Programs*, we talked about George Bool and his Boolean algebra. This defined how we can combine values of `true` and `false` with `and`, `or`, and `not`. To be able to use these values in our programs, we have a type that is named after Bool, called Boolean. A variable that uses this type can only have one of two values—`true` or `false`. For languages that have these types, we use the actual `true` and `false` words.

Languages that have this type either call it `Boolean` or just `bool`.

Numeric type

Numeric types fall into one of two categories—integer types and floating-point types. We will look at them in detail, next.

Integer data types

The first question you could ask yourself here is why are we talking about types in plural when it comes to integers? You could argue that data is either an integer or not. As it turns out, many languages will have several types for representing integer values and the reason for this has to do with how much memory is used for the data and how that data should be interpreted.

As we saw earlier in this chapter, a language will define how much memory to use when storing data in a variable. When working with integers, we might only work with small values in a predefined range, such as the age of a human, or the values might be huge, such as the distance between stars.

If we think about the characteristics of the data we are working with, we will discover that it has natural limitations. The age of a human, for example, will never have a negative value, and if we take the highest human age recorded (122 years, at the time of writing) and add some years to be on the safe side, we could state that a valid human age will fall into the range of 0 to 150. One byte—remember that one byte is 8 bits (8 zeros or ones)—can work with numbers in the range 0 to 255, so that is more than enough to store human age.

If we instead talk about the distance between us and other stars, we have a different range of values. The closest star, except for our own sun, are the two stars in the Alpha Centauri system. They are just over 4 lightyears away. The furthest star that we have observed, known by the name MACS J1149+2223 Lensed Star 1, is 9 billion lightyears away. So, if we are working with these values, we still would not need any negative numbers and the range would be between 4 and 9,000,000,000.

Sometimes, we need to work with both negative and positive numbers—for example, if we are writing some accounting software.

This means that integer values can have different properties, and for that reason, we have more than one integer type so that we can find one that fits our needs. As we don't need any negative numbers and the maximum won't ever exceed 150 as a value for human age, a type that can work with huge or negative numbers would be a waste of the computer's memory.

With this knowledge, programming languages are often implemented with several different integer types that differ in how much memory (measured in bytes) they will use to represent a value. The programmer's task is to pick one that matches the properties for the data that will be handled by the variable that has this type.

Different languages will have a different set of integer types, but here are some typical integer types, their sizes, and the range of values that they can handle:

Name	Size in bits (1 byte = 8 bits)	Minimum value	Maximum value
byte	8	-128	127
word or short	16	-32,768	32,767
int	32	-2,147,483,648	2,147,483,647
long	64	-9,223,372,036,854,775,808	9,223,372,036,854,775,808

Table 6.2

As you can see, all the preceding types include negative as well as positive values. Representing both will limit how a type can serve large numbers. Taking human age as an example again, we will see that the byte type wouldn't really work as although it has a maximum value of 127, it has 128 negative values that we would never use.

The reason why we have this restriction has to do with how negative numbers are represented.

Signed and unsigned integers

If we look at the smallest type in the preceding table—the byte—and think about how negative numbers can be represented, we will see that we have a problem. When working with binary numbers, we have several bits that can store either 0 or 1, but we don't have any other values, so we can't just insert a minus sign to indicate that this is a negative number. Instead, one of the following three methods can be used.

Let's see how they work.

Signed Magnitude Representation (SMR)

Even if the name is a bit complicated, this is the easiest way to represent negative values in binary form. Imagine that we are working with one byte that gives us eight bits to represent a value. However, if we assign one of the bits to represent whether this is a positive or negative value, we are left with just seven bits for the actual value:

128	64	32	16	8	4	2	1
0	1	1	1	1	1	1	1

Figure 6.5 – A byte using only 7 bits to represent a value—127, in this case

If we use the bit to the left in the preceding diagram—often referred to as the most significant bit as it is the bit representing the highest value—to represent whether the rest should be considered either positive or negative, the rest of the bits can form a maximum value of 127:

128	64	32	16	8	4	2	1
0	0	0	1	1	1	0	1

Figure 6.6 – Using the most significant bit to represent a positive value—29, in this case

If we designate the first position to indicate whether this is a positive or a negative value, we can use 0 to show that this is a positive value and 1 to show that this is a negative one:

128	64	32	16	8	4	2	1
1	0	0	1	1	1	0	1

Figure 6.7 – Using the most significant bit to represent a negative value, -29, in this case

Using this technique, we have a range of values from -127 to 127 using a single byte. We will also have two representations for 0—positive and negative. This is one disadvantage of this method and a reason why it is not used so often.

Another problem with this technique is found when performing mathematical operations, such as addition, on two values that use SMR.

Figures 6.8 to 6.12 illustrate what happens if we add 3 and c together if we have used SMR to represent a negative value. To understand the diagrams, imagine that you add two decimal numbers. If you want to add 495 and 572, we will put one above the other and start to add them column by column:

```
  495
 +572
 --------
    7
```

We then do the same for the next column, but as we get a value larger than 9, we have to carry:

```
   1
   495
 + 572
 --------
    67
```

When adding the last column, we use the carried number as part of the numbers we add:

```
   1
   495
 + 572
 --------
  1067
```

We can apply the same principle for adding binary numbers. The only difference is that we now work with just two digits. So, instead of 10, we will need to carry a value as soon as the result is greater than 1. Now, when adding two bits that can be either 0 or 1, we only end up with three different results—0, 1, or 2 (in decimal). If we consider that we need to add two values and one potential carried value, the maximum will be $1 + 1 + 1 = 3$. Now that we know the maximum value we can possibly get (3), we can translate it into binary. 3 in binary is 11. This means that our possible results will be 0, 1, 10, and 11. 0 and 1 fit within a single bit, but 10 and 11 do not, so here, we will need to carry 1.

As guidance, let's use a table to convert between decimal and binary values:

Decimal value	Binary value
0	0
1	1
2	10
3	11
4	100
5	101
6	110
7	111
8	1000
9	1001
10	1010

Table 6.3

Let's also see another table that helps us understand how binary addition works:

Operation	Total result	Result in current position	Carry
0 + 0	0	0	0
1 + 0	1	1	0
1 + 1	10	0	1
1 + 1 + 0 (when having to carry)	10	0	1
1 + 1 + 1 (when having to carry)	11	1	1

Table 6.4

As you can see, the last three operations resulted in two digits, so all of them will result in a carry.

Let's see how we can apply this principle when adding binary numbers:

128	64	32	16	8	4	2	1
0	0	0	0	0	0	1	1

+

128	64	32	16	8	4	2	1
1	0	0	0	0	0	1	1

=

128	64	32	16	8	4	2	1

Figure 6.8 – Adding two values, 3 and -3, where the negative number is represented using SMR

When we want to add two binary numbers, we do the same thing that we did with decimal numbers. The only difference is that we can only handle results that are 0 or 1. If the result is 2, we need to carry 1 to the next position:

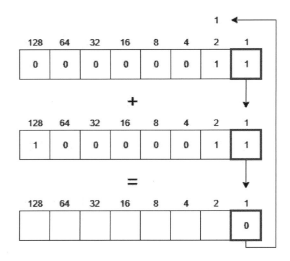

Figure 6.9 – Step one is to add the two rightmost bits—1 + 1 = 2

From the preceding diagram, we can see that as 2 in binary is 10, we insert 0 at this location and carry 1.

This means that in the next step, we have three values—1 + 1 + 1. As the result will be 3, which is 11 in binary, we insert a 1 in this position and carry 1 to the next round:

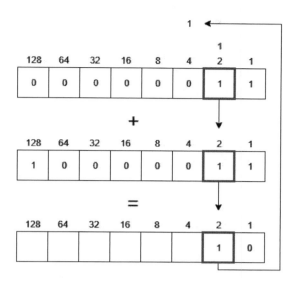

Figure 6.10 – Repeating the operation for the next two bits

In this example, we now have several positions where we add zeros together, but we must remember that we have carried 1 the first time:

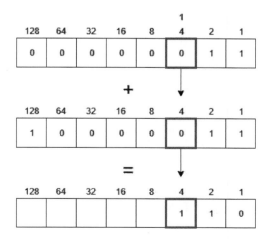

Figure 6.11 – For the third pair of bits, we are adding two zeros with the carry

We can now repeat this all the way to the last position. This is our sign bit:

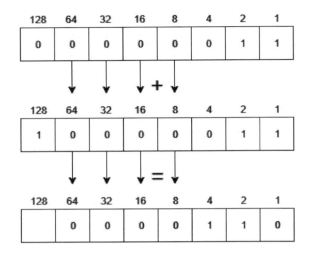

Figure 6.12 – The next four bits are just zeros with no carry, so they will all result in zeros

As we are adding a positive value (3) with a negative value (-3), we have 0 at this position for the first value and 1 in the second to indicate that the value is negative. As 0 + 1 is 1, this indicates that the result is negative:

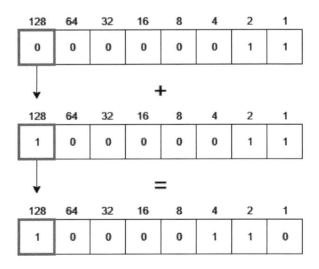

Figure 6.12 – When we add the bit used as a sign bit, the result will be 1, indicating that the result is negative

To our surprise, we discover that the result of adding 3 and -3 is not 0 as we expected but -6, as we have 4 plus 2, which is 6, and 1 at the first position, indicating that this is a negative number.

This is another reason why this method is not used that often.

Ones' complement

Another approach to representing negative numbers that will address the problem we saw when we tried to add a positive and a negative value is the use of something called ones' complement. It also uses the most significant bit (the leftmost bit in our illustrations) as the sign bit but stores negative numbers differently compared to SMR.

If we have a positive value, we can use 3 again as an example, and if we store it in a byte, we get 0000 0011, as we can see here:

128	64	32	16	8	4	2	1
0	0	0	0	0	0	1	1

Figure 6.13 – Storing positive 3 in a byte

To store -3, we flip all the bits, so 0 becomes 1 and vice versa, as follows:

128	64	32	16	8	4	2	1
1	1	1	1	1	1	0	0

Figure 6.14 – Storing -3 using ones' complement. All values are the opposite of when we store positive 3

As we can see, all the bits are the opposite compared to when we stored a positive 3. When this number is interpreted, the sign bit is checked first. If it is 1, all the other bits are then flipped to form the actual value. This might seem like a strange thing to do, but let's see what happens when we add the two together:

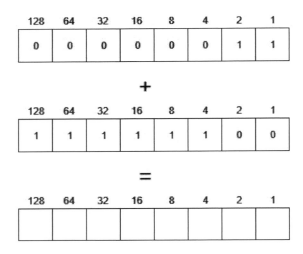

Figure 6.15 – Adding 3 and -3 where the negative number is represented using ones' complement

As we can see in the preceding diagram, we add 1 and 0 for each location. The result will, therefore, be 1 in every position, as we can see here:

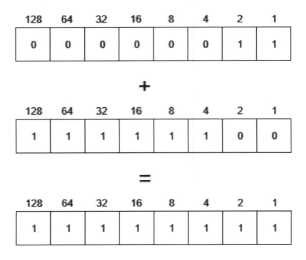

Figure 6.16 – The result of adding the two bytes will be 1 in all locations

As we have 1 for the signed bit, this means that we have a negative result, so all the other bits need to be flipped and the result will be -0. Now, this is better as 3 + (-3) is 0, but negative 0 does not mean anything. This means that this method also has the same problem as SMR, where we have two representations of the value 0—one positive and one negative:

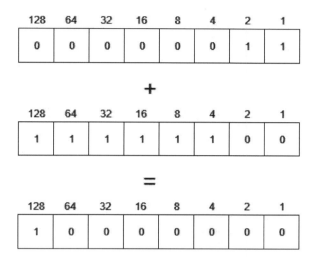

Figure 6.17 – As the sign bit is 1, all the other bits need to be flipped, forming negative 0

Let's see whether we can tackle this problem and find a representation that works.

Two's complement

To solve the problem of two zeros in ones' complement, a third method for representing integer values exists, which is called two's complement. It works in the same way as ones' complement but with a twist.

The first step is to use ones' complement to represent a negative number, which takes the positive value and flips all the bits. But when that is done, we add 1 to the result. Now, this might seem like we are messing the result up totally, but as we will see, it solves the problem with the double zero representation.

See *figures 6.18 to 6.21* to see how this works:

128	64	32	16	8	4	2	1
0	0	0	0	0	0	1	1

Figure 6.18 – Representing the value 3 in a byte

Representing a positive value is done just the same as before. However, when dealing with negative numbers, we do things differently:

128	64	32	16	8	4	2	1
1	1	1	1	1	1	0	1

Figure 6.19 – Representing -3 in the two's complement form

Here, we take all the bits from the positive representation and flip them, so 0 becomes 1 and vice versa:

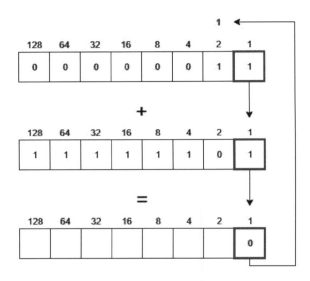

Figure 6.20 – When adding 3 and -3, we do what we did before. 1 + 1 = 10, so 0 goes to this position and 1 is carried

Adding the bits together is done in the same way as before:

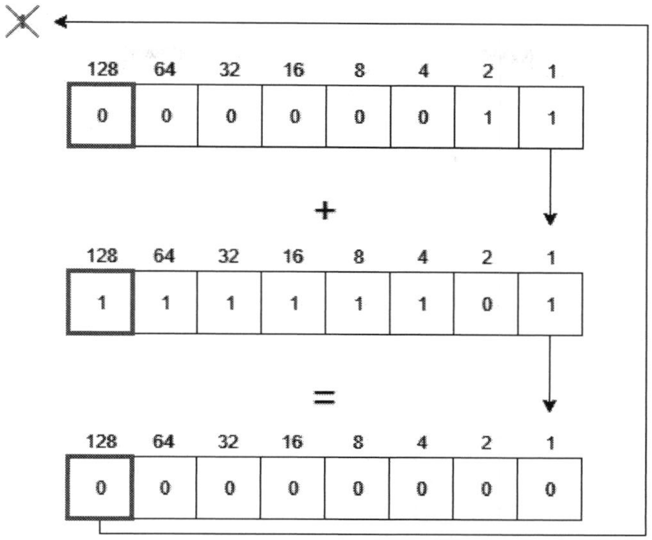

Figure 6.21 – For all positions, we have 1 carry, so we will add 1 + 1 + 0 = 10

When adding the sign bit to the left, we get a carry. The two's complement method states that this carry should be discarded.

We can see that the result of this operation is a byte with only zeros, giving us a single representation of 0 as a result.

As two's complement solves both the problem with the binary representation of zero and the problem of adding two values together, this is the one that is most frequently used.

Unsigned integers

Some languages will let us work with integer types that use all bits as values. This allows us to work with only positive integers, but they can, on the other hand, be twice as big because we use all the bits to store values.

Not all numerical values are integers, so let's now look at another group of numerical data types—floating-point types.

Floating-point types

Representing floating-point numbers using the binary form is tricky, and as a programmer, we soon discover some oddities that relate to this. Let's look at the following code:

```
result = 0.1 + 0.2
```

We would expect the result stored in the variable result to be 0.3, but in many languages, this will instead be something like 0.30000000000000004.

The reason we get odd results like this is that we try to represent a decimal floating-point number as a binary floating-point number. We will not go into too much detail about how floating-point numbers are represented in a computer as it will get a bit complicated. If you want to learn how this is done, you can search for it online and see lots of detailed explanations for how it works.

But what we will do is to think about the problem the computer faces when dealing with a binary representation of a decimal number.

In our decimal positional system, each position in a number has a value, as we saw earlier. This is just as true for floating-point numbers as for integers. For a floating-point number, the positions have values, as illustrated:

Figure 6.22 – The values that the different positions have in the decimal system, to the left and right of the decimal point

Using this system makes it easy for us to store a value—for example, one-tenth can be written as 0.1. In binary, the positions are as follows:

Figure 6.23 – The values that the different locations have in the binary system, to the left and right of the decimal point

As we can see, no value represents one-tenth, so something else needs to be done. What computers do is store floating-point values in scientific notation. Representing the 300 decimal value in scientific form come to 3×10^2. The computer does this but in binary form and divides the value into three parts. The first is the sign, just as we saw for integer values. The second part is the exponent used and the last part is called the mantissa. The mantissa is the decimal part of a logarithm to base 10 (that is, a decimal number). If that means nothing to you, don't worry. You don't need to understand the math to be able to use floating-point numbers. However, we must understand why numbers don't always come out the way we expect them to.

To illustrate this, we can think about what happens if we calculate 1/3. We will get 0.333333333..., where we will have an infinite number of threes. The same thing happened when we tried to represent 0.1 using binary numbers. The result will be a value that goes on forever in the binary form. The problem is that the computer does not have an infinite amount of memory, so when the amount that is assigned to this type runs out, it will just stop, which means that we will not have an accurate representation of the number. That is why we got 0.3000000000000004 instead of 0.3 when we added 0.1 and 0.2 together in the preceding example.

Without going into the math of how floating-point numbers are represented, we need to understand the two most frequent types for representing them that we find in programming. They are usually called **float** and **double**.

The difference between them is that a float will usually use 32 bits and a double will use 64 bits. This means that the double has more memory to use before it chops off a number. It is named double because it has double precision compared to the float type.

What we can learn from this is that if precision matters in our application, we should use a double, but if not, we can use a float. If, for example, we want to store outside temperatures, a float will be fine to use as we never deal with that many decimals.

We can now work with integer and floating-point numbers, but sometimes we want to represent other kinds of values, such as complex numbers.

Some programming languages have a special type for working with complex numbers. Some examples of languages that use this type are Go, C++, Python, and Ruby.

There is also another numeric type, even if we often think of it as something else—the character type.

A character that is a letter, a punctuation mark, or any other character that we can come up with can be represented as a number. Many programming languages will provide a special type that is meant to handle a single character, but under the hood, it is an integer type. It is treated in a different way than the other numeric types that we have seen, as we can assign not only numbers to it but also characters, surrounded by some quotation marks—often single quotes. It can look something like this:

```
character_a = 'a'
```

Here, we assign the a character to a variable called character_a. The character is surrounded by single quotes to indicate that this is a character and not a variable named a. What happens is that the numerical value for this character is assigned to the variable. The character value for lowercase a is 97, so in this case, that is what will be stored in the variable.

To print the content of the variable to the screen, type the following code:

```
print character_a
```

We will see a printed, not 97, as the programming language will know that this is a character type and not a normal numeric type and will translate the numerical value back to the character representation again.

Sometimes, we need to store more than one value at a time. Then, we can use what are called **composite types**.

Composite type

A composite type is a data type that is made up of more than one value. There are situations when keeping several related values together makes sense. In our everyday life, we do this often. A shopping list is an example. Instead of having several papers, each one having one item we need to buy, we store all the items on one piece of paper and call this a list.

This is how a composite type works in programming as well. We have several types that all have some specific characteristics. The first one can be used when we want to represent a sequence or list of things. This is often called an array.

An array—also called a vector, list, or sequence—is a data type that stores several elements. This number can be fixed or flexible.

Fixed array

When we have a fixed size array, we say how many slots we want it to have when we create it. This size will not change. If we create an array that can store 10 integers, it will reserve space for 10 integers, even if we only use 3 or 5.

Typically, we would create a fixed-size array as follows:

```
numbers[10]
```

Here, we say that we want an array that can store 10 integers and we call it `numbers`. We are not storing any values in the array, so we say that these 10 locations are unassigned, but we have space in memory reserved for us, and we have a name that we can use to access this space.

We can see this as if we have 10 different variables. The only difference is that we store all 10 variables under the same name.

We will now need a way to address these variables individually. This is done by indexing.

We can index into the array by using its name and an index value:

```
numbers[2] = 44
```

Here, we store 44 at position 2 in the array. You might think that position 2 is the second value in the array, but it is actually the third. The reason for this is that the index starts at 0, as shown:

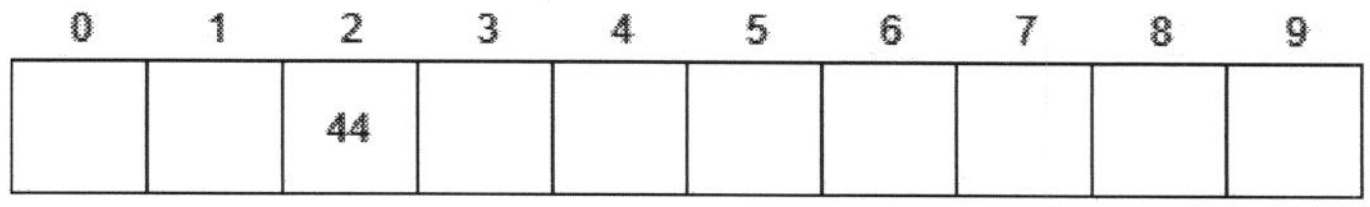

0	1	2	3	4	5	6	7	8	9
		44							

Figure 6.24 – Inserting 44 at index 2 will place the value in the third position of the array

The reason that the indexing starts at 0 and not 1 is that we can think of the name that we used for this array as a reference to the first location in the array. When using an index, we say how many places we should move forward. So, `numbers[2]` means we start at the first location and move forward 2 integers in memory. That is the location you should store the value at.

We can also retrieve a value from a given index, as follows:

```
print numbers[2]
```

The preceding code prints the value that is located at index 2, which is the third value in the array.

Having an array of a fixed size can be problematic as it is not always the case that we know how many values we need to store. If this is the case, then we can use another type of array that can grow and shrink as we use it. This is sometimes called a dynamic array.

Dynamic array

A dynamic array (or list, vector, or sequence) is an array that can grow and shrink as we use it. Initially, this kind of array will be empty when we first create it, but we can then add and remove things from it as we go along. How we create these arrays will differ from language to language, but it can look something like this:

```
numbers = []
```

Here, we are creating an empty dynamic array.

We can now add and remove things from this array:

```
numbers.add(10)
numbers.add(11)
numbers.add(12)
numbers.remove(11)
```

Here, we first add three values—10, 11, and 12. Values are usually added at the end, so they will be stored in the 10, 11, 12 order.

On the last line, we remove the 11 value. The array now has the 10 and 12 values.

Often, we will have different ways to dictate where in this array new values should be added and removed. We might, for example, be able to do something like this:

```
numbers.addBack(10)
numbers.addFront(11)
numbers.addBack(12)
numbers.addFront(13)
```

From the preceding code, we can see the following:

1. We add the 10 value to the back of the empty array.
2. Then, we add the 11 value to the beginning of the array. We now have 11, 10.

3. Then, we add 12 to the back, giving us 11, 10, 12.

4. In the last line, we add 13 to the front of the array. We now have the 13, 11, 10, and 12 values.

We can often use an index, just as with a fixed size array, to retrieve individual values from a dynamic array. The problem is that we need to keep track of how many items we currently have in the array. This is important because if you have an array of let's say five things and you say that you want to get item number 10, you are looking outside the array and your programming language will most likely halt the execution of the program as you are doing something that is considered illegal (according to your language, that is.)

Dynamic arrays come at another cost as well. When we create a fixed-size array, a big enough chunk of memory will be found, and we can then go ahead and use this. All the items in the array must come sequentially in memory because that is what makes indexing work. As we saw, the name of the array will tell us the starting location for this array, and we then use an index to say how many steps into the memory we need to move to come to the correct place.

When using a dynamic array, this might be a problem. If we add item after item, we will eventually hit a memory location where something else is located. Our array will now need to move to another location that is big enough for all the values we already had in it, plus the new value that we want to add. As a programmer, this is not a usual task. The language does this for us, but copying all the old values from the original location to this location will take time. This is the cost we pay for the freedom of having a structure that can grow and shrink depending on our needs.

Most programming languages will only let you store data of the same type in an array. There are a few, however, that will allow you to mix the types as you wish.

Sometimes, we want to store values that are related in another way—let's say information about a person. Then, we can use what is called a record.

The record type

If you are writing an application and you want to represent information about, say, customers, you will first need to decide what information you want to handle. This might be the customer's first and last name, a street address, a city, a ZIP code, and so on. This might include data of different types. It would also be handy if you could retrieve the different items with the help of a name.

Records are sometimes called structures or structs. To use them, we first need to define what they look like. This can look something like this:

```
struct Person
    firstName,
    lastName,
    streetAddress,
    city,
    zip
end_struct
```

What we are doing here is defining a new type called `Person`. One variable of this type can store a first name, last name, street address, city, and ZIP code.

Creating a variable of this type might look something like this:

```
Person person1
```

We now have a variable called `person1`, but we do not store any data in it yet. Doing so might look like this:

```
person1.firstName = "Anna"
person1.lastNamme = "Smith"
person1.streetAddress = "34 Main Street"
person1.city = "Home Town"
person1.zip = "123 456"
```

All the information we have about this person is now stored in the `person1` variable. We can now create other `person` variables to store information about other people:

```
Person person2
Person person3
person2.firstName = "Bob"
person3.firstName = "Colette"
```

We can also retrieve the data stored within these variables, as follows:

```
print person1.firstName
print person2.firstName
print person3.firstName
```

The output of this will be as follows:

```
Anna
Bob
Colette
```

Here, we have a relationship between a variable name, `firstName`, for example, and some data—`Anna`, `Bob`, and `Colette`. We know about this relationship beforehand, so the record structure is perfect for us. Sometimes, we might not know what we will get, but the data might still come in pairs. Then, we can use another data type known as a dictionary.

The dictionary type

A dictionary (also known as a map, hash map, or associative array) is a collection type that uses key-value pairs. The key needs to be a unique value that we can use to retrieve the value that is associated with it.

A colon often separates the key and the value.

They might look something like this:

```
dictionary books
    "Pride and Prejudice": "Jane Austen",
    "David Copperfield": "Charles Dickens",
    "Madame Bovary": "Gustave Flaubert"
end_dictionary
```

Here, we are using the name of some famous books as the keys, and the value associated with each key is the author of that book. As we stated before, the key needs to be unique. If we reuse the key and assign another value to it, the old value will be overwritten by the new one.

We can access the values—the names of the authors, in our case—by using the key as an index:

```
print books["David Copperfield"]
```

This will give the following output:

```
Charles Dickens
```

As it is only the key that needs to be unique, we can have multiple items that have the same value. We can, for example, add a book to the dictionary as follows:

```
books["Oliver Twist"] = "Charles Dickens"
```

We now have two values containing Charles Dickens, but they are associated with two different and unique keys.

Sometimes, we have other reasons for storing unique values. We might want to represent what in mathematics is known as finite sets. For that, we also have the set type.

The set type

A set is a composite type that will store unique values without any order. As this type is unordered, we cannot retrieve items from it with an index. This is usually not a problem as this type is often used to test for membership. You might, for example, have two sets with some values in them and would like to know which values occur in both sets.

Let's see how we might create these two sets and then print the values that occur in both:

```
firstSet = {2, 5, 7, 9}
secondSet {2, 3, 4, 8, 9}
print firstSet.intersection(secondSet)
```

In set theory, an intersection between two sets are the values that exists in both sets.

The output of this will be as follows:

```
2, 9
```

This output is represented as follows:

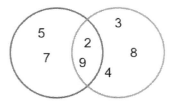

Figure 6.25 – Representation of two sets that has an intersection of 2 and 9 as these two values exist in both sets

Sometimes, we want to create a new type so that we can dictate what values can be assigned to variables that are of this type. For this, we have enumeration.

Enumeration

Enumeration, often called just **enum**, is an enumerated type with distinct values. We can use this to create our types and dictate what values can be assigned to a variable that has this type.

It can look something like this:

```
enum TrafficLight
    red,
    yellow,
    green
end_enum
```

TrafficLight is now a type and we can use it to create variables:

```
TrafficLight light1
TrafficLight light2
```

As both light1 and light2 are of the TrafficLight type, we can only assign the things we described inside this type:

```
light1 = yellow
light2 = green
```

Behind the scenes, there are numerical values associated with each of the items in the enum. In our case, red will be 0, yellow is 1, and green is 2.

Now, we have seen that we can work with Boolean values, numbers, characters, and different composite types, but you might notice that we're missing one type. We have still not seen a type that can handle text. It is time to look at strings.

Strings

A string is a composite type as it is stored as an array of characters. Most languages will use double quotes to designate that something is a string and will use single quotes for single characters. Some languages will let you use either single or double quotes for both types. Here, we will use double quotes for strings and single quotes when we only have a single character.

Usually, we will not consider a string an array. We can create a string as follows:

```
greeting = "Hello there"
```

Here, we created a variable of the string type, called `greeting`, and assigned a `Hello there` value to it. Behind the scenes, an array of characters will be created and each character in the string will be assigned to one location in this array, as shown:

0	1	2	3	4	5	6	7	8	9	10
'H'	'e'	'l'	'l'	'o'	' '	't'	'h'	'e'	'r'	'e'

Figure 6.26 – The Hello there string stored as an array, where each item is a character

As a string is an array of characters, we can use an index to access individual characters. As an example, let's print the character at position 7, which is the eighth character:

```
print greeting[7]
```

The output will be as follows:

```
h
```

Now that we can handle data in different formats, we can move on to do something with this data. It is time to look at operators.

Operators – things we can do with variables

In *Chapter 5, Sequence – The Basic Building Block of a Computer Program*, we talked about how a statement is made up of expressions and that expressions can be made up of operations or operands.

Let's see an example of this. Here, we will create two variables and assign a value to each of them. Then, we will add the two values together and store the result in a new variable:

```
number1 = 10
number2 = 15
result = number1 + number2
```

In line one, we created a variable called `number1` and assigned a value of `10` to it. We now know that this means several things:

- The variable name is `number1`.
- As it is assigned an integer, it must be of an `integer` type.
- The = sign is an operator, taking whatever is on the right and assigning it to what we have on the left.

- Somewhere in the computer's memory, enough space for an integer has been reserved.

- The name, number1, will act as an alias for this address.

We then do the same thing in line two, the only difference being that we have another name for the variable, number2, and we assign it another value, 15.

On the third line, we use the addition operator. This operator has two operands—number1 and number2. It will now extract the values in these two variables, add them together, and return the result.

This operation will result in a value of 25, which is what will be assigned to the variable result. As a result of the addition operation giving us another integer, we now also know that the variable result will also have the integer type.

Let's look at some operators for basic arithmetic.

Arithmetic operators

Most programming languages share the symbols used for basic arithmetic operations. Refer to the following table to see the most common ones:

Name	Symbol	Example	Description
Addition	+	6 + 2	Adds two values
Subtraction	-	6 - 2	Subtracts two values
Multiplication	*	6 * 2	Multiplies two values
Division	/	6 / 2	Divides two values
Modulus	%	6 % 2	Returns the remainder of an integer division

Table 6.5

The last one, the modulus operator, might not be familiar to you. It is often used in programming as it has some features that can be handy when working with numbers. We can illustrate what it does with a simple example. If we calculated 16/13, we would get a result of 1.230769.... The integer part, 1, tells us that 13 goes once into 16. What the modulus operator does is tells us how much there is left to get to 16. So, if 13 goes once into 16, we must add 3 to 13 to get to 16.

We would express that with 16 % 13 and get a result of 3. If you have not worked with modulus before, I suggest you search it up online to get an understanding of how it works as it is something that you will find very useful as a programmer.

Next up, we have some operators that we can use to compare things.

Relational operators

Relational operators are used when we want to compare two values. They can be equal or not equal. We might want to know whether one value is greater than the other. The following table lists the relational operators that are typically found in programming languages:

Name	Symbol	Example	Description
Equal	==	age == 13	Compares two values and returns true if they are equal
Not equal	!=	age != 13	Compares two values and returns true if they are not equal
Greater than	>	age > 13	Returns true if the left operand is greater than the right one
Less than	<	age < 13	Returns true if the left operand is less than the right one
Greater than or equal to	>=	age >= 13	Returns true if the left operand is greater than or equal to the right operand
Less than or equal to	<=	age <= 13	Returns true if the left operand is less than or equal to the right operand

Table 6.6

With these operators, we can compare two values, but sometimes we have more values to compare. In this case, we will need logical operators.

Logical operators

These operators are used to represent and, or, and not. Some languages will use these exact words to represent them, but others will have special signs for them. They are used in statements such as if the age is greater than 12 and age is less than 20. In code, that would look something like this:

```
if age > 12 && age < 20 then
```

The three operators we can use are as follows:

Name	Symbol	Example	Description
And	&&	`age > 12 && age < 20`	The things on both sides of the `&&` operator must be true for the whole statement to be true.
Or	||	`age < 13 || age > 19`	At least one of the things on each side of the `||` operator must be true for the statement to be true.
Not	!	`!raining`	This will reverse a Boolean value, so if it is true, it will become false, and vice versa.

Table 6.7

Most languages will have more operators than the ones we have seen here. We will not cover them here as some are combination operators, which is a combination of two of the operators we have seen here, and others are specialized for one or a few languages.

Next up, we will look at two different ways that variables can be stored in memory and why that concerns us.

The concept of values and reference variables

There are two ways that a variable can store its value in memory. We could think of these ways as direct and indirect. This might sound strange, but let's use an analogy to explain.

The variables that directly store their data are like boxes. When we create them, we can think of them as a box that has the name of the variable stuck to it with a label. We can store the value inside the box and look in the box later to see what value is in there. Variables that store their values like this are called **value variables**:

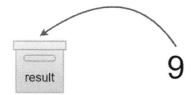

Figure 6.27 – A variable that stores its data by value is like a box

Variables that use indirect storage will act as an index card in a library. It will not store the book but will have the location where it is stored, so it only contains the address to where in memory the actual value is. Variables that store values like this are called **reference variables**:

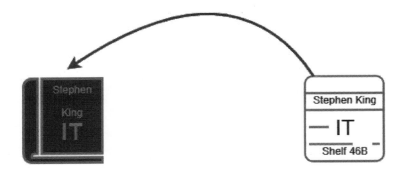

Figure 6.28 – Variables that store data by reference are like a library index card

Let's see how they both work.

Value variables

When we create a variable—or declare it, as we would usually say—of a type, several things will happen, as we saw at the beginning of this chapter. Let's see what will happen when the following code line is executed:

```
x = 10
```

As we now know, a chunk of memory that is large enough to host an integer is located, and this location has an address. The name we give the variable—x, in the preceding example—is just an alias for this address. It is much easier for us to remember that a variable called firstName stores a name instead of having to remember that the first name was at the 38892819283 address.

When our code is interpreted or compiled, the variable name is changed to the actual address, but that is luckily not anything that we will ever see. As this is a variable that stores its data by value, there is a direct relationship between where the data is and the variable name.

Reference variables

When it comes to reference variables, there is an extra step between the variable name and where the data is. Let's see what happens when we create a reference variable with another code example:

```
weather = "Sunny"
```

In this example, the data will still need to be stored somewhere, so a memory location for it is found and as before, the address of where this is is noted. However, the difference is that the variable name is not an alias for this address. Instead, the address for where the data is is stored at another location in memory and the variable is an alias for that location. The following diagram illustrates this:

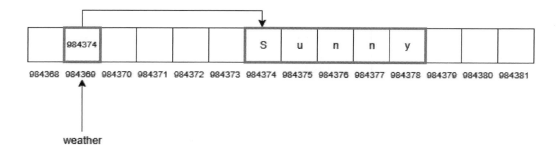

Figure 6.29 – A variable named weather as a reference variable

This might seem pointless. Why can't we store the text string at the location pointed out by the `weather` variable? What is the point of this extra step? The answer is efficiency. In a program, we need to pass data around. The data that we have in a variable in one part of the program needs to be passed along to another part. Imagine that the data stored is much larger than the short text string in the preceding example; the actual passing of the data would mean that we need to make a copy of all the data. This takes some time, and we will now have two copies of the data, which will use twice as much memory. If a variable is of this reference type, we will not need to copy all the data. In the preceding example, this will mean that we will not need to copy `Sunny`. Instead, the `weather` variable contains the address to where this data is, so it can just pass the address.

How a language uses these two types will differ from language to language. When learning a new language, it is vital to learn how it works with value and reference variables.

Now that we have covered lots of things related to variables, we are now ready to use them. We will now see how we can work with numbers, and after that, we will look at text strings.

Working with numbers

Numbers are essential in computer programs. We use them to represent real-world concepts, such as the number of items in a shopping cart, the weight of a package, and the distance to a location. We also use them to represent internal things within our program, such as the number of characters in a name so that we can calculate whether it will fit on an address label if we print it. The point is, we use numbers all the time, so let's see what we can do with them.

First, we can do basic arithmetic, such as addition, subtraction, multiplication, and division, as in the following code snippet:

```
age1 = 34
age2 = 67
mediumAge = (age1 + age2) / 2
```

In this example, we have two ages and we are calculating the medium age.

We often use numbers as counters of things. What this means is that we will use them to keep track of how many times we have done something. This means that we need to increase (and sometimes decrease) them by 1. We could do this as follows:

```
count = count + 1
```

To understand what happens here, we need to look to the right of the = sign first. Here, we have a variable called count. As this is just a line that is ripped out of its context, we can assume that it already has a value stored. This value is now used, and we add 1 to it. The result of this addition is then stored back in the variable count, and we have increased its value by 1.

As this is such a common thing to do in programming, some shorthands for this have been developed. As we are using the same variable on both sides of the = operator, we can skip one of them and instead use a different operator that looks something like this:

```
count += 1
```

This is the same as in the last example, but just shorter. We can read it as taking the value that is stored by the count variable, adding 1 to it, and storing the result back in count.

Some languages have taken this further and shortened this even more:

```
count++
```

Again, the result will be the same as the other two. We can read this as increasing the value stored in count by 1.

All of the three examples we just saw can, of course, be done with subtraction too, as shown:

```
count = count - 1
count -= 1
count--
```

When working with numbers, they can either be stored in a variable, as with `count`, or digits directly in the code, as is the case with `1` in the preceding examples.

Sometimes, we will work with more complex mathematical formulas and do several things in one single line.

We could have something like the following:

$$x = \frac{a + 3}{7 - b}$$

How would we write that in a program?

First, x, a, and b are variables in mathematics and will be variables in our program, too. `a + 3` and `7 - b` must be done before we can divide. We use an equation such as this as a recipe to calculate something. To use it, we insert some values for a and b. Then, we do the math, and x will be the result.

In our program, we can, therefore, assume that a and b have some values given to them earlier in the program. So, let's see how we can let the computer do the math for us:

```
x = (a + 3) / (7 - b)
```

Adding parentheses means that what is inside of them will be calculated first. So, if we imagine some values for a and b—let's say a = 3 and b = 4—then a + 3 will be calculated first, so we have 3 + 3 = 6. Then, 7 - b will be calculated, so 7 - 4 = 3. At this point, we can imagine that a + 3 is replaced by 6 and 7 - b by 3; we are left with 6 / 3. The result, 2, will be stored in x.

If basic algebra is not enough for us, most programming languages come with a vast library of mathematical functions that we can use, such as cosine, tangent, square root, and absolute value.

Another data type that programmers use a lot is strings. Let's look at some of the things we can do with them.

Manipulating strings

A string is a sequence of characters, and a character does not have to be a letter, it can be punctuation marks, a space, a hyphen, or any other character we can produce using a computer. A string can also contain digits.

The first thing we must understand is that a string only containing digits will not be the same as if it were an integer. Look at the following code:

```
numberA = 1234
numberB = "1234"
```

Notice the quotation marks around the digits in the last number. This turns it into a string. The first one, numberA, will be of the integer type, so it can be used for counting and other mathematical operations. For the computer, the second one is just as much a number as the word dog is—that is, not at all.

When working with strings, there are several typical things we can do with them. Let's look at some frequent string operations.

String concatenation

When we take two strings and add them together to form a new string, we call it concatenation. How this is done will differ a bit from language to language, but often, we can use the + operator, as in the following example:

```
word = "day" + "break"
```

Here, we have two strings—day and break. The quote marks tell us that they are strings. They will now be concatenated into a new string that is stored in the word variable. This variable will contain the daybreak word.

Splitting strings

Sometimes, we want to split a string into multiple strings. To do this, we will often use a delimiter inside the string, which we can use to indicate where the string should be divided. Let's assume that we have a string that contains a first name and last name and that the names are separated by a comma, such as Sue, Smith.

If that is stored in a variable called name, in some languages, we could do something like this:

```
firstName, lastName = name.split(",")
```

As usual, we will begin by looking at the right side of the = operator. Here, we say that we have a string in a variable called name. We want to break up this string into two parts, so we use split. Inside the parentheses, we see a string. Again, we know that it is a string because it has quote marks and contains a comma. This is the character that will be used for the split. All characters that precede the comma inside the variable name will be sent to the first variable to the left, firstName. Everything after the comma will be sent to the second variable, lastName. The comma itself that is inside the variable name will be discarded.

It is also important to note that the content of the variable name has not changed, so if we peek into the variables after this line has executed, we can see that they contain the following:

```
firstName = Sue
lastName = Smith
name = Sue,Smith
```

The result can also be an array that contains the two strings. This would look something like the following:

```
splitName = name.split(",")
```

The splitName variable will now be an array that contains two strings. Remember that the first position in an array is 0, and in that location, we will find the Sue string, and at position 1, we will find Smith.

Substrings

Substrings are used when we take part of a string to form a new string. How this is done will change from language to language. Here are some examples of what it might look like if we want to extract the car substring out of the phonocardiogram string.

First, we store phonocardiogram in a variable, as follows:

```
word = "phonocardiogram"
```

In some languages, we can then do something like this:

```
newWord = word[5:8]
```

This will begin extracting the substring from location 5 in the string. Just as with arrays, the counting will start at 0. As the letter c is the sixth letter, the index we use will be 5. Then, as per the code given, we end at 8. But that looks like we went one letter too far. Commonly, we use two values as the start and end index. The first will state where to start and the second will point out the first things that are outside the range. We can read the preceding example as starting at location 5 and stopping at location 8 without including it.

After this line has executed, the newWord variable will contain the car string, and as before, the word variable will be unchanged.

Other languages will do something like the following instead:

```
newWord = word.substr(5,8)
```

Here, we use substr instead of square brackets. Also, note that 5 and 8 are separated by a comma here and that we used a semicolon in the first example.

A third variant would look something like this:

```
newWord = word.substr(5, 3)
```

In languages that use this form, the second value indicates how many characters we want instead of the end index. However, the result will be the same.

Case conversion

Converting string casing is something we often want to do. The reason for this can, for example, be so that we can ask the user of our program to enter a text command, and then we will need to check what command the user entered. As an example, we can imagine that they entered the following commands:

- Start
- Pause
- Stop

We will need to compare what the user wrote against these strings, but we have a problem. When we compare strings, they need to be cased the same to be equal. This means that start, Start, and START will all be different.

We can't compare all the combinations as they would be rather too many. For just the start word, we have the following variants:

- start
- Start

- STart
- StArt
- STArt
- SRArT
- sTART
- starT

We could go on, but instead, let's just convert a string into either all uppercase or all lowercase. Then, we will know what form the string has.

We can do this as follows:

```
answer = answer.lower()
```

Alternatively, the string can be converted as follows:

```
answer = answer.upper()
```

lower and upper will not change the original string that is inside the variable answer, but instead will create a new lowercase or uppercase version of this string. We will store this new version back into the variable, and by doing so, we will overwrite the old string with the new version where we know how it is cased.

We have seen a few examples of things we can do with strings. This not all we can do, but consider these as some examples of some frequent operations that we can perform on strings.

Summary

In this chapter, we covered one of the two main pillars that programming rests on—how we can store, retrieve, and change data in the computer's memory using variables.

We learned that a variable has a name and a data type and that the type of the variable dictates what can be stored in it and how much memory it will use. We also learned how we could concisely name our variables and that there are naming conventions that we can use for guidance.

With that covered, we then talked about primary or primitive data types and saw that numbers are handled either as integers or floating-point numbers, which are further divided into different sizes, so we can pick a type that suits our needs and make sure we don't waste memory space.

Some data naturally comes in a sequence or in natural groups. For this data, we used a composite data type, and we saw that this type lets us work with groups of data.

We then talked about what operators are and how we can perform operations on variables using them, as well as what common operators are and some examples of how to use them.

A variable can be stored in memory either as a value or reference type. We learned that when it is stored as a value, the data it stores is located at the memory address of the variable. A reference variable does not save its value directly but stores an address to where the data can be found.

We used variables with numbers and performed some basic operations on them using our operators. In the end, we turned our attention to strings and looked at how we can manipulate them.

In the next chapter, we will introduce logic to our programs with proper selection so that we can do things only if a condition is met. We will also see how we can repeat the same thing several times with the help of loops.

7
Program Control Structures

If all of our code was simply executed in sequence, our programs would always do the same thing, no matter what data we provided them with. We must be able to control the path through the program so that some part of the code executes at the designated time, and other parts at other times, depending on the values provided by the data. For instance, only if it is cold outside do you put on warm clothes, not always. The same thing applies to our code. When things are a certain way, we want something to happen.

In a way, we can say that we, by this, will introduce some sort of intelligence, or at least some decision-making capabilities into our code. If things are this way, do this, if not, do that.

In this chapter, you will learn the following topics:

- Controlling the execution path of the program
- Making decisions with the help of `if` statements
- Selecting one out of many options with `switch` statements
- Repeating code execution with `for` loops
- Iterating over code until a condition is false using `while` and `do while`
- Going over a sequence of data, one item at the time using `for each`

In this chapter, we will dive into some real programming. In the topics that we will cover here, we will be able to control the execution path of the program. Let's first explore what that means.

Controlling the execution path

In *Chapter 5, Sequence – The Basic Building Block of a Computer Program*, we learned that the code within a program is executed in sequence.

A sequence is one of the three basic logical structures we have in programming. So, in this chapter, we will cover the other two, *selection* and *iteration*.

Selection statements

There are situations when we only want to execute some code if a condition is met. For example, if you recall our application from *Chapter 5, Sequence - The Basic Building Block of a Computer Program* which turned on the outdoor light, we had a condition that said if our phone detected that we were within a given range from our house, it should send a signal to the home computer. To refresh your memory, let's take a look at some images you have seen before. *Figure 7.1* was used to illustrate the action of us entering the range:

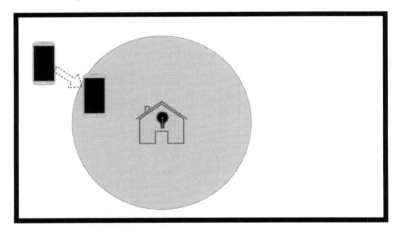

Figure 7.1: The phone detects that it is within a given range from our house

Then, we have a condition. We used the illustration shown in *Figure 7.2* to indicate that when the condition was true, that is, we are within the range, a signal should be sent to the home computer:

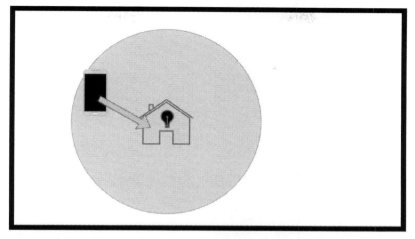

Figure 7.2: The condition is met, so the code for sending the message can be executed

Let's break it down a bit more and consider the actual steps involved. The application on the phone would need to do the following:

1. Ask the GPS on the phone for the current position.
2. With the help of the given coordinates, calculate the distance to our home.
3. If the distance is within a given range from our house, then send a signal to the home computer.

As you can see, in *step 3*, we have a condition that states that the signal will only be sent if the condition is true. So, here, we have some code that will not always be executed. We call this selection. We could define selection like this: *selection is the ability to execute a section of code only if a condition is met.*

Now we can ask ourselves another question. What should we do if the condition is false, that is, we are not within the range? Well, for this application, the answer is nothing. If we are not in the range, then we won't need to do anything.

The phone app also had another feature that is interesting to us now. When we have finished checking whether we are within the range or not, we will either send a signal to the home computer or do nothing. After that, we will go back to the beginning and repeat everything again so that we can be ready to check whether, after the movement, we are in the given range. We call this an *iteration*. We will learn what this is next.

Iteration statements

An iteration is when we want to repeat something several times. It can also be referred to as a loop. The number of times we want to iterate something can be in the range of 2 to infinity. Now, in programming, infinity has a somewhat different perspective on things than you and I would usually have. Infinity in programming does not mean forever and ever, but more like as long as the program is running. So, in programming, infinity ends when the program ends.

In the outdoor light app, we had an iteration. The following diagram illustrates the sequence for our phone app, and here we can clearly see the iteration:

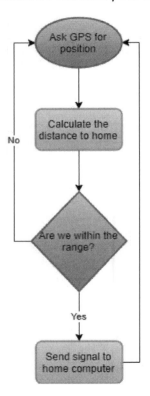

Figure 7.3: The two arrows pointing at the top item indicate iteration

The diamond shape in the diagram is a condition. If the condition is true, that is, the answer is yes, that we send the signal. We can also see that no matter whether the condition was true or false, we will go back to the beginning. This app will continue to repeat these steps over and over an infinite number of times, that is, until you close the app or turn off your phone.

Sometimes, we only want to iterate a fixed number of times. Let's say that you are implementing an e-commerce solution, and a customer wants to check out all of the items that are currently in the shopping cart. You would need to iterate over all of the items in the cart to calculate the total price. If there were 5 items in the cart, then you would need to iterate 5 times.

Both selection and iteration use conditions, so before we look at the different kinds of selection and iteration statements, let's take a closer look at what a conditional statement is and how it works.

Conditional statements

We have covered the basics of this in several chapters already. A conditional statement is just a statement that can result in either true or false. The following is a list of examples:

- It is raining today.
- Your age is below 20.
- Your credit card has expired.
- Your coffee cup is empty.

All of these will result in either true or false. There are no maybes. It is either raining or not; you are either below 20 or not, and so on.

We have also seen that conditional statements can be combined with logical AND, or logical OR, to form a new, compound conditional statement. Here are some examples:

- It is raining today, and I have blue shoes.
- Your age is below 20, or it is above 60.
- Your credit card has expired, and you have no cash.
- Your coffee cup is empty, and your coffee machine is broken.

These compound, or full, statements are made up of two individual statements. *It is raining today* is one part, and *I have blue shoes* is another part. The two now need to be combined to form a full statement that can be either true or false. In the preceding example, we use *and* to combine them. This means that both individual statements need to be true for the whole statement to be true. It must be raining, *and* I must have blue shoes.

If we look at the second statement, the two smaller statements are combined with an *or*. This means that, for the whole statement to be true, at least one of the parts must be true. Either your card has expired, *or* you have no cash. It could also be unfortunate that both are true, and then the entire statement will be true.

Now we know that we have selection and iteration statements and that they work with conditions, so let's see how we can write code that uses them. Let's start with the most common selection statement, if.

Selection with the if statement

When using selection in our programs, we could argue that the application uses some sort of *intelligence* because it can now make decisions and do different things depending on various conditions. So, how can we make our applications smart? Well, the easiest way is with the use of if statements, which are, sometimes, just referred to as *conditions*. In most languages, they will have a similar structure.

If we write a small program that asks the user for their age, the first part might look something like this:

```
print "Enter your age: "
input age
```

Here, the program prints Enter your age: on the screen. The user then enters an age and presses the *Enter* key to confirm the input. The value entered will be stored in the age variable.

Now we want to give different feedback depending on the age entered:

```
if age < 18 then
    print "You are young"
end_if
```

Here, we have the condition where we check whether the age is below 18. If so, we will print the message, You are young. The condition is that the age must be below 18. If it is 18 or above, nothing will happen, as the program will skip everything between them and end the if statement.

If, instead, we want to check for an interval, we could create a compound conditional statement, as follows:

```
if age >= 13 and age <= 19 then
    print "You are a teenager"
end_if
```

As you can see, we are combining the two parts that make up the condition with an `and`. This means that both conditions must be true for the whole condition to be true. The age must be greater or equal to `13`, and, at the same time, it must be less than or equal to `19`. This will give us a range between 13 and 19, with both values included. If the age falls into this range, we will enter the `if` statement and print the text. If it is either less than 13 or greater than 19, nothing will happen.

The `if` statement comes with an optional part. This section is called `else` and marks a block of code that will be executed only if the condition in the `if` statement is false. This is shown in the following code:

```
if age >= 13 and age <= 19 then
    print "You are a teenager"
else
    print "You are not a teenager"
end_if
```

The difference here is that, now, we will always have something printed on the screen. Either the condition is true, and the message will be printed, or the condition is false and the section between `else` and `end_if` will be executed. Additionally, note that the part that will be executed when the condition is true now ends with the `else` keyword.

We can have more than one statement in each of the sections if we want to:

```
if age >= 13 and age <= 19 then
    print "You are a teenager"
    print "I hope you are having fun."
else
    print "You are not a teenager"
end_if
```

Now, if the age falls into the teenage range, we will print two lines. And, if it is false, we will still only print one line.

If we want to have more complex logic, we can have nested `if` statements. That means we can have new `if` statements either in the section that executes if the condition is true or on the part that only executes if the condition is false.

For example, if the condition in the preceding code is false, we know that you are either younger or older than the teenage years. If we want to distinguish this further, it is in this section of the code that we can check it:

```
if age >= 13 and age <= 19 then
    print "You are a teenager"
    print "I hope you are having fun."
else
    if age < 13 then
        print "You are a child"
    else
        print "You are getting old"
    end_if
end_if
```

Now the logic is a bit more complicated. If the user of our program responded with an age that is between 13 and 19, nothing has changed. However, if the age is anything else, we have a new if statement. As this one is located within the else section of the first one, we know that the age is either below 13 or above 13. The second if statement checks whether it is less than 13. And, if so, prints the You are a child message.

Now, think about what condition we have if we enter the second else section. First, we know that age is not between 13 and 19, or we would not be in this part of the program at all. We also know that the age is not below 13 because, if it was, we would have executed the You are a child part. We only have one option left; the age must be above 19.

To have an if statement directly following an else statement, like we just saw, is so common that some languages have a special construct for it, called elif. In such a language, the same code would look something like this:

```
if age >= 13 and age <= 19 then
    print "You are a teenager"
    print "I hope you are having fun. "
elif age < 13 then
    print "You are a child"
else
    print "You are getting old"
end_if
```

The logic of the program is the same, but the code is more compact. As you can see, we have the second condition, if the age is below 13, on the same line as the old `else` statement, and the `else` statement has now changed into an `elif` statement. The word, `elif`, is just made up of the two words, `else` and `if`.

Additionally, note that, in the first example, the program ended with two lines containing `end_if`. The second version just has one.

If you look at the second program, you can now clearly see that there are three different sections and that only one of them will be executed:

- If the age is between 13 and 19, we enter the first section and execute the code within that block. After that, we are done, and the rest of the code will be skipped.

- If the age is below 13, we will first skip the first part and go to the `elif` part. The condition here is true, so we will enter this part and execute the code within. After that, we are done and can, again, skip to the end.

- Finally, if the age is greater than 19, we will first skip over the first section and go to the `elif` part. The condition found here will also be evaluated to false, so we skip ahead to the `else` part. As this part does not contain any condition, we will always end up here if none of the preceding conditions were true.

Even if the language we are using does not have an `elif` statement, we can create the same logic anyway. Consider the following code:

```
if age >= 13 and age <= 19 then
    print "You are a teenager"
    print "I hope you are having fun. "
else if age < 13 then
    print "You are a child"
else
    print "You are getting old"
end_if
```

You can see that the only thing that has changed here is that the `elif` statement has been replaced with the two words, `else` and `if`. The rest is the same and the logic is also unchanged.

To use this idea with nested `if` statements such as this can be very efficient. First, we must understand that we can have as many of these as we need. The structure can then look like this:

```
if condition1 then
    do option1
elif condition2 then
    do option2
elif condition3 then
    do option3
elif conditon4 then
    do option5
else
    do option6
end_if
```

If you look at this structure, you can see that this looks like a fork, where we only can choose one of the tines:

Figure 7.4: Nested if statements are like a fork

When we have one out of many things that can be true, we do have an option. It is another fork-like structure that works pretty much the same way as the nested `if` statement we just saw. It is called a `switch` statement. We will study this next.

Selection with the switch statement

One alternative, when we have one option out of many that can be true, is the `switch` statement. It also works with conditions even if they are not as apparent as they are in an `if` statement.

Another difference is that a `switch` statement only compares values for equality. The reason for it is that it is not suitable for the age logic we used when we explored the `if` statement, as we wanted to see whether the age was between two values. Instead, it is perfect if we're going to match it to a value that is fixed. We will soon look at a real example. However, first, let's explore the structure of a `switch` statement.

What a `switch` statement looks like depends on what language we use. What we will see here is a structure that is rather common, but when applying it, you will need to look up the correct syntax for your language.

A `switch` statement begins by stating what variable we want to check. It is common for languages to use the `switch` keyword for this.

The structure looks something like this:

```
switch(variable)


end_switch
```

In this example, the name, `variable`, is just a placeholder for the actual variable we want to work with. Between the `switch` keyword and `end_switch`, we will need to specify each value we want to compare the variable to. It could look something like this:

```
switch(variable)
    case 1:
        ...
    case 2:
        ...
    case 3:
        ...
end_switch
```

Each case specifies the value that we compare the variable to. The first case compares it to 1, the second to 2, and so on. The ellipsis (. . .) marks the location where we will insert the code for each option. The first ellipsis is to indicate which code will be executed if the variable is 1, the second for when the value is 2, and so on.

In many languages, we have something that is called a *fallthrough*. What this means is that when the right value is found, the code within that `case` statement will execute, but then the code in all the `case` statements that follow will also execute. So, if the value of the variable is 2, the code for both 2 and 3 will execute. The reason it does that is so that we can have multiple `case` instances following each other and just one code block for them.

To indicate that we want the fallthrough to stop, we must give an instruction that we are done, and we can now jump to the end of the switch statement. This instruction is, usually, break. It is shown in the following example:

```
switch (variable)
    case 0:
        print "Zero"
        break
    case 1:
    case 3:
    case 4:
    case 7:
    case 8:
        print "Odd value"
        break
    case 2:
    case 4:
    case 6:
    case 8:
        print "Even value"
        break
end_switch
```

Normally, we have one value for each case block, so the code will look like this:

```
switch(variable)
        case 1:
            ...
            break
        case 2:
            ...
            break
        case 3:
            ...
            break
end_switch
```

If the value of the variable is 2, the code within that block will execute, and when the `break` statement is reached, the execution of the whole `switch` statement will end. This is good, as only one of the options can be true. So, if one has been executed, we know that we are done.

You could argue that the `break` statement in the `case` block for the value of 3 is unnecessary as we don't have any more statements that we can fall through to. However, it is a good practice to have it there because we might add more options in the future, and then we wouldn't want to take the risk of forgetting to add that `break`.

`switch` statements also have something that resembles the `else` part of an `if` statement, that is, a block that would execute if no other values evaluated to true. In a `switch` statement, this is called `default`. It usually comes at the very end, after all of the `case` statements. It can look like this:

```
switch(variable)
        case 1:
            ...
            break
        case 2:
            ...
            break
        case 3:
            ...
            break
        default:
            ...
            break
end_switch
```

Again, the last `break` statement is optional, but we keep it there for consistency. Note that now we can appreciate that we had a break within number 3, since, without it, a value of 3 would first execute the code in the 3 block and then fall through to the default block.

Now we have all the parts of a `switch` statement in place, so let's look at an example of when and how it can be used.

Here, we will ask the user of our program to input the numeric value for a month, that is, 1 for January, 2 for February, and so on. We will store the number the user entered in a variable we call `month`. We can now use this variable in a `switch` statement to figure out the name that matches the number the user gave us. Consider the following code:

```
print "Enter a month number: "
input month

switch (month)
    case 1:
            month_string = "January"
            break
    case 2:
            month_string = "February"
            break
    case 3:
            month_string = "March"
            break
    ...
    case 12:
            month_string = "December"
            break
    default:
            month_string = "Invalid"
            break
end_switch

print "The name of the month you entered is " + month_string
```

In the preceding code, months 4 to 11 are left out, but they are repeated using the same pattern.

Let's say the user enters 8. The program will start at the top and check case 1. If this has been an `if` statement instead of a `switch`, case 1 would be equivalent to this:

```
if month == 1 then
```

Since the user entered 8 and not 1, this is false, so the program will go to the next case, case 2, and try again. There is still no luck, so it will continue all the way down to case 8, where it finally gets a match. It will now enter this block and create a variable called month_string and assign the value of August to it.

On the next line, it hits a break. This means, "get me out of here," so the program will now skip all of the other tests because it knows that it is done.

If the user entered an invalid month, say 14, all cases will first be checked, but as none will be true, the code in the default block will execute and the month_string variable will get an Invalid value.

On the very last line, the text, The name of the month you entered is, will be printed, and the value we have in our month_string variable will be appended to the end.

The execution of the program would look something like this:

```
Enter a month number: 8
The name of the month you entered is August
```

With the help of the selection structures, if and switch, we can build complex logic.

When designing a solution, you should keep a couple of things in mind:

- It is easy to get a bit confused as the logic will, at times, feel entangled and hard to understand. It is, therefore, essential to remember what we said earlier in this book: try to zoom in to one small subproblem, understand it, and design a solution for it. When that is in place, you can zoom out a bit and examine how it works in a bigger context. Then, you can repeat this process. This might sound very abstract but keep it in the back of your mind, and try to use this approach when you feel that a problem is getting too complex.

- Always remember that the readability of your code counts. What this means is that if you have a solution that works but the code is very complex and hard to read, you should go back and try to rewrite it, making sure that it still works but also that another programmer (or you in the future) easily can read and understand what the code does.

Now that we have covered two of the three fundamental pillars that programming rests upon, sequence and selection, it is time to tackle the last one, iteration.

Iteration with the for loop

The first type of iteration we will look at is the `for` loop. This is a kind of loop when we, in one way or the other, know how many times we want to repeat something. This can be a fixed number of times, such as iterating over a list using the days of the week. We know it is always 7. It can also be that we have values in an array. We might not know precisely how many items there are in the array at any given time; however, as we will see, there are ways to ask the array how many objects it is currently holding.

When using a `for` loop, we will work with a variable that keeps track of how many times we have iterated. We can decide what value this variable shall start on. It is this variable that helps us to know when to stop iterating. Let's look at an example:

```
for i = 0 to 10
    ...
end_for
```

Here, we create (or declare, as a programmer would say) a variable called i. The name, i, is frequently used as the name for this variable since it is often used as an index. However, we will discuss that in more detail later. After the assignment operator (=), we say that we want to give i a starting value of 0. We will then repeat the code within the `for` block and i will be increased by one for each iteration. The value of 10 is the stop condition. When i has reached this value, it should stop repeating and continue executing the code that comes after the loop.

If we print the value that i currently has inside the loop, the code will look like this:

```
for i = 0 to 10
    print i
end_for
```

Most languages will print the values of 0 to 9 and not 0 to 10. That might seem strange, but if we look at the logic that the `for` loop uses, we can understand why that is.

When we first hit the line with the `for` loop, the variable, i, is created and initialized with the value of 0, since we said that we want this as our starting value.

It will then compare the value that i has with the second value we gave, 10. If they are equal, the loop will stop. As this is the first iteration, the value is 0 and they are not equal; therefore, the code inside the loop will execute. When we come back up to the line with the for loop again, the value in i is incremented by one, that is, 0 + 1 = 1. This value is now compared to our end value, 10. This is still not a match. It will continue like this until the value of i is 9. When returning to the line with the for loop again, it will increase i by 1, making it 10. Now, when the values are compared, they will be equal and the for loop will end. So, we will never enter the loop when i has the value of 10 and that is why we only see the values of 0 to 9 printed.

As mentioned before in this book, the C programming language has had a huge impact on the syntax of many other languages. The way in which for loops are written is such an example. Let's examine what the same for loop would look like in C:

```c
int i;
for (i = 0; i < 10; i++)
{
    printf("%d", i);
}
```

On the first line, we declare the variable, i, also stating that it shall work with the data type, int. In the C language, statements end with a semicolon. That is why we have one after the i variable.

Then comes the for loop. In C, we have three sections in a for loop. They are separated using semicolons. The first is the initialization. That is where we say i = 0. This means that i will have a value of 0 in the first iteration.

The second part is the condition that states how long we shall continue to loop. Here, we say i < 10. We can read this as *continue as long as i is less than 10*.

The last section indicates how i will change in each iteration. Here, we say i++. This is C's way of saying, *take whatever is in the variable, i, right now and increase it by one, then store the new value in i*.

The line inside the loop might look a bit strange. But there is no need to go into all of the details of how C handles printing values, as it is far more complicated than in most languages. The only thing we need to know is that it will print the current value of i.

The output will be the same as in our earlier example, 0 to 9. Here, we can see why the value of 10 is not printed because the condition says i < 10. When i is 10, this is no longer true, and the loop will exit. If we, instead, had i <= 10, the value of 10 would be included.

The languages that use this style include C++, C#, Java, JavaScript, PHP, and Go. With slight variations, they all have for loops that use the three sections that we saw in the C loop.

For simplicity, we will not use the C-style loops in this book but stick to the first version we looked at instead. This will help us to focus on how for loops work without being distracted by the syntax for writing them.

If we want to change the loop variable in any other way than just increasing it by one, we can do that as follows:

```
for i = 0 to 10 step 2
    print i
end_for
```

Here, we will increment the value that i has by 2 each time. The output of this program will be similar the following:

```
2
4
6
8
```

It still starts at 0, but as we increment by 2, all the odd numbers will be skipped. Just like earlier, we are exiting the loop when i reaches 10.

Sometimes, we want to put a for loop inside another for loop. This is called a nested for loop. We will need two different variables for these loops so that they don't interfere with each other. As an example, we might want to go over all 7 days of the week. We will print the days such as day 0, day 1, and so on. We will start at 0 for simplicity, but we could, of course, have started at 1 if we wanted to.

For each day, we want to print all of the hours of that day. If we think about it, we will need a loop for the days. When we are inside this loop, we can imagine that we are working with one single day. For this day, we will need to print all of the hours. Then, when we are done, we will need to repeat the process for the next day. Instead of using the variable name, i, we can use more meaningful names for the two loops. We will use day for the loop that handles the days and hour for the loop that controls the hours.

This is what the program should look like:

```
for day = 0 to 7
    print "day " + day
    for hour = 0 to 24
        print "hour " + hour
    end for
end for
```

The output would look something like this:

```
day 0
hour 0
hour 1
hour 2
...
hour 23
day 1
hour 0
hour 1
hour 2
...
day 6
...
hour 21
hour 22
hour 23
```

> **Note**
> We are leaving out parts of this long output. The parts left out are indicated by an ellipsis.

If we follow the logic of this program, we can see that we first start out with the outermost loop, that is, the one that handles the days. We have a variable called day and assign it to the starting value of 0.

Then, we print the text, day, and append the value stored in the variable named day. Note that day within quotes is a string that will be printed as it is, and day without quotes is the variable.

Then, we come to the innermost loop. This will handle the hours. This also starts out with a value of 0 and uses a variable called `hour`. It will print the current hour in the same way that we did with the days.

The program will run inside the inner loop until we get a value of 24 inside the variable, `hour`. Then, it will exit. The program will now go back to the beginning of the outer loop, the one handling days. It will increase the `day` variable by one, and check whether it is less than 7. And, because it is, we will enter the loop, and the process will repeat.

It is also possible to go backward in a `for` loop. We just need to switch the starting and end values and decrease the loop variable instead of increasing it. It can look something like this:

```
for i = 10 to -1 step -1
    print i
end_for
```

Here, we will count down from 10 to 0. Since we want the value of 0 to be printed, we have set the stop value to -1. We can see the stop value as the first value that should not be part of the range. Since we are decreasing the variable by 1, the first value after 0 is -1. We have also changed the step to -1. This will cause the variable to decrement by 1 each time.

Sometimes, we don't know how many times we want to repeat something. We can use another type of `for` loop, that is, the `while` loop. Let's explore what that is.

Iteration with the while loop

Let's assume that we want to write a small dice-guessing game. The user will need to enter a guess between 1 and 6. The computer will then roll a dice and let the user know whether their guess was correct or not. The program will then allow the user to guess again, and again, and again. However, if the user enters a value of 0 as their guess, we will let them exit the game.

We have no way of knowing how many times the user wants to play the game. They might give up after the first try or go on for hundreds of attempts (which is not that likely as this is a rather dull game, but you get the point).

A `for` loop would not work that well for us here as we would need to say how many times the user would need to play before we let them out of the loop. Instead, another type of loop that is perfect for this scenario is the `while` loop. This loop works on a condition instead of a count. If the condition is true, it will continue to loop.

The structure looks like this:

```
while condition
    ...
end_while
```

If the condition is true, we will continue looping. This means that somewhere within the loop, the condition must be able to change or it will never get out of the loop.

We will still need a variable to use in the condition. For example, we could use a Boolean variable for this. Recall that a Boolean variable only can hold the values of `true` and `false`, and a condition is something that will be evaluated to either true or false. It can look like this:

```
continue = true
while continue
    ...
    some code that eventually sets continue to false
end_while
```

Here, we declare a variable called `continue` and set it to `true`.

The `while` loop will look at the content of this variable, and, since it is `true`, it will enter the loop.

It will now continue to loop as the variable has the value of `true`. It is, therefore, vital that we, at some point inside the loop, assign a value of `false` to the variable so that we can get out of the loop.

Let's now build our guessing game using a `while` loop:

```
continue = true
while continue
    print "I will roll a dice. Guess the result(end with 0): "
    input guess
    dice = random(1, 6)
    if guess == 0 then
        continue = false
    else
        if guess == dice then
            print "Yes, you got it!"
        else
```

```
        print "Sorry, better luck next time."
    end_if
  end_if
end_while
print "Thank you for playing this exciting game."
```

Before going over the program and how it works, take a look at the following output from a potential game:

```
I will roll a dice. Guess the result(end with 0): 4
Sorry, better luck next time
I will roll a dice. Guess the result(end with 0): 2
Sorry, better luck next time
I will roll a dice. Guess the result(end with 0): 6
Yes, you got it!
I will roll a dice. Guess the result(end with 0): 0
Thank you for playing this exciting game.
```

Looking at the code, we can observe the following:

- We can see that we first create our variable that will keep track of when to stop looping. Since the `while` loop runs if something is true, we set this variable to `true`. If it is set to `false`, we will not enter the loop and the game will be over before we even had a chance to play.

- Then comes the actual loop. Since the variable initially is set to `true`, we will enter the loop.

- The first thing that happens in the loop is that there is some text that provides instructions to the user. This is an excellent idea to let the user know how to exit the game.

- We then take the input from the user and store it in a variable called `guess`.

- Now it is time to roll a virtual dice. The `random(1, 6)` will give us a random number between 1 and 6. We store that random number in a variable named `dice`.

Before we check whether the user made a correct guess or not, we will examine whether the user has entered 0 to indicate that the game is over. The reason we do that before we check whether the guess is correct or not is because if the user wants to end the game, we don't want to check their guess as we know 0 will indicate a wrong guess. We don't want to treat the input of 0 as a guess.

If guess is equal to 0, we want to exit the loop. We do that by assigning false to the continue variable.

As the rest of the content of the loop is in an else block, we will skip that if the input was 0. When we move to the line with while, continue will now be false, and we will exit the loop and print the thank you line at the end of the program.

If the user has, instead, entered something other than 0, we will enter the first else block.

The first line inside of this block is where we check whether the user made a correct guess. If the value we store in guess and the value that is in the dice variable is equal, we have a winner.

If so, we will print a message congratulating the user. If not, we will let the user know that the guess was wrong.

Looking at the code, we can see that the indentation of the code helps us to see which part belongs to which block. Note the block that starts with the following line:

```
if guess == dice then
```

This can only be reached if the user did not enter a value of 0 since it is within an else block.

As you can see, a while loop is a handy feature. It has a sibling, the do while loop, which is almost identical to the while loop but with a little twist. Let's examine that next.

Iteration with the do while loop

The do while loop has the same features as the while loop. do while works on a condition and can be used when we don't know how many iterations we will need to make.

The difference from the while loop is that where a while loop might never execute because the condition could be false the first time we test it. In comparison, the do while loop is guaranteed to run at least once. The reason for this is because the condition is moved from the beginning of the loop to the end of it.

This can be good for several reasons, and it can make our guessing game slightly less complicated. However, before we do that, we should look at what a do while loop looks like:

```
do
    ...
    some code that eventually sets the condition to false
while condition
```

The do keyword marks the beginning of the loop. As you can see, there is nothing more on this line, so the program must run through the code inside the loop at least once to reach the condition at the very end.

Just as with the while loop, we must have some code that somehow modifies the condition so that we can get out of the loop.

One interesting aspect, when compared with the while loop, is that we don't need to create a variable outside the loop to hold a value that we can use for our condition. The reason for this is that, since we are checking the condition at the very end, we might be able to perform the condition check using a variable that we create inside the loop. To see this in action, let's modify our guessing game to use a do while loop. Take a look at the following snippet:

```
do
    print "I will roll a dice. Guess the result(end with 0): "
    input guess
    dice = random(1, 6)
    if guess != 0 then
        if guess == dice then
            print "Yes, you got it!"
        else
            print "Sorry, better luck next time."
        end_if
    end_if
while guess != 0
print "Thank you for playing this exciting game."
```

The program is a bit shorter. This is because the continue variable is gone. If you look at the condition found on the penultimate line, you will see that we are using the guess variable directly to check whether it is not 0 (remember that the != operator means, does not equal to). This means if the user does not input 0, we will repeat.

We have also changed the if statement inside the loop. It now checks whether the guess variable is not equal to 0, and only if it is, we will treat it as a proper guess.

If we have a sequence of things, such as an array, for example, it can be handy to go through that sequence one item at a time. We do have a loop for that too, which is the for each loop. Let's explore how that works next.

Iterating over sequences using for each

When we have a sequence of things, we often want to go through it item by item. We can, of course, do that using a `for` loop, like this:

```
names = ["Anna", "Bob", "Carl", "Danielle"]
for i = 0 to names.length
    print "Hi " + names[i]
end_for
```

On the first line, we declare an array of strings containing some names. We are using a variable called `names` to store the values.

Then, we use a `for` loop, starting at 0. To find out how many times we will iterate, we ask the array how many items it currently has stored. We do that by using the `names` variable, and, by using a dot, we can get what is known as a property from the array. This property is a value that stores how many items the array currently has. The way we can ask a sequence how many items it has will differ from language to language, but it will most likely be something like what we have done.

We need to remember two things here:

- When using an index to retrieve a value from the array, we start at 0. This means that we need to give our loop a start value of 0, since `Anna` will be stored at that index.

- We need to make sure that the ending value is one that is greater than the last index in the `for` loop. Our array has four values, so when we ask it for its length, that is the value we get. However, when indexing into the array, we need to use the values of 0, 1, 2, and 3. This is four values, and the counting starts at 0, not 1. Since we know that the second value we give in the `for` loop is the ending value, and it is the next value outside the range we want, then saying that we want to end at `names.length` ensures that we only get the values of 0, 1, 2, and 3.

Inside the loop, you can see that we are using the `loop` variable to index into the array. The first time, we will get `Anna`, the next time, we will get `Bob`, and so on.

An easier and safer way to do this is by using something known as a `for each` loop. What this will do is it will go through a sequence and give us one of its items, one at a time. Taking the same previous code and using such a loop will now be like the following:

```
names = ["Anna", "Bob", "Carl", "Danielle"]
foreach name in names
    print "Hi " + name
end_foreach
```

Now, this is much nicer. We can read this as follows:

- From the sequence names, give us the first item and store its value in the name variable.

- In the first iteration, name will contain Anna. The loop keeps track of where it is in the sequence. So, in the next iteration, name will be given the value of Bob.

  Additionally, note that we don't need to keep track of how many things there are in the sequence, and we don't need to use any indexing, since indexing starts at 0 and not 1.

This kind of loop gives us cleaner and more readable code that also reduces the risk of us inserting any errors into the code.

We can use this loop to iterate over any sequence. As a string is a sequence of characters, using this loop on a string will give us each character that the string is made up of. Consider the following code example:

```
print "Please enter your name: "
input name
foreach character in name
    print character
end foreach
```

Here, we ask the user for a name and store the answer in a variable called name. We will then iterate through the variable, one character at the time. The current character will be stored in a variable called character. Inside the loop, we will just print that character.

Running this program will give us an output like this:

```
Please enter your name: Charlotte
C
h
a
r
l
o
t
t
e
```

We have looked at four different ways to make iterations and all of them have their different use cases. View them as a set of tools that we have at our disposal and can pick and use as needed. Add to that the tools for selection that we looked at earlier in this chapter and the toolset will keep improving!

Summary

Sequence, selection, and iteration are the three pillars that programming rests upon, and, in this chapter, we have covered the latter two.

Selection is when we test values in variables using a condition that can be either true or false. If our test turns out to be true, we can let the program execute a block of code. If it turns out to be false, we can have another block that only runs if in the case. This is done with the help of `if` statements.

Sometimes, we have multiple options to choose from, and we need to pick one. We could then use a `switch` statement. Using it instead of an `if` statement can make your code less verbose and easier to read.

The common task of repetition can be done in at least four ways, with the most common being the `for` loop. This loop will let us iterate a fixed number of times.

When we don't know how many times we want to iterate, we can use either a `while` loop or a `do while` loop. They will both iterate as long as a condition is true. This will let us write very flexible applications that might repeat something twice.

The difference between the `while` loop and the `do while` loop is where the condition is located. In a `while` loop, it comes at the beginning, and, in a `do while`, it comes at the end.

If we have a sequence of something, using a `for each` loop is the best choice, since it will go through the sequence and give us one of its objects at a time. It is a safe structure to use because it makes sure that we actually get all the values and don't miss out on the first or the last one.

In the next chapter, we will structure our code with the help of functions. They are a great way to make our code easier to read, understand, and maintain. They are also perfect for helping us to reuse the code that we have written.

8
Understanding Functions

There are a number of useful concepts that we, as programmers, always should follow. One is to write code that is easy to read and understand. Another is to avoid duplicating code. When you start out your career as a programmer, you will find yourself copying and pasting code and just changing some small things here and there. This is a bad habit as it nullifies the first concept of code that is easy to read because reading more or less the same lines over and over is tedious and it is hard to spot the tiny differences.

A better solution is to package code that we want to reuse several times into a function. A function is a way for us to give a name to a block of code and then, with this name, the code block can be called over and over every time we want it to execute.

In this chapter, you will learn the following:

- Deciding what goes into a function
- Writing a function
- Returning values from a function
- Passing arguments to a function
- Working with local and global variables

Deciding what goes into a function

A function is a way for us to package a code block and give it a name. This is a good idea for several reasons. Back in *Chapter 4, Software Projects and How We Organize Our Code*, we talked about software modules and that dividing our code into small parts is wise as it will give us code that is easier to read, update, and maintain. The same reason applies to functions as they, too, package our code into smaller units. Another reason we want to use functions is so we can easily reuse parts of our code.

When deciding what will go into a function, we can have one rule of thumb. A function should always do only one thing and it will be named after what reflects that. What this means is that if we have a function called `send_email_and_print_invoice`, we are doing things wrong. This function does two distinct tasks and should, therefore, be two separate functions. We can rephrase this rule with a quote by Robert C. Martin, the author of an excellent book on writing clean code:

"A function should do something or answer something, but not both."

What this means is that a function either should have a very well-specified task and only do that task and nothing else or it should answer a well-specified question and only answer that question and nothing else, and a single function should absolutely not do both of these things.

Another quote from Robert C. Martin about functions is as follows:

"The first rule of functions is that they should be small."

This is an interesting quote because it raises some questions. What if I have a very well-defined problem that I would like to package within a function so it follows the first quote, but the problem is rather complex and the resulting function ends up being several hundred lines of code? Would that not contradict the second quote? Yes, it would and we will need to deal with it. We can take this long function and find subtasks and move these subtasks into separate functions. How we split a function into several smaller functions might not be that obvious at first glance, but this is something we will see in the *Splitting the code further* section.

If we create a function with the first quote in mind, it does only one thing, and if this is true, would not breaking it up into smaller things contradict the second quote, meaning that the function does several things? No, not necessarily. Think of something you often do, such as making breakfast. That is one single thing, but it can be broken down into several smaller things that together make up the tasks of cooking breakfast. You would make coffee or tea, toast some bread, boil an egg, and so on.

Observe the following figure:

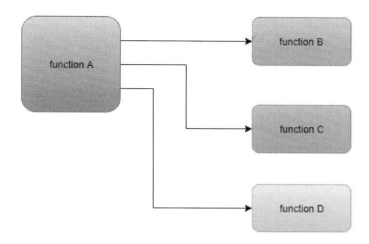

Figure 8.1 – A function that uses other functions to fulfill its task

The preceding figure illustrates how a function, here called **function A**, has been broken up into several smaller functions, and to accomplish its task, it uses subtasks of **function B**, **function C**, and **function D**. Compare this to the following figure, where we illustrate making breakfast in the same way:

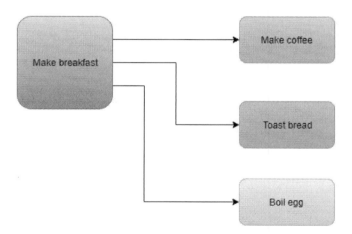

Figure 8.2 – The task of making breakfast broken down into subtasks

Functions are an important building block of computer programs; let's see how we can write them. So, after understanding what comprises a function, let's see how to use it.

Writing a function

Let's see what a function looks like in code:

```
function name()
    code within this function
    more function code
end_function
```

Here, we see that a function has a name, just like a variable. The conventions used by a language for naming functions are usually the same as those used for variables. If you don't remember what those were, you can find them in *Chapter 6, Working with Data – Variables*, in the *Naming conventions* section.

After the function name, we find open and close parentheses. Whenever we refer to this function, they will be included after the name. They will also have another use, which we will see later in this chapter.

After that, we see a code block, the body of loops and `if` statements, for example. This is the code that will be executed when the function is called.

A function can be called just by using its name, and we must not forget the parentheses. Calling the preceding function would look like this:

```
name()
```

All of the code within this function will now run. Once this is done, the program execution will return to where the call occurred and continue from there.

The following program illustrates this:

```
function say_hi()
    print "Hi there!"
end_function

print "Before the function"
say_hi()
print "After the function"
```

Even if the code for the function is above the rest of the function, it will not execute until we call the function, so the output when running this program will be this:

```
Before the function
Hi there!
After the function
```

We can now call the function as often as we like, and all of the code within it will run each time. So, for example, check the following code:

```
function say_hi()
    print "Hi there!"
end_function

print "Before the function"
say_hi()
say_hi()
say_hi()
print "After the function"
```

We can see that we are making three calls to the function. This is reflected in the output, as follows:

```
Before the function
Hi there!
Hi there!
Hi there!
After the function
```

Now that we know what a function looks like, we can try to write a more realistic one and see how it can make code easier to read and better structured.

Moving code into a function

Assume that we are writing a program that calculates how many seconds have passed since midnight.

The code for this might look like the following:

```
time_now = now()
time_midnight = Date(time_now.year, time_now.month. time_now.
    day)
time_diference = time_now - time_midnight
seconds_since_midnight = time_difference.total_seconds()
```

This code will first get the current date and time. Note that it is the full date-time, that is, the year, month, day, hour, minute, and second. All of this is stored in the time_now variable.

On the second line, we create an object that will hold the date and time for the previous midnight. We are using the current year, month, and day. As we have the current date and time in the time_now variable, we can use it to get the current year, month, and day. This will set the hour, minutes, and seconds to 0 as we did not provide a value for them. The idea is that today's date with hour = 0, minute = 0, and second = 0 is the previous midnight.

Then, we take the current date and time and subtract the date and time for midnight. This will give us the time difference between now and past midnight.

Finally, we use this difference and convert it into the total number of seconds. In this case, the time_difference variable is an object that can hold time information, that is, how many hours, minutes, and seconds have elapsed since midnight. How this works will differ from language to language. Here, this object provides the functionality to give us this time in the total number of seconds. Now we have a variable called seconds_since_ midnight that contains the number of seconds since the last midnight.

But if we want to do this now and again in a number of places in our program, we will end up with something like this:

```
time_now = now()
time_midnight = Date(time_now.year, time_now.month. time_now.
    day)
time_diference = time_now - time_midnight
seconds_since_midnight = time_difference.total_seconds()

do some other stuff
do some more stuff

time_now = now()
time_midnight = Date(time_now.year, time_now.month. time_now.
    day)
```

```
time_diference = time_now - time_midnight
seconds_since_midnight = time_difference.total_seconds()
```

As we can see, the four lines that calculate the time get repeated. And we would need to do this every time we want to get the number of seconds that has passed since midnight.

A better solution would be to move the code where we perform the calculation into a function. It would look something like this:

```
function calculate_seconds()
    time_now = now()
    time_midnight = Date(time_now.year, time_now.month. time_
        now.day)
    time_diference = time_now - time_midnight
    seconds_since_midnight = time_difference.total_seconds()
end_function
```

Every time we need the calculation, we can now call the function and we no longer need to repeat the code.

The full program will now look like this:

```
function calculate_seconds()
    time_now = now()
    time_midnight = Date(time_now.year, time_now.month. time_
        now.day)
    time_diference = time_now - time_midnight
    seconds_since_midnight = time_difference.total_seconds()
end_function

calculate_seconds()
do some other stuff
do some more stuff
calculate_seconds()
```

As we can see, this is much better as we only need to code for calculating the time once. But we do have a problem. The result from the calculation is *trapped* within the function. By trapped, I mean that we calculate the correct number of seconds but the value obtained can't get out of the function so there is no way for us to use this value outside of it. To solve this problem, we will need to return the result back out to the caller. Let's see how that works.

Returning values from a function

The idea behind a function is that it not only can be used to package code so we can reuse it over and over but can also do something that will produce some sort of value. In our example with the time calculator, the function has calculated a result, the number of seconds that have elapsed since midnight, and we now want that value at the location where we called the function. Functions have the ability to return data, and this is a feature we can use to get the value.

In its simplest form, returning a value from a function works like this:

```
function greet()
    return "Hello my friend"
end_function

result = greet()
print result
```

Here, we have a function called greet. All it does is return a string containing the greeting, Hello my friend. Remember that the code within a function is not executed until the function is actually called. The call happens below the function. Consider what happens when the following row is called:

```
result = greet()
```

Things work as they always do. The thing to the right of the assignment operator (=) is executed first. This is the call to the function.

Now the program will jump to the actual function, executing the code within it. The only thing inside the function is this:

```
return "Hello my friend"
```

We must understand two things about this line. First, a line with the return keyword will exit the function, even if there is more code following it. This might sound strange, and we will soon come back to that. Secondly, it will return whatever follows the word return back to the location that called the function.

This will take us back to this line:

```
result = greet()
```

We are now done with the operation on the right of =, and that has returned the Hello my friend string. That string is now assigned to the result variable.

On the last line, the content of that variable is printed.

Now, this is a silly program, as the function always returns the same thing, but it illustrates how `return` works. We can now use this in our function that calculates the number of seconds since midnight, as follows:

```
function calculate_seconds()
    time_now = now()
    time_midnight = Date(time_now.year, time_now.month. time_
        now.day)
    time_diference = time_now - time_midnight
    seconds_since_midnight = time_difference.total_seconds()
    return seconds_since_midnight
end_function
```

We did this by just adding one line at the end that returns the content of the `seconds_since_midnight` variable.

As this variable is created on the line just above `return`, we could actually remove it and instead return the result immediately like this:

```
function calculate_seconds()
    time_now = now()
    time_midnight = Date(time_now.year, time_now.month. time_
        now.day)
    time_diference = time_now - time_midnight
    return time_difference.total_seconds()
end_function
```

We can now call this function over and over and get the current number of seconds since midnight, as follows:

```
seconds_since_midnight = calculate_seconds()
print "Seconds since midnight: " + seconds_since_midnight
do some other stuff
do some more stuff
seconds_since_midnight = calculate_seconds()
print "Seconds since midnight: " + seconds_since_midnight
```

Here, we take the result returned back from the function and store it in a variable called `seconds_since_midnight`. We then print a text together with the result. The output might look something like this:

```
Seconds since midnight: 36769
```

This is great because now we can package a piece of code and we can call it whenever we want that code to run. We can also get data back from the function. But there is one piece missing. What if we would like to send data to the function? We can do that with the help of function arguments.

Function arguments

Often, we want our functions to be somewhat flexible, so they don't do exactly the same thing every time we call them. Consider the following two functions:

```
function add_2_and_3()
    return 2 + 3
end_function

function add_5_and_9()
    return 5 + 9
end_function
```

These two functions add two numbers and return the result. The first one adds 2 and 3, and the second one does the same but with 5 and 9. Now, these are just two pairs of numbers. If we would like to have a function that could add any numbers, we would need to create an endless number of functions.

But if we look at what the functions do, we can see that they are actually doing the same thing. They add two numbers and return the result. The only thing that changes are the numbers that are used in the addition operation.

What we want is to be able to pass the numbers we want to be added to the function so it can use them in the calculation, and by that, only have one function that can add any two numbers.

We can pass data to functions. We say that the function can accept arguments. For a function that can add two numbers, this can look like this:

```
function add(number1, number2)
    return number1 + number2
end_function
```

Here, we can see that we now have made use of the parenthesis that has followed the function name. This is where we can specify variables that will receive the data we want to pass to the function. Now we can use this function like this:

```
result = add(73, 8)
print(result)
result = add(2, 3)
print result
result = add(5, 9)
print result
```

The output, when running this program, will be this:

```
81
5
14
```

As we can see, we can now serve any two numbers using only one single function. Let's examine this a bit closer to really understand how this works.

Let's remove two of the calls to the function and only focus on what happens when we call the function the first time. We will have this code:

```
function add(number1, number2)
    return number1 + number2
end_function

result = add(73, 8)
print result
```

When we make the call to the function, we are passing in the values, 73 and 8. These are called arguments. On the receiving side, that is, in the add function, these two values will be assigned to two variables, number1 and number2. These are called the parameters of the function. The first argument that we pass in, the value, 73, is assigned to the first parameter, number1, and the second argument, the value, 8, will be assigned to the parameter called number2.

When we enter the function body, we now have these two variables and they are assigned the values that were passed to the function. So, this time, the variables will have the values 73 and 8 respectively.

When we call the function with the values, 2 and 3, then number1 will get 2 and number2 will get 3. This means that the parameters in the function will receive data in the same order as the paramters are passed to the function:

```
add(4, 5)
```

Here, number1 will get the value 4, and number2 will get the value 5:

```
add(5, 4)
```

Here, things are reversed as number1 gets 5 and number2 gets 4.

Now we can create functions that can take arguments and return values. Let's put all of this together and use it in a more realistic application, our automatic light app.

Now, having a function that adds two numbers together is pointless as we already have an operator that performs addition. It is only used here to illustrate the concept of arguments.

Functions in action

If we again go back to our application for turning on the lights outside our house and focus on the application running on our phone, we will see that we have at least two distinct things we need to do over and over again.

We will need to get our current position and we need to calculate our distance to home so we know whether it is time to turn on the lights or not.

These are two distinct tasks, and they are very well suited to being packaged up into two different functions, namely, `get_current_position` and `calculate_distance_to_home`, as shown in the following figure:

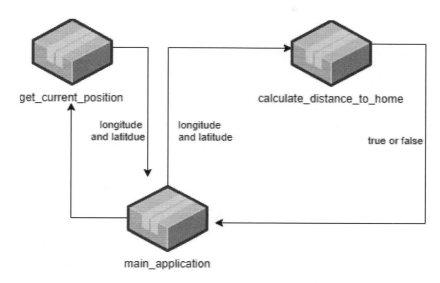

Figure 8.3 – main_application calls two different functions

This diagram shows that we have a block that we call `main_application`. This is a function, and it calls a function called `get_current_position` that will return the longitude and latitude, indicating the current position of the phone. Equipped with this information, `main_application` can now make another function call, this time, to a function called `calculate_distance_to_home`, and pass the longitude and latitude just obtained to it. This function will do some calculations and return either `true` or `false`, indicating whether we are within the range or not.

The question is, how did I decide to divide the code into these functions? Would we even need to have them, or could this program be written without the use of them? The answer is yes, it could, and we will now see why it is a good idea to use functions instead of just having all of the code in one place.

In *Chapter 7, Program Control Structures*, we had the following figure:

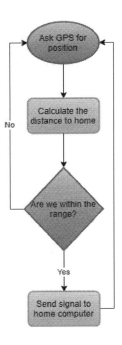

Figure 8.4 – Flowchart of the phone application

Here, we can see that we have a loop that runs forever (remember that forever in programming means as long as the program is running). We also have a selection statement that checks whether we are within the range and if we are, the signal is sent. After that, no matter whether we sent a signal or not, we will go back to the beginning and ask for our current position again.

Now, imagine the code for this application. It might look something like this:

```
while true
    some code that connects to the phone GPS
    some code that asks the GPS for the current position
    some code the calculates the distance to our home
    if distance_to_home < range_limit then
        some code that connects to the home computer
        some code that sends a notification to home computer
    end_if
end_while
```

Every line that starts with some code will most likely be made up of several code lines in the real application.

If we read the code, we can see that we start ours with a while loop that runs as long as true is true. true will always be true so this is how we can create an endless loop that will just go on and run forever.

If you compare the program to the flowchart in *figure 8.4*, you can see that the logic is identical:

- The oval at the top is the two lines in the code, which is connecting to the GPS and communicating with the GPS.

- The rectangle that follows the oval is represented by the code that calculates the distance.

- The diamond shape is the if statement and the code within the if statement is the final rectangle in the flow chart.

- The two arrows that bring us back to the top is the while loop that encapsulates the rest of the code.

Looking at the code, it might not look that bad, but remember that this is just an outline of what needs to be done.

If we now start to change this to see what the program actually might look like, we can change the two first lines into something like this:

```
location = Location
my_latitude = location.get_latitude()
my_longitude = location.get_longitude()
```

The first line creates some sort of location object that can be used to communicate with the GPS. Note that we store this object in a variable called location, with all lowercase letters. Location with a capital *L*, to the right, is the thing that creates this object for us. To see how this is actually done, we will need to read the documentation for the programming language we are currently using. Most likely, it will be done in a line that resembles this.

We can then use this location variable to get the current latitude and longitude.

Calculating the distance between two geographical coordinates is something that most of us can't even imagine how we should do. Searching online might scare us. What we will get back is that we must use something called the *haversine formula* (there are other ways to accomplish this too, but for this example, we will stick with this formula). Then, we get something like this that will explain the formula:

$$a = sin^2(\Delta\varphi/2) + \cos\varphi_1 \cdot \cos\varphi_2 \cdot sin^2(\Delta\lambda/2)$$

$$c = 2 \cdot atan2\left(\sqrt{a}, \sqrt{(1-a)}\right)$$

$$d = R \cdot c$$

Here, ϕ is latitude, λ is longitude, and R is the Earth's radius (the mean radius is 6,371 km). Note that all angles need to be in radians.

Don't be scared if you don't understand any of that. Most likely, someone else has already looked at that formula and translated it into source code for the language you are using. This is good as we can use it without actually understanding the formula. We must make sure, though, that the calculations done with it match other tools that do the same things. We will soon do such a test, but first, let's just see what such an implementation can look like.

In this example, we pretend that we are at the *Musée des Lettres et Manuscrits* in Paris and that we rent a home on *Avenue Victor-Hugo* in the same city. Musée des Lettres et Manuscrits is located at latitude 48.855421 and longitude 2.327688. Our pretend home on Avenue Victor Hugo is located at latitude 48.870320 and longitude 2.286560:

```
my_latitude = 48.855421
my_longitude = 2.327688
home_latitude = 48.870320
home_longitude = 2.286560
earth_radius = 6371
my_lat_radians = radians(my_latitude)
my_long_radians = radians(my_longitude)
home_lat_radians = radians(home_latitude)
home_long_radians = radians(home_longitude)
lat_distance = home_lat_radians - my_lat_radians
long_distance = home_long_radians - my_long_radians
a = sin(lat_distance / 2)**2 + cos(my_lat_radians) *
    cos(home_lat_radians) * sin(long_distance / 2)**2
distance = 2 * earth_radius * asin(sqrt(a))
print "The distance is " + distance + " km"
```

Wow, scary stuff, but the good thing is that we don't need to understand it to use it. We must just make sure that it works. As we can see at the top, we have the coordinates to the museum (that we pretend that we are visiting), followed by the coordinates to our home (that we pretend that we are renting). Running this program will give us the following output:

```
The distance is 3.4345378351411333 km
```

Plugging these same coordinates into an online geo coordinate distance calculator will give us the result shown in *figure 8.5*:

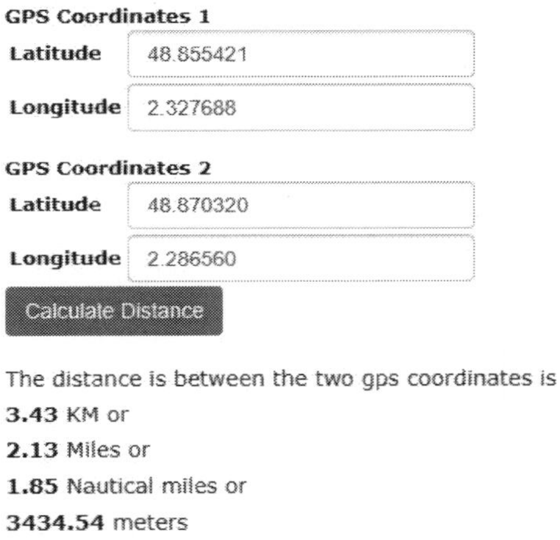

Figure 8.5 – Online geo coordinate distance calculator

As we can see, the result matches ours. We should perform more tests by trying other coordinates, both in our program and the calculator, to verify that the results match.

Great, now we can perform this calculation even if we don't understand all of the details for how it works.

We now have a distance that tells us how far we are from our Paris home. Now we need to decide how close we need to be to our home before we turn on the light. Maybe 500 meters is a good distance as we don't want to turn it on too early and not too late; 500 meters is 0.5 kilometers, so this is the value we can compare our distance to:

```
if distance < 0.5 then
    some code that connects to the home computer
    some code that sends a notification to home computer
end if
```

For now, let's ignore the code that connects to the home computer and sends the notification, and just put everything together that we have so far:

```
while true
    location = Location
    my_latitude = location.get_latitude()
    my_longitude = location.get_longitude()
    home_latitude = 48.870320
    home_longitude = 2.286560
    earth_radius = 6371
    my_lat_radians = radians(my_latitude)
    my_long_radians = radians(my_longitude)
    home_lat_radians = radians(home_latitude)
    home_long_radians = radians(home_longitude)
    lat_distance = home_lat_radians - my_lat_radians
    long_distance = home_long_radians - my_long_radians
    a = sin(lat_distance / 2)**2 + cos(my_lat_radians) *
        cos(home_lat_radians) * sin(long_distance / 2)**2
    distance = 2 * earth_radius * asin(sqrt(a))
    if distance < 0.5 then
        some code that connects to the home computer
        some code that sends a notification to home computer
    end_if
end_while
```

Reading this code is hard and confusing. What can we do about it? Functions are the answer. Let's see how that works.

Splitting the code further

When breaking a long code into small functions, we must remember that a function should do one thing or answer one question.

One trick we can use to identify separate tasks within the code is to read it from beginning to end, and when we feel that the application shifts its focus from one thing to another, we can insert a blank line into the code. Let's do that for the application that we have used so far:

```
while true
    location = Location
    my_latitude = location.get_latitude()
    my_longitude = location.get_longitude()

    home_latitude = 48.870320
    home_longitude = 2.286560
    earth_radius = 6371

    my_lat_radians = radians(my_latitude)
    my_long_radians = radians(my_longitude)
    home_lat_radians = radians(home_latitude)
    home_long_radians = radians(home_longitude)
    lat_distance = home_lat_radians - my_lat_radians
    long_distance = home_long_radians - my_long_radians
    a = sin(lat_distance / 2)**2 + cos(my_lat_radians) *
        cos(home_lat_radians) * sin(long_distance / 2)**2
    distance = 2 * earth_radius * asin(sqrt(a))

    if distance < 0.5 then
        some code that connects to the home computer
        some code that sends a notification to home computer
    end_if
end_while
```

As we can see, there are now blocks of code separated by blank lines. Let's study them closely.

There is nothing we can do about the first line with `while`, at least not at this point. It will just sit at the top and make sure that we repeat the code over and over.

After the line with `while`, three lines follow that all have to do with establishing our location. When reading the code, we should ask ourselves, what task does this line help us to accomplish? For all of these lines, the answer will be, answer the question where we are. But when we hit the line that begins with `home_latitude`, this is no longer true. We are now in a block of code that does something else. The code has shifted focus, so we insert a blank line.

We now have two lines that answer the question "where do we live?". They obviously belong together. But after these two lines, there is a line defining the radius of the earth. This is a noticeable shift in the focus so why did I not insert a blank line here?

The answer can be found if we look closer at these three lines. All three do have something in common. They all have fixed values that will never change. We say that these are constant values. We will deal with them later, but let's move on.

Then, we come to a larger block that deals with the distance calculation. That is a single task.

In the end, we have the `if` statement containing the signaling to the home computer that we have left unimplemented so far.

To begin with, we have two strong candidates for becoming functions here and that is where we get our current location and the distance calculation. Let's try to turn them into functions and we start with the part that tells us where we are.

Currently, that part of the code looks like this:

```
    location = Location
    my_latitude = location.get_latitude()
    my_longitude = location.get_longitude()
```

We can move these three lines into a function like this:

```
function get_current_position()
    location = Location
    my_latitude = location.get_latitude()
    my_longitude = location.get_longitude()
end_function
```

Now, we must check two things. First, does this function need any data as input? The answer is no. To accomplish its task, it does not need any more data. This means that this function will not take any arguments.

Secondly, will this function need to return any data back to the location where we called the function? The answer to this is yes, but it is a bit tricky.

The current longitude and latitude are now created inside a function and this makes it inaccessible outside it. These are called *local variables*, a topic we will discuss in more detail at the end of this chapter. We had the same problem with the function that calculated the number of seconds since midnight. We solved it then by returning the result using the return keyword. We will need to do that here too, but most programming languages will only let us return one single value from a function, but we need to return two values, both the latitude and longitude.

We can get around this limitation by putting the two values inside an array. Remember that an array is a sequence of things, and an array is treated as one single item, even if it contains many values.

We can change our function so it looks like this:

```
function get_current_position()
    location = Location
    my_latitude = location.get_latitude()
    my_longitude = location.get_longitude()
    return [my_latitude, my_longitude]
end_function
```

Note that the two values are inside square brackets. This creates an array and inserts latitude as its first value and longitude as its second.

We must now call the function and receive the coordinates in location in the code where we previously fetched the location. The while loop now looks like this:

```
function get_current_position()
    location = Location
    my_latitude = location.get_latitude()
    my_longitude = location.get_longitude()
    return [my_latitude, my_longitude]
end_function


while true
    position = get_current_position()

    home_latitude = 48.870320
    home_longitude = 2.286560
```

```
        earth_radius = 6371

    my_lat_radians = radians(my_latitude)
    my_long_radians = radians(my_longitude)
    home_lat_radians = radians(home_latitude)
    home_long_radians = radians(home_longitude)
    lat_distance = home_lat_radians - my_lat_radians
    long_distance = home_long_radians - my_long_radians
    a = sin(lat_distance / 2)**2 + cos(my_lat_radians) *
        cos(home_lat_radians) * sin(long_distance / 2)**2
    distance = 2 * earth_radius * asin(sqrt(a))

    if distance < 0.5 then
        some code that connects to the home computer
        some code that sends a notification to home computer
    end_if
end_while
```

On the first line inside the `while` loop, we are now making a call to the function. We will get the array containing the latitude and longitude and we store them in a variable we call `position`.

We have a problem now as, later on, when we calculate the distance, we will be using the variables, `my_latitude` and `my_longitude`. These two now only exist inside the function, so when we reach the lines that convert them into radians, we will get an error saying that `my_latitude` is undefined. This is how a programming language will tell you that it has no idea what `my_latitude` is.

The problem here is that we have packaged the coordinates inside an array that we have named `position`. We could solve this by replacing the two problematic lines with this:

```
    my_lat_radians = radians(position[0])
    my_long_radians = radians(position[1])
```

Remember that we can access individual items within an array by using the index to the position that the item has within the array. Also, remember that the indexing starts at 0.

> **Note**
>
> If you need a reminder on how arrays work, we talked about them in *Chapter 6, Working with Data – Variables* in the *Composite types* section.

As we added the latitude as the first element in the array, it can be found at index 0 and the longitude at index 1. This code is harder to read through as we must know how the array was created within the function to know that the latitude came before the longitude.

Another option that would make our code easier to read would be to unpack these two values into variables again like this:

```
position = get_current_position()
my_latitude = position[0]
my_longitude = position[1]
```

Now, after we are making the call, we insert the first value into a variable called my_latitude and the second into a variable called my_longitude. As we picked the same name that was later used in the calculation, we will not need to change it at all if we use this option.

I will go with a third option and will leave the variables in the array for now and not change the code in the calculation. We will soon see why.

We can now turn our attention to the calculation code and turn that into a function. This function will now look like this:

```
function calculate_distance_to_home()
    my_lat_radians = radians(my_latitude)
    my_long_radians = radians(my_longitude)
    home_lat_radians = radians(home_latitude)
    home_long_radians = radians(home_longitude)
    lat_distance = home_lat_radians - my_lat_radians
    long_distance = home_long_radians - my_long_radians
    a = sin(lat_distance / 2)**2 + cos(my_lat_radians) *
        cos(home_lat_radians) * sin(long_distance / 2)**2
    distance = 2 * earth_radius * asin(sqrt(a))
end_function
```

Again, we will now check to see whether this function needs any more data to fulfill its task. Yes, as this is written, we are missing several things. This function does not know about our latitude and longitude. It does not know the home latitude and longitude either and earth_radius is also unknown to it.

Let's turn the attention back to the three lines where we defined the home location and the radius of the earth. Who will need this data? When we think about it, the answer is, only the function we just created. This means that we can move these three lines into the function like this:

```
function calculate_distance_to_home()
    home_latitude = 48.870320
    home_longitude = 2.286560
    earth_radius = 6371

    my_lat_radians = radians(my_latitude)
    my_long_radians = radians(my_longitude)
    home_lat_radians = radians(home_latitude)
    home_long_radians = radians(home_longitude)
    lat_distance = home_lat_radians - my_lat_radians
    long_distance = home_long_radians - my_long_radians
    a = sin(lat_distance / 2)**2 + cos(my_lat_radians) *
        cos(home_lat_radians) * sin(long_distance / 2)**2
    distance = 2 * earth_radius * asin(sqrt(a))
end_function
```

We add them at the top, so they are all defined when they are needed later on in the function.

Now, we are only missing the latitude and longitude for our current position. This function must accept them as their arguments. We can now either say that this function takes two arguments, latitude and longitude, as separate parameters like this:

```
function calculate_distance_to_home(my_latitude, my_longitude)
```

Another option is that we can let this function accept an array with the values. This suits our needs as we know that we will get an array back from the other function we wrote. So, let's use that option.

It will look like this:

```
function calculate_distance_to_home(current_position)
```

We now accept an array, and we call it `current_position`. We must now make one change inside the function on the lines where we use `my_latitude` and `my_longitude`. We can do the same as we saw before and index into the array as follows:

```
my_lat_radians = radians(current_position[0])
my_long_radians = radians(current_position[1])
```

The full function now looks like this:

```
function calculate_distance_to_home(current_position)
    home_latitude = 48.870320
    home_longitude = 2.286560
    earth_radius = 6371

    my_lat_radians = radians(current_position[0])
    my_long_radians = radians(current_position[1])
    home_lat_radians = radians(home_latitude)
    home_long_radians = radians(home_longitude)
    lat_distance = home_lat_radians - my_lat_radians
    long_distance = home_long_radians - my_long_radians
    a = sin(lat_distance / 2)**2 + cos(my_lat_radians) *
        cos(home_lat_radians) * sin(long_distance / 2)**2
    distance = 2 * earth_radius * asin(sqrt(a))
end_function
```

Putting it all together

Now we must check whether this function needs to return something. It calculates the distance and we need that outside the function, so that value needs to be returned.

Again, we have two options. We can either return the value contained inside the variable distance like this:

```
distance = 2 * earth_radius * asin(sqrt(a))
return distance
```

Or, if not the previous option, we can make this shorter, though, as the `distance` variable is only used to hold the distance for one line. So, instead of using it to hold the value we want to return, we can return the result from the calculation directly and get rid of the `distance` variable. It would look like this:

```
return 2 * earth_radius * asin(sqrt(a))
```

That is better. The function is now finished and looks like this:

```
function calculate_distance_to_home(current_position)
    home_latitude = 48.870320
    home_longitude = 2.286560
    earth_radius = 6371

    my_lat_radians = radians(current_position[0])
    my_long_radians = radians(current_position[1])
    home_lat_radians = radians(home_latitude)
    home_long_radians = radians(home_longitude)
    lat_distance = home_lat_radians - my_lat_radians
    long_distance = home_long_radians - my_long_radians
    a = sin(lat_distance / 2)**2 + cos(my_lat_radians) *
        cos(home_lat_radians) * sin(long_distance / 2)**2
    return 2 * earth_radius * asin(sqrt(a))
end_function
```

We will now need to call it. Our `while` loop is now much cleaner and its main responsibility is to call our two functions. The loop now looks like this:

```
while true
    position = get_current_position()

    distance = calculate_distance_to_home(position)

    if distance < 0.5 then
        some code that connects to the home computer
        some code that sends a notification to home computer
    end_if
end_while
```

We call the new function by passing the `position` array to it, and we will get the distance back and store it in a variable called `distance`.

Now, this is more pleasant to look at. If you think about it, you can treat this as a table of contents in a book. On the first line, we call a function called `get_current_position`. The name of the function is chosen to reflect what it does. So, reading this line explains what happens. We can now decide whether we are interested in seeing what happens when we get the current position or not. If not, we can just accept that we get the current position back. If we do want to know how it works, we can go to the function and read the code there.

We can then treat the next line in the same way. The name tells us what the function does, so there is no need for us to go and read that. We can trust that it does its job and that we get a distance back.

The code is easier to read, maintain, and update, thanks to the use of functions. Another benefit is that complex distance calculation is hidden away in a function and we don't need to see it if we don't want to.

We now only have the part inside the `if` statement left. To communicate with the home computer, we can use something called *sockets*. The concept of sockets is rather advanced, and we will not go into any details of it here. We can just say that all of that code will go into a function of its own and we can call that function from within the `if` statement by using a final `while` loop that looks like this:

```
while true
    position = get_current_position()

    distance = calculate_distance_to_home(position)

    if distance < 0.5 then
        notify_home_computer()
    end_if
end_while
```

Compare this to the code we started with, which looked like this:

```
while true
    location = Location
    my_latitude = location.get_latitude()
    my_longitude = location.get_longitude()
```

```
        home_latitude = 48.870320
        home_longitude = 2.286560
        earth_radius = 6371
        my_lat_radians = radians(my_latitude)
        my_long_radians = radians(my_longitude)
        home_lat_radians = radians(home_latitude)
        home_long_radians = radians(home_longitude)
        lat_distance = home_lat_radians - my_lat_radians
        long_distance = home_long_radians - my_long_radians
        a = sin(lat_distance / 2)**2 + cos(my_lat_radians) *
            cos(home_lat_radians) * sin(long_distance / 2)**2
        distance = 2 * earth_radius * asin(sqrt(a))
        if distance < 0.5 then
            some code that connects to the home computer
            some code that sends a notification to home computer
        end_if
    end_while
```

This is a major clean up of the code and is indeed very helpful, not to mention less scary and more pleasing to the eye!

In this section, we have seen that when we create a variable inside a function, it becomes inaccessible for all of the code outside that function. We will now discuss this further with local and global variables.

Local and global variables

A variable declared (created) inside a function is called a local variable, and it can only be accessed from within the function. Outside the function, it is as if the variable never existed at all. Check the following code:

```
function my_function()
    name = "Lisa"
end_function


my_function()
print name
```

Here, we create and assign a value to the name variable inside the my_function function. Outside the function, we first call the function, and then we try to print the name. The program will crash with an error on the line where we try to print the name. The reason is that the name variable is unknown in this part of the program. It is only valid as long as we execute code inside the function.

This is a local variable. It is local as it is created inside the function.

If we instead change the program so it looks like this, things will be different:

```
name = "Bill"

function my_function()
    name = "Lisa"
end_function

my_function()
print name
```

It might be hard to see what happens here. To understand this, we must read the code as the compiler/interpreter will read the code when it executes it:

- It will start at the first line and see that we create a variable called name and assign the Bill string to it.
- It will then continue and see the function. It will not run the function; just remember that it exists.
- Then, we call the function, so the execution of the program will now jump up and run the code inside the function.
- Here we find a line where we assign the Lisa string to a variable called name. As it already knows about this variable, it will change its content and will store Lisa in it and the Bill string is now gone.
- The end of the function is now reached, so the execution jumps back down to where it came from.
- On the last line, the content of the variable name will be printed, which is Lisa.

From the working of the preceding code, we saw that as we moved the declaration of the variable out of the function, it turned global (for use in code) and so it is now a global variable. A global variable can be accessed from any location.

Some programming languages will not let us modify a global variable, as we did in the preceding example, but instead of the assignment of Lisa within the function, it will create a new variable with the same name.

It might sound as if global variables are the way to go. But it is actually the opposite. We shall always strive to use local variables as often as we can. The reason is that it is hard to control global variables.

Imagine that you have a program that is thousands of lines long, and all variables are global. They get changed here and there and all over, and then you discover that one of the variables has a value that would be impossible for it to have. Somewhere, a code line has changed this variable in a bad way. This is an error in our program, and we need to find it and fix it. But where is that line? As all parts of the program can change that variable (and all of the others that are declared global), it can be extremely hard to find that location. It might also be so that the reason this variable has a bad value is that some other variable had a bad value and that we discovered the error was just a side effect.

Code like this is called *spaghetti code*. The reason it is called this will be obvious if you look at figure 8.6, which illustrates how five functions change four global variables. Look at it and try to figure out how changed what and when:

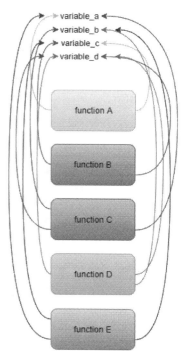

Figure 8.6 – Five functions changing four global variables

By using local variables, we will make things much cleaner and easier to understand. We can do this by passing data into a function using arguments and returning results from the function to the location that called it.

We should also note that function parameters are considered local variables. What this means is that if we look at the `calculate_distance_from_home` function that we created earlier, we can see that we have a parameter called `current_position`:

```
function calculate_distance_to_home(current_position)
```

It will be treated as a local variable within this function.

Summary

In this chapter, we have seen that functions are a powerful tool we can use to organize and structure our code to make it more readable and reusable.

We saw how functions have a name, and that name can be used to call them. Calling a function makes the code inside it to execute. This is something we can do over and over again as often as we need to.

Sometimes, we want functions to produce a value as a result of its operations. In those cases, we can let the function return something. We can then use that value in the location where we called the function.

Then, we learned that we can also pass data into a function. This can be done using function arguments. The function receives these arguments in local variables called parameters.

With the introduction of functions, we also have the concepts of variables being either global or local. We saw that global variables can be accessed from any location within the program and local variables can only be used within the function where they are created.

Sometimes, things will not go according to plan, and we will discover that our program either produces the wrong results or simply crashes. In the next chapter, we will see how we can identify bugs in our programs and handle errors that can be harder to predict.

9
When Things Go Wrong – Bugs and Exceptions

Writing software can be hard, and when we write it, we will make errors. We will, unintentionally, introduce bugs to our application.

Some of them will be rather trivial to find and fix, but some can set us off on a wild goose chase through the code where we try to understand the reasons as to why things are not working the way we expect them to.

It is not unheard of that people spend days, and sometimes weeks, attempting to track down a bug. To be able to find bugs in our applications, we will need to understand what kinds exist and how they affect the way our applications run. This chapter will help us recognize them.

In this chapter, you will learn about the following topics:

- Understanding software bugs

- Finding bugs using a debugger

- Working with exceptions

- Handling exceptions

In this chapter, we will also talk a bit about variables and data types. Look back at *Chapter 6, Working with Data – Variables*, if you need to refresh your memory about these.

Understanding software bugs

When writing software, things will not always go according to plan. The programs we create will contain bugs.

The term *bug* to describe an error, flaw, or fault in a program dates way long before we had any computers. It has been recorded as a part of engineering jargon since the 1870s. In a letter, dated 1878, to an associate, Thomas Edison wrote the following:

> *"It has been just so in all of my inventions. The first step is an intuition, and comes with a burst, then difficulties arise—this thing gives out and [it is] then that "Bugs"—as such, little faults and difficulties are called—show themselves and months of intense watching, study, and labor are requisite before commercial success or failure is certainly reached."*

The first mechanical pinball game, Baffle Ball, was advertised as being *free from bugs* in 1931, and in 1944, Isaac Asimov used the term *bug* to describe issues with a robot in the short story **Catch That Rabbit**.

One story that has often been given tribute for being the origin of the term bug in software comes from Grace Hopper. In 1946, she joined the Harvard Faculty at the Computation Laboratory, where she continued her work on the Mark I and Mark II computers.

The Mark II computer produced errors and, after some searching, the operators found that the cause was a moth trapped in a relay. The moth was carefully removed and taped to the logbook. Under the moth, the following was written:

> *"First actual case of a bug being found."*

The date in the logbook was September 9 1947, and that was the first time we had the term *bug* used in computer science:

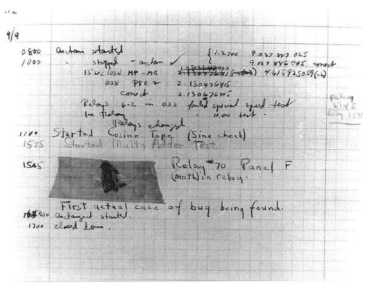

Figure 9.1 – The moth found in the Mark II computer in 1947 – US Naval Historical Center Online Library Photograph (Public Domain [PD])

The likelihood that an actual bug will make our programs produce the wrong output is almost nonexistent. It is much more likely that the source of the error is ourselves.

There are many different types of bugs. To understand some of them, and to see what damage a bug can cause, we'll look at two incredibly expensive software bugs.

NASA's Mars Climate Orbiter

This is one of the most famous bugs in the history of computing. The Mars Climate Orbiter was a space probe that was launched by NASA on December 11, 1998. Its mission was to study the Martian climate, atmosphere, and surface changes. On September 23, 1999, all communication with the spacecraft was lost. It is not known if it was destroyed in the Martian atmosphere or if it continued existing in space.

On November 10, 1999, the Mars Climate Orbiter Mishap Investigation Board released a Phase I report. In it, it was made clear that the reason for the disaster was a bug in a piece of ground-based software provided by one of NASA's contractors. This software produced a result in the United States customary units (units used in the US, such as inch, foot, and mile) while the NASA software expected the input to be in SI units (the metric system).

The cost of this mistake was estimated at 125 million US dollars.

The Morris worm

In 1988, a Cornell University student named Robert Morris released a computer worm that was designed as a harmless experiment. It exploited some flaws in the Unix operating system's sendmail program that were spread from computer to computer. When a new computer was found, the program checked to see if this computer was already infected. Morris understood that this would be an easy way for system administrators to stop the spread and help the system identify if it was infected already. To compensate for this, Morris designed his worm so that it infected any computer that responded with a yes 1 out of 7 times.

This was the big mistake that made the worm not only spread rapidly across the internet but also infect the same computers multiple times, disrupting the target machines. The Morris worm was the first known internet worm, and the cost of cleaning up the mess it created was an estimated 100 million US dollars. Morris was fined 10,000 US dollars but made a good career later; he is now a professor at the Massachusetts Institute of Technology. A disk with the source code of the worm is on display at the Computer History Museum in California.

Both of these examples show us that even a small error can have enormous consequences. In the first example, one single programmer made an error that went unnoticed in the final product. The biggest problem here is not the error that was introduced but that no one saw it and stopped it before it was too late.

As for the second example, here, we had a person who created something on his own. The nature of this program was that no one should know about the program. The problem here is that he had no organization behind him with other developers who could help him make a plan for how the program should work. It is extremely hard to think about all the consequences one decision will have if you are alone and don't have anyone else to discuss your ideas with. In the latter case, having other people around him would hopefully result in them telling him that the idea as a whole was bad and should never have been done in the first place.

Here, we have seen two examples of what a bug is, but there are so many other kinds around. Due to this, the first thing we should do is attempt to define what a bug is.

Defining a software bug

To understand what a software bug is, we can first look at Techopedia's definition:

"A software bug is a problem causing a program to crash or produce invalid output. The problem is caused by insufficient or erroneous logic. A bug can be an error, mistake, defect, or fault, which may cause failure or deviation from expected results."

As we can see from this definition, a bug is caused by software that is not functioning correctly. This can result in incorrect or unexpected results. We can understand this if, say, we provide a program with some well-defined data. Here, we expect a certain result back. If the result is not what we expect, the reason can either be that there is something wrong with the data we provided or there is something wrong with the program. Let's say we, for example, provide a calculator app with the following data:

```
3 + 4
```

Here, we will expect the following result:

```
7
```

If we get anything else, we can say that there is a bug in our application.

The definition also says that a program can behave in unintended ways. This is when we expect a program to do one thing, but it turns out that it does something completely different. If we have a program that should turn down the thermostat in our home when it's reached a certain temperature, but it turns it up, then that would be a bug.

Why do we have bugs in our software? There isn't a single answer to this. To understand this, we will need to define some different types of bugs.

Understanding types of software bugs

There are many different ways we can classify bugs. Here, we will look at some common types, see what they are, and see what they can look like.

Arithmetic errors

Arithmetic bugs, as the name suggests, have to do with arithmetic operations. There are a few things we should look out for, as outlined in the following sections.

Division by zero

One such thing is division by zero. This is not only related to computers as we can also never perform a division where the divisor is zero. In mathematics, dividing by zero has no meaning, because if we do $\frac{6}{2}$, we will get 3. If we multiply 3 and 2, we will get 6 back. But if we take $\frac{6}{0}$, there is no number we can multiply by zero to get back to 6.

This might seem simple enough, but sometimes, it happens anyway, especially when we are working with variables.

Let's assume that we have two variables that get their value somewhere in our application, like this:

```
x = 3
y = 14
```

Later on in the program, we perform some calculations, maybe with some other variables, it might look like this:

```
y = y - current_temperature
```

If the `current_temperature` variable now has the same value as y, which is 14 in our case, we will store the result, 0, back in y.

If we then did something like this, our application will crash:

```
result = x / y
```

The reason for this is that we are dividing by zero. It might not be obvious that y is zero, so the problem is not easy to spot.

Arithmetic overflow/underflow

In *Chapter 6, Working with Data – Variables*, in the *Primitive data types* section, we talked about integer types and that they could have a fixed size. What that means is that some integer types have a predefined size that describes how much memory they will use. This also gives a variable of this type a maximum and minimum value. As long as we are storing values between the maximum and minimum value, there will be no problem, but what happens if we try to store a value that is larger or smaller than these values? Let's look at an example.

We will now assume that we are using a programming language that has a data type called byte. This data type can store values between -128 and 127.

We can create a variable of this type and assign it a value as follows:

```
my_byte = 127
```

Now, what would happen if we increased this variable by one?

```
my_byte = my_byte + 1
```

Naturally, we expect 127 + 1 will result in 128. To our surprise, it is -128.

The reason for this is that when we are at the maximum value a data type can handle and increase it by one, we will end up at the smallest number it can handle; in this case, -128. If we had increased it by 2 instead of 1, we would have ended up with -127.

This is an overflow error. If we were at the lowest value the data type can handle and decrease the value by one, we would go to the largest value of this data type. This is called an underflow error.

Loss of precision

As we mentioned in *Chapter 6, Working with Data – Variables,* floating-point numbers are something that is tricky for computers to work with, and we are always faced with the risk of losing precision when it comes to rounding off a value.

In some languages, this can become obvious.

Let's assume we have this code:

```
x = 1.3
y = 1.1
print x + y
```

The expected output of this program would, of course, be this:

```
2.4
```

To our surprise, some languages will instead give us this:

```
2.400000000000004
```

This is the computer showing the problems it has with floating-point numbers. If you need a refresher on how this works, go back to *Chapter 6*, *Working with Data – Variables*, and read the section about floating-point numbers under the *Numeric type* heading.

We could argue that an error of 0.0000000000000004 is not much, but what if we were working with several of these results and added them together? This error would now accumulate and soon, we will have a value that is way off.

These three are the most common arithmetic errors we will find in software. The next group of errors are not as fun for us programmers as they are introduced when our logic is incorrect.

Logical errors

A logical error will usually not make a program crash but produce an unintended result. Unfortunately for us, there are a lot of opportunities to make logical errors.

We could, for example, accidentally use the wrong operator. An example would be if we wanted to check if somebody's age was above 18, but we did this:

```
if age < 18 then
    ...
end_if
```

Another common thing is to forget to use less than or equal to or greater than or equal to. Here, we could write something like this:

```
if age > 18 then
    ...
end_if
```

This is incorrect as we actually wanted to check if the age was greater or equal to 18, like this:

```
if age >= 18 then
    ...
end_if
```

Another common error is to use one equals sign instead of two. Some languages will let us do something like this:

```
if age = 20 then
    ...
end_if
```

Here, we intended to use the equal to operator, ==, but instead, we used the assignment operator, =. Some languages will interpret this as assigning value to age. This will give us two problems. First, we might enter the `if` statement, even if, in reality, we shouldn't. The other problem is that the value that was in the `age` variable now will be overwritten by the value 20.

One thing that has always amazed me is how hard it can be to get the logical operators right. Even though they are only two, it is very common that we use one instead of the other. Yes, even I do that at times.

If we intend to check if the age is above 12 and below 20, we might write this:

```
if age > 12 or age < 20 then
    ...
end_if
```

However, what we wanted to do was this:

```
if age > 12 and age < 20 then
    ...
end_if
```

The first example will always be true, as age will always be either greater than 12 or less than 20.

These are just some examples of logical errors. They can be hard to find as the code is valid, meaning that the program will run, but its behavior will be unexpected.

An easier group of errors to amend is when the code is written so it can't run because we are breaking the language syntax rules. Let's take a look at these in more detail.

Syntax errors

The rules that tell us how code should be written in a particular language are called its syntax. When we write code that does not follow the syntax rules, we get what is called a syntax error.

These are rather easy to spot compared to many other errors as the compiler or interpreter will tell us where the problem is and also give us a hint about what the error is.

Let's look at some syntax errors and investigate what message we get back that can assist us in fixing the error.

Here is one syntax error. Can you spot it?

```
print "Hello
```

Here, we are trying to print a string, but we forgot the closing quote. Languages will report this error differently. As we will see, the message we get back does not always direct us to the real error.

Here are four examples from four different programming languages – Python, Go, C#, and JavaScript, respectively:

```
SyntaxError: EOL while scanning string literal in line 1 column
12
```

```
1:12 syntax error: unexpected newline
```

```
Compilation error (line 1, col 12): Newline in constant
```

```
error: unknown: Unterminated string constant (1:12)
```

The second and third are talking about newline, while the first and last ones are talking about strings. We will need to learn the messages we get back from the language we are using. All of them will also direct us to where the error was discovered. In different formats, we are directed to line 1, column 12.

The location that's given is not always where the actual error is, it is where the compiler/interpreter discovered the error. If you don't find anything at the location given, look at the line above or sometimes some lines above this location.

We know from earlier chapters that we cannot name variables with a number as its first character. Let's do that anyway and do something like this:

```
1apple = 1
```

This will give us messages like the following:

```
SyntaxError: invalid syntax in line 1 column 2
```

```
1:2 syntax error: unexpected apple at end of statement
```

```
Compilation error (line 1, col 2): Identifier expected
```

```
error: unknown: Identifier directly after number (1:2)
```

As we can see, some languages call these errors syntax errors, while others will name them things such as compilation errors. Again, we will need to learn what the language we are using is calling these errors as it will help us identify them.

Often, our editor will assist us in finding syntax errors by marking them even before we run the application. It uses the same technique as a spellchecker in a MS Word processor – a wiggly red line below the error.

Look at the following screenshot. Here, we can see that the editor had marked a syntax error before we tried to run the program:

Figure 9.2 – An editor showing a syntax error in the programming language Python

Syntax errors are, as mentioned previously, rather easy to find as the program will not run and we will be directed to a location close to where the error is. But how do we find bugs when we have logical errors? We have tools for this called debuggers.

Finding bugs using a debugger

A debugger is a tool that can help us see what happens when a program is running. As we have already mentioned, some bugs can be hard to find and understand just by running the program. Often, we will discover a strange behavior in the program, but it might not be obvious what the reason behind this behavior is.

A debugger is an application that is tailored for a particular programming language and can be used to pause the application at a specified code line. At this point, we can inspect what values all the variables have.

We can also resume the execution of the program or execute it one line at a time to see what happens.

Let's try using a debugger. To do this, we first need to pick a language and then write a small program that contains a logical error. We can take one of the errors that we previously looked at:

```
if age > 12 or age < 20 then
    ...
end_if
```

Remember that in this example, we accidentally used or instead of and.

Let's write this program in Python. In the following screenshot, we can see what it looks like:

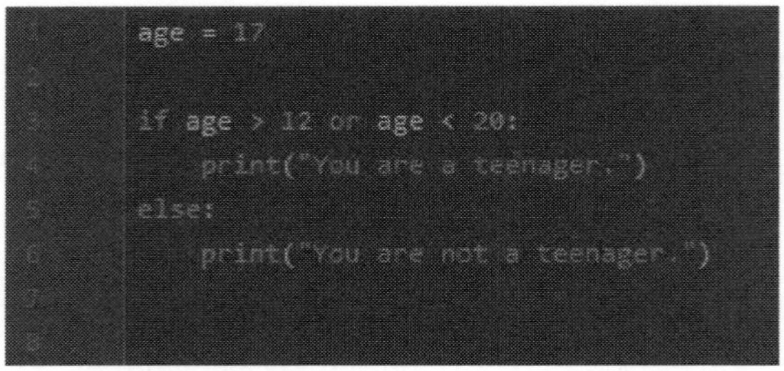

```
age = 17

if age > 12 or age < 20:
    print("You are a teenager.")
else:
    print("You are not a teenager.")
```

Figure 9.3 – A small program written in Python that contains a logical error

On the first line, we declare (remember that declaring a variable means that we are creating it) a variable called age and assign the value 17 to it.

Then comes our if statement, where we're checking if the age is greater than 12 or less than 20. The error here is that we used or.

When running this program, we get the expected output:

```
You are a teenager.
```

If we now change the program, that is, we assign another value to age, say 24, and run it, it will not give us the predicted result:

```
You are a teenager.
```

You can see the changed program in the following screenshot:

```
age = 24

if age > 12 or age < 20:
    print("You are a teenager.")
else:
    print("You are not a teenager.")
```

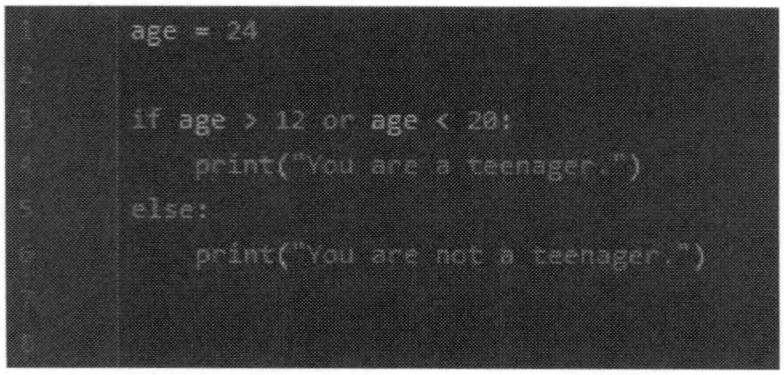

Figure 9.4 – The same program with another value for age

Now, let's use a debugger and explore this error. The first thing we need to do is set a breakpoint.

Breakpoints

A breakpoint is a way for us to say, run the program to this point, then pause it and show me the status of the program.

In the following screenshot, we can see that we have a breakpoint on the line containing an `if` statement:

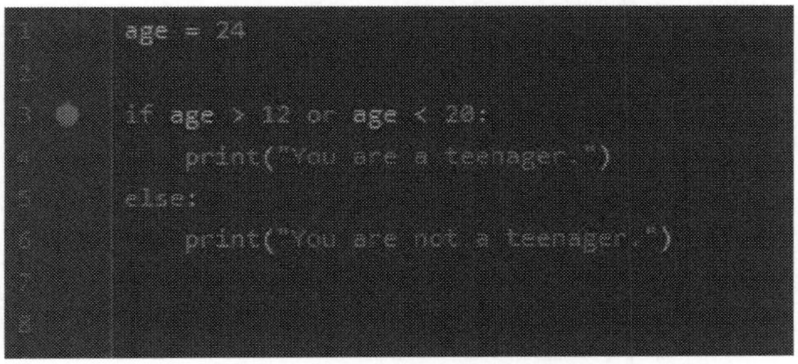

Figure 9.5 – A program with a breakpoint on line 3

If we now run the program, it will stop when it reaches this line. At this point, the line that contains the breakpoint has still not executed. It will look like what's shown in the following screenshot:

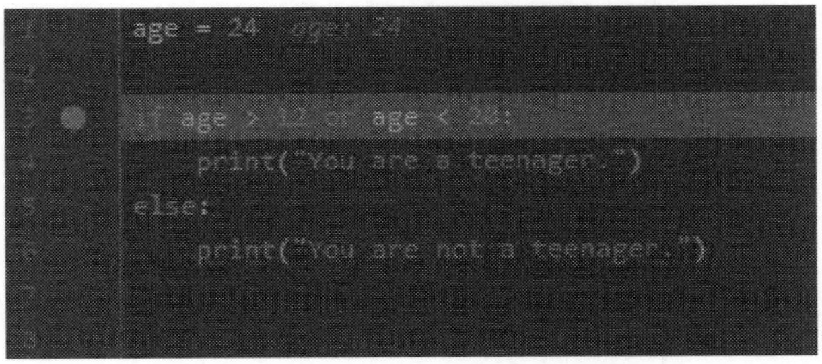

Figure 9.6 – The debugger has stopped at the breakpoint

The line we are about to execute is marked with a blue line. Also, note that this debugger is showing the `age` value in gray on line 1. This helps us understand what value it currently has.

If we zoom out a bit, we will see that we have some other tools that have popped up as the program paused at this line. We can see what it looks like in the following screenshot:

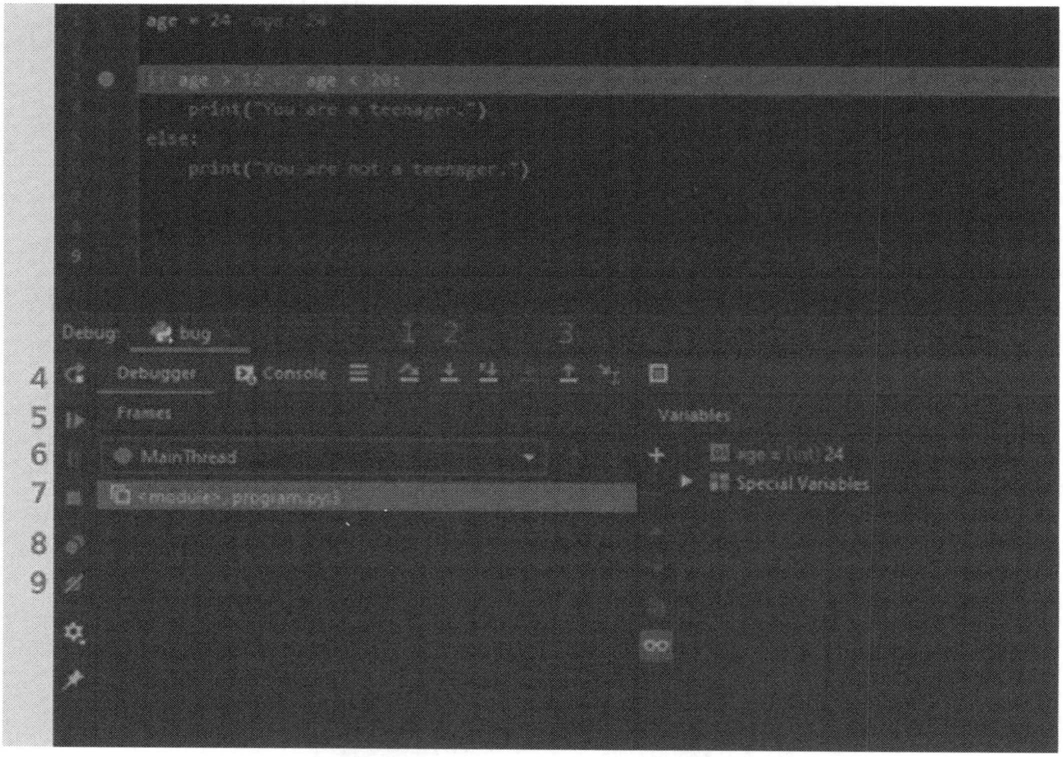

Figure 9.7 – The debugger tools

What we see here there are several tools that are provided to us by the debugger application. Let's understand what they consist of:

- To the right, we see a section marked **Variables**. Here, we can see all the variables that are currently defined and what values they have.

- Above this window, we can see some arrows pointing in different directions. They are used to advance the program one step. We have some options here. The first one is the arrow that first goes up and then goes down (marked as **1** in the preceding screenshot). This is called step over. If we have a function call on this line, step over will not jump to that function. Instead, it will call that function, run all the code within it, and then stop again when it returns to where we currently are.

- The next arrow, the one pointing straight down, is step into (marked as **2**). This will, if we have a function on this line, jump to that function and let us step through it.

- We can ignore the two arrows that follow and instead look at the one pointing straight up (marked as **3**). This one is called step out. We can use this one if we have stepped into a function and changed our minds. It will run all the code in the function and stop again when we go back to the location we came from.

- To the far left, we have some other tools that will restart the program (marked as **4**), resume the execution of the program (marked as **5**), pause a running program (marked as **6**), stop the program (marked as **7**), allow us to view all the breakpoints we currently have in the program (marked as **8**), and ignore all the breakpoints and continue to run (marked as **9**).

For our problem, none of these tools will be able to help us. We know that the program will enter the `if` statement as the output was as follows:

```
You are a teenager.
```

Instead, there is another tool that might help us. In the following screenshot, we can see it marked with a rectangle:

Figure 9.8 – The evaluate expression button

This tool, which looks like a small calculator, is the evaluate expression tool. If we click it, we will see a window like the one shown in the following screenshot:

Figure 9.9 – The evaluate expression window

In the top field, we can enter an expression. This can help us understand what is happening. We are currently on this line:

```
if age > 12 or age < 20:
```

If we enter a part of this expression into the evaluation expression tool, it will show us the result. Let's take the first part of this if statement. Entering it into the tool will look as follows:

Figure 9.10 – Evaluating an expression

Here, we can see that this part of the if statement is true.

If we now do the same with the second part, we will see that the result is false, as shown in the following screenshot:

Figure 9.11 – Evaluating another expression

We can now take both of these statements, since we have written them in the code, and check the result, as shown in the following screenshot:

Figure 9.12 – Evaluating the full expression

Here, we can see that the result of the full expression is true, even though the value is greater than the last part of the condition, 20.

We can now suspect that the culprit is or. Let's change it to an and and see the result.

In the following screenshot, we can see that the result is now evaluated to `false`, which is the value we expected:

Figure 9.13 – Evaluating the expression with and instead of or

We can now stop the debugger and change our code.

This was one example of when the debugger can help us understand a problem. We will frequently run into errors like this one, and what the problem is might not be obvious to us right away. As a programmer, we should learn to use the debugger, what features it has to offer, and how we can use it.

Sometimes, we have other types of errors where the syntax is correct, but still, the program will crash. These are called exceptions. We will move on to those next.

Working with exceptions

An **exception** (short for **exceptional event** or **exceptional condition**) is an error or an unexpected event that occurs while a program is running. It is caused by a condition in the software where the program has reached a state where it can no longer run.

There are many reasons we can get an exception. One example could be if our program needs to read data from a file, but the file is not where it is supposed to be. Since the program has a reason to read the data from this file, a failure to do so will put the application in a state where it can no longer guarantee that its output will be correct. The best option, in this case, is just to halt the program and give back an error that hopefully instructs us about what the problem is so we can fix it.

No software developer wants to write an application that crashes. It can make the users of the application lose unsaved work, though the consequences might be even worse, depending on the nature of the program.

Soon, we will talk about how we can handle exceptions so that they don't crash our program. But before we do that, let's explore exceptions a bit so that we have an understanding of how they work.

Let's look at some common reasons we get exceptions.

Common reasons for exceptions

As we saw, a missing file can be one reason we get an exception. Another common reason is that when we are trying to index into a sequence, we use an index that is larger than the sequence. Let's take a look at an example:

```
names = ["Anna", "Bob", "Cara", "David"]
```

Here, we have an array (you can read more about array's in *Chapter 6, Working with Data – Variables*, in the *Composite type* section). It contains four values; in this case, four names. We can index into this array to retrieve a single value, as follows:

```
print names[2]
```

This will give us the following output:

```
Cara
```

Remember that the index value for the first item is 0, not 1, so the third item, `Cara`, has index 2.

What will happen if we use an index value that is greater than the number of items we have, like this?

```
print names[6]
```

There is no value at this location, so the program cannot fetch it for us. The syntax is correct, and if we had enough values, it would work perfectly fine. But this time, it won't, as we have used an index for something that does not exist.

The program cannot continue at this point as it cannot guess what it should do. We have given an instruction that says that we want a value from this location. The programming language cannot just come up with a value for us. The most sensible thing to do at this point is to just end the program and wait for it to give us an error. This error might look something like this:

```
IndexOutOfRangeException: Index was outside the bounds of the
array at line 2.
```

This is an exception. We can see it in the output as it clearly says `IndexOutOfBoundException`.

How much we use exceptions, and how many different exceptions we will need to deal with the different issues available, will differ greatly between languages. Some, such as Java, make heavy use of exceptions. C++, on the other hand, has just a handful of built-in exceptions. Then, we have languages such as Go that don't have exceptions at all, but instead will let a function return an error type alongside the real return value from the function.

Some of the errors that we already have seen in this chapter will also generate exceptions. One such exception will happen if we divide something by zero.

Most languages support exceptions. Even if the number of exceptions a programming language has differs, the way they work will be pretty much the same, no matter what language we are using. The names will differ, as well as what kinds of exceptions we have, but the way we work with them will be the same.

At times, it can be hard to understand the output we get from an exception. The reason for this is that when we get an exception, something called the call stack is also printed.

Exceptions and the call stack

Imagine that we have a program and that in it, we have a main function. This function is calling another function that calls another function, and so on. We will have something like the following:

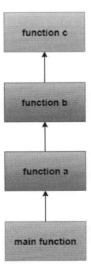

Figure 9.14 – A function that calls a function that calls a function, and so on

Keeping track of where we are in this chain of function calls is called the call stack, and that is handled by the programming language when we run the program.

Now, imagine that we get an exception in the last function called **function c**. This function will now exit immediately and return to where it was called. That is **function b**. This function will also exit as soon as the control gets handed back to it, and we will be returned to where we came from. This time, it is **function a**. Again, this function will be terminated immediately, and we are returned to the **main** function. The last thing that will happen is that this function will also end. Since this was the first function that was called in this application, the application as a whole will end.

The reason why all the functions will exit is that none of them handle the exception.

Now, we will get not only the exception information printed to the screen but also the call stack.

To illustrate this, let's use a very simple program like the following one:

```
function c()
    result = 10 / 0
end_function

function b()
    c()
end_function

function a()
    b()
end_function

function main()
    a()
end_function
```

This is a rather silly program, but it will illustrate what will happen. At the bottom, we have a function called main. The main function will be called automatically when we run this program.

Inside the main function, we call the function named function a. This function will call function b, which calls function c.

When we enter function c, function b is still running and is waiting for function c to finish. The same thing is true for function a, which waits for function b. The main function is waiting for function a to finish, so at this point, we have four active functions.

Now, inside `function c`, we perform a division by zero, causing an exception to go off.

At this point, `function c` will exit immediately. Control will be handed back to `function b`, which will exit, giving the control back to `function a`, which exits back to `main`, and finally, the program will exit.

The output we'll get will look something like this:

```
Callstack
function c() at line 2
function b() at line 6
function a() at line 10
function main() at line 14
ZeroDivisionError: division by zero
```

As we can see, all the function calls are there. How this is displayed will differ from language to language. Some will print all the functions in the opposite order. Again, this is something we will need to learn when we pick up a new language.

The reason we get all this information is that it can help us figure out where things went wrong. Even if the error occurred in `function c`, the reason it happened might originate somewhere else. Let's assume that the program looked as follows instead:

```
function c(x, y)
    result = x / y
end_function

function b()
    c(10, 0)
end_function

function a()
    b()
end_function

function main()
    a()
end_function
```

Now, function c takes two arguments, and it uses these to perform the calculation. This happens when function c is called from function b. The problem arises when we pass in 10 and 0 as arguments to the call.

Since the data has its origins in function b, this is where the problem came from. function c does not know the origins of these two values. They might come from some user input, they might have been read from a file, or they may have come from any other source.

To fully understand the origins of this problem, we will need the information that we get from the call stack as it tells us how we ended up in function c when the error occurred.

But what if we don't want the program to crash? No problem. We can write code that will handle exceptions. Let's look at that next.

Handling exceptions

To understand how we can handle exceptions, we must first understand what the origins of a problem might be. It is only when we have understood this that we can insert measures to handle them correctly.

Let's return to our function that divides two values. Let's say this function takes two arguments, as it did in our previous example:

```
function c(x, y)
    result = x / y
end_function
```

We should assume that this function does something more than just print this single line. We can mark it out with some comments, as follows:

```
function c(x, y)
    // The function does some things ere
    result = x / y
    // And even more things here
    // It might even return a value
end_function
```

We know that as this function divides two values, we might get an exception if y is given a value of 0.

The first thing we should ask ourselves is if this is the best place to handle the problem. It could be, but most likely, it is not. This function is getting two values sent to it as arguments. Several parts of the application might use the function, so it has no way of knowing the source of the data that is being sent to it.

What we can do, though, is check if y is equal to zero before we perform the division. Let's do that now. At the same time, we can change the function's name to calculate as it better reflects what the function does:

```
function calculate(x, y)
    if y == 0 then
        // y is zero, so we cannot perform the division
    end_if
    // The function does some things ere
    result = x / y
    // And even more things here
    // It might even return a value
end_function
```

But what should we do if y is zero? We cannot continue running the function as we would then perform the division anyway. We cannot change y to something else either, because what would we even change it to?

We need a way to signal to the caller of the function that we cannot accept a value of zero for y.

One way to do this would be to let the exception happen and remove the if statement again. If we did that, the caller could handle the error.

Let's see how we can handle an exception when we call a function. The call to the function would then need to be within a special block of code called a try statement. It could look something like this:

```
try
    calculate(10, 0)
catch ZeroDivisionError
    // We will end up here if we get a ZeroDivisionError
    // exception
end_catch
```

Here, we can see that the call to the calculate function is located within a try block.

If everything is fine and we return from the function without any exception, the program will jump to the line after end_catch and resume its execution.

But if we get an exception and that exception is of the ZeroDivisionError type, we will end up in the block below, which begins with a catch.

Exceptions can be caught, but we need to specify what exception it is we want to handle. If we get another exception, one that does not have a matching catch, the program will crash as before.

Calling the function like this could be a solution for us, but is it a good solution? Not really. Imagine that the calculate function is located in a different module that is in a different file. It might even be written by somebody else. In this situation, how do we know that it will perform a division and that it will use the second value we pass to it as the divisor in that division? We will most likely not know anything about that, or we should at least assume that the users do not know anything about how the function is written.

Therefore, we could not assume that they will use a ZeroDivisionError exception in their catch statement. Instead, we could give them another exception that might make more sense.

Let's change our calculate function, as follows:

```
function calculate(x, y)
    if y == 0 then
        throw ValueError("Second argument cannot be zero")
    end_if
    // The function does some things ere
    result = x / y
    // And even more things here
    // It might even return a value
end_function
```

throw will create another exception; this time, one called ValueError. We are also passing a string to this exception. If someone now calls our function and gives us a value of zero for y, they will get this exception with the message we provided.

When they call our function, they could now check for this exception instead:

```
try
    calculate(10, 0)
catch ValueError
    // We will end up here if we get a ValueError exception
end_catch
```

Since this is the location where the bad value for y originated, it is much more likely that this is where we can change it. If this, for example, was a value that was given to us by the user of the program, we could give a nice error message back, saying that they cannot enter a value of zero.

We can say that this is the location that *owns* the data and therefore has the opportunity to change it.

If we use try...catch blocks around calls to functions that can throw exceptions, the program will no longer crash. In this case, the calculate function will still exit as soon as we throw the ValueError exception, but since we are catching it right after the call to the function, we might be able to correct the problem and call the function again with a correct value.

Exceptions are a great way to handle conditions when we can't decide what to do due to a condition that we could not predict when we wrote the program. Without them, it would be very difficult to signal to other parts of the program that something is wrong. We should use them when we need to, but also ensure proper care. Exceptions always send a clear message regarding what is wrong and assist the author of the code that receives the exception with understanding what the problem is.

Summary

In this chapter, we realized that we, as humans, make mistakes, but we can go back and fix them as well.

A software bug is an error in an application that can have several causes. Depending on what is behind the bug, we must approach it differently when trying to fix it.

In some cases, as with syntax errors, we will be told what the cause of the bug is right away, and even be directed to the correct location in the code.

Other bugs will be harder to find. When the programming language syntax is correct, but the logic is not, the program will behave in unexpected ways. To be able to find these bugs, we can use a tool called a debugger. It helps us track down the bugs by letting us pause the execution of the program and see all the values the variables have; it will even let us step through the execution one line at a time.

An exceptional event is when things that should not happen still happen. In programming, they are referred to as exceptions. When they happen, they will immediately halt the execution of the program if they are not handled. Fortunately, we can handle them by inserting code that will only run if the exceptional event occurs so that we can try to fix the problem.

In the next chapter, we will look at different ways to approach a problem and create a solution with code. This is called a paradigm. A programming language will use one of these. As we will see, some languages will use concepts from more than one paradigm.

10
Programming Paradigms

If we look at all the programming languages, we can see patterns and similarities between them, and we can use these to classify them into different paradigms. The word **paradigm** means a typical example or pattern of something, and this is precisely what we are looking for in programming languages when grouping them.

The reason we want to do this classification is because the way we write a program in one of these groups will differ significantly from how we do so in languages belonging to another group.

A computer program will almost always, in one way or another, model something in the real world. We are solving real-world problems using software. The question is how best we can model and represent real-world things in code and how best we can structure the solution we have to this real-world problem.

In this chapter, you will learn about the following topics:

- Understanding structured programming
- Understanding object-oriented programming
- Understanding functional programming
- Understanding logic programming
- Understanding other paradigms
- Understanding multi-paradigm languages

Let's begin with the paradigm that we are most familiar with: structured programming.

Understanding structured programming

Structured programming is what we have looked at in this book. Loops, conditionals, and functions define the flow of a program that uses this paradigm. If you have read the previous chapters of this book, then they should all be familiar to you by now.

Structured programming is a branch of a family of paradigms called **imperative programming**. Languages that use the concepts of imperative programming use statements to change the program's state.

If we look at that definition, we must first learn what statements and program state are.

Statements

In the first part of this definition, we'll talk about statements. A statement, as described in *Chapter 5, Sequence – The Basic Building Block of a Computer Program*, in the *Understanding statements* section, this can be viewed as a command that we give to the application. In natural language, we have something that is called the imperative mood. The imperative mood is something that forms a command, such as *Move!*, *Don't be late!*, or *Work hard!*. In imperative programming, we give instructions to the computer with something that is like the imperative mood; that is, a command that is expressed in the form of a statement.

That is the first half of the definition of imperative programming. The second part talks about changing the program's state.

Program state

A program is said to have a state if it remembers previous events that have occurred. A program stores data in variables. At any given point, during the program's execution, we can look at the data that is currently in all the variables we have defined. The combined value in all these variables is what makes up the state of the program.

If we change one variable, the state of the program will also change. When we are talking about imperative programming, we mean that as soon as a statement changes the content of a variable, it has changed the program state.

This is what forms the memory of preceding events. When an event – a statement, in our case – occurs and it changes a variable, it will affect the behavior of the program. If we have an application that will launch a rocket, we might have a function that takes care of the countdown. To keep track of what number we are currently at, we need to have a variable. Changing this variable during the countdown will change the state of the application. When the variable reaches zero, it will trigger the event of sending the start signal to the rocket.

If this is imperative programming, how are things different in structured programming? Let's compare them.

Comparing imperative and structured programming

Programs written in assembly language use a concept known as GOTOs. It is a technique that's used to control the flow in a program. To use them, we insert labels into the code, and we can then instruct the program to jump to one such label and resume its execution there.

A small code snippet of assembly language can illustrate this:

```
        mov eax,3
        jump exit
        mov eax,123   ; <- not executed!
  exit:
        ret
```

Here, we have a label called `exit`. On the first line, we move the value 3 into a register (remember that a register in an assembly is like a variable) called `eax`. On the second line, we do an unconditional jump to our label, `exit`. The jump being unconditional means that we will always do this jump. In the assembly language, there are also conditional jumps where we only jump if a register is equal to, less than, or higher than some value.

Since the jump is unconditional, line three will never execute as we will always jump past this line.

Many languages that came into existence in the 60s and 70s also had the same concept of an unconditional jump. Here, we can find languages such as BASIC and C. In these languages, it is not called a jump. Instead, the term *GOTO* is used. The programming language C++ is based upon C, so it also uses GOTO. The same program written in C++ will look like this:

```
    int x = 3;
    goto quit;
    x = 123;         // <- not executed!
quit:
    return x;
```

Today, it is, under most circumstances, considered a bad practice to use GOTOs as the code will be hard to read, understand, and maintain. There is hardly ever any need to perform a GOTO as languages such as BASIC and C support constructs that can let us achieve the same result and maintain good code quality.

Using this style of programming was what first defined imperative programming. As programming languages developed and we got other tools, such as loops, `if` statements, and functions, there was a need to distinguish these more modern languages from the older style. Even though these programming languages use the same ideas as assembly language, these statements will change the state of the program. This is because they no longer rely on jumps or GOTOs to accomplish this. This was when we got the definition structured programming. A language that supports structured programming is a language that modifies the state of the program using statements and has functions, loops, and `if` statements as tools to accomplish this.

We will sometimes also hear the terms *procedural* and *modular* languages. There is no need to go into the details of what the difference is between these as this is mostly academic. We can safely consider all these the same thing.

Some well-known languages that support structured programming or their relatives, procedural and imperative programming, are as follows:

- Ada
- ALGOL
- BASIC
- C

- C++
- C#
- COBOL
- Fortran
- Go
- Java
- JavaScript
- Pascal
- Perl
- PHP
- Python
- Ruby
- Rust
- Swift
- Visual Basic

Structured programming is a popular paradigm, as this long list of languages proves. In the 90s, another paradigm gained popularity and is still one of the essential paradigms in use. It is called object-oriented programming. Let's see what this is about.

Understanding object-orientated programming

The main idea within object-oriented programming is to model the code in the same way as we as humans look at the world.

Even if you've never thought about it, we are always classifying things and grouping things together using abstraction. We can talk about vehicles, and we have shared knowledge of what is included in this group. Cars, bicycles, boats, and airplanes are, while pencils, ducks, and swimsuits are not.

I could say, *I need to go to town. Can anyone lend me a vehicle?*

You will interpret this in such a way that the actual kind does not matter, but it must be something that can transport me to town. It could just as well be a car as it could be a skateboard.

Grouping things into these abstractions make our lives easier as we will not go into details every single time, we talk about something. I can ask for a vehicle instead of describing that I need a device that can transport me from my current location to town.

Things within such an abstraction can be very different, but if they share some key characteristics, we will understand it. Take a look at the following image. Here, we have two items that can both be grouped into something that we can call remote controls.

One of them will control your TV and let you change channels and change the volume. The other one will let you lock and unlock your car:

Figure 10.1 – Remote controls

Even though they work with different devices and the result of pushing their buttons will be very different, they share the behavior in that they control something from a distance wirelessly. We have labeled these devices remote controls to make our communication more convenient.

What if we could do the same when writing software? This is where object orientation comes in. It will let us use the same approach.

If we are going to write a program that keeps track of the warehouse inventory and we want to do so object-oriented style, we can look at a real warehouse and describe it just as we see it.

In the warehouse, we have things such as the following:

- Products
- Shelves
- A coffee machine
- Warehouse employees
- A dead flower in the window

Our system will need to know about some of these things, but not all of them. In the preceding list, we can ignore the flower and the coffee machine, but the other three are good candidates for making it into our program.

If we look at one of these products, we will see that it can be several things, all the way from tiny screws and bolts to machines or devices of some sort. But from the perspective of a warehouse, they share the same characteristics. They are all items that we store, and we can describe them using the same attributes. They have a name, a weight, and manufacturer; we have a certain amount of them; and so on.

In object-oriented programming, we try to preserve this way of describing things and represent them in a way that is not too different from how we just described them here.

To understand how object-oriented programming works, we will need to break it down into some main concepts that we will need to understand. Let's check them out.

Classes and objects

In object-orientated programming, a class is like a blueprint, or description, of something. Let's take the concept of a person as an example. How can we describe a person? We can start to make a list of things that apply to all people. It might look something like this.

A person has the following attributes:

- A name
- An age
- A gender
- Height
- Weight
- Hair color

- Eye color

- Shoe size

- Nationality

- Address

- Telephone number

The list can go on. We can now decide that these are things that apply to all people. If we think about it, this is all data about a person. We have not described any behavior. We could make another list that describes things a person can do.

A person can do the following:

- Jump

- Run

- Walk

- Sit

- Stand

- Sleep

- Chill

- Work

- Play

- Dance

The same thing applies here – this list can be very long.

If we are going to represent a person in a program, we won't need all the available data and behavior. Instead, we need to make an abstract of a person in such a way that we can represent them with the things that are interesting for us. Name, age, and sex might all be such things, but shoe size will most likely not be unless we are writing an application for a shoe store. Let's focus on the data and pick some things that might be interesting enough to implement in an application. We might pick the following:

- Name

- Age (most likely in the form of date of birth)

- Gender

- Address

- Nationality
- Phone number
- Email address

Now, we'll learn how to define a blueprint – called a class in object-oriented programming – for a person since we have a list of data that applies to all people.

We give it a descriptive name and list the things we are interested in. It might look something like this:

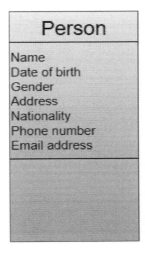

Figure 10.2 – A class called person

The preceding image depicts a class in a simplified way; that is, a rectangle with three sections. In the top section, we have the name that we have given this class. In the middle section, we've described the data we want to use to describe a person. The last section is for behavior, which is something we will come back to soon.

Object-oriented programming is very focused around data, so when we're deciding what a class will look like, this is often where we start. The data that makes it into our class will often dictate what kind of behavior we want it to have. This behavior often dictates the operations we need to perform on the data.

The behavior we identified for a person earlier, such as jump, run, and sleep, will most likely not be something we will need to represent. Instead, we will usually find things that will modify the data, such as changing the address.

For now, we will leave the third section of the class empty, but we will come back to it later.

Now, we have a class and the blueprint for a person, but we haven't represented any actual people yet. A representation of a thing – in our case, a person – is called an *object*. An object will always belong to a class. Now that we have a class, we can create an object from it, and each object will represent one person.

If we have a group of people that we want to represent in our application, a representation of them could look as follows:

Figure 10.3 – Four objects from the person class

As we can see in the preceding diagram, all four objects have their own set of data; a name, a date of birth, a gender, an address, a nationality, a phone number, and an email address. The data in one object is independent of the data in other objects that belong to the same class. If we change the address in one object, it will not affect any other object.

To summarize this, we can state that a class is a model or the blueprint for the objects. The data that is defined within the class is often referred to as **member variables** or **attributes**.

Member variables

A member variable is just like any other variable, with one key difference: it lives inside of an object.

To illustrate this, we can consider a very minimal class for a person. It could look something like this:

```
class Person
    name
    age
end_class
```

Here, we're defining a class called Person. It has two variables inside it: name and age.

At this point, no actual variables exist in the computer's memory as this is just a blueprint for what a person object will look like. To make them come into existence, we need to create objects, often referred to as instances, from this class.

This can be done like this:

```
p1 = Person("Dipika", 34)
p2 = Person("Manfred", 58)
```

This creates two objects. We use the variable names p1 and p2 to reference them. The interesting part is what happens when we create these objects. If we take a closer look at line one, we will see that a chain of events will occur:

1. The first thing that happens is that, somewhere in the computer's memory, an object from the Person class is created with a set of two variables called name and age, as shown in the following image

Figure 10.4 – An object from the person class

2. The next step is that the member variables get initialized with the data we passed in when we created the object. This is illustrated in the following image:

Figure 10.5 – The member variables in the object are initialized

3. The last step is that the p1 variable now points out where in memory this object is located, as illustrated in the following image:

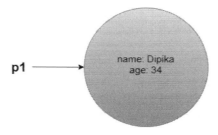

Figure 10.6 – The object is referenced by the p1 variable

Then, this process is repeated for the object that contains the name Manfred. By doing this, we get something that looks similar to the following:

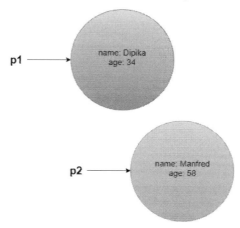

Figure 10.7 – Two objects from the Person class

Now that we have two objects, we can see that we have two variables called `name` and `age`. One of each is inside the `p1` object and the `p2` object. For every object we create from the `Person` class, we will get a new set of these two.

We will soon change this class, but as it looks now, we can access these variables like this:

```
p1 = Person("Dipika", 34)
p2 = Person("Manfred", 58)


print p1.name
print p1.age
print p2.name
print p2.age
```

This will give us the following output:

```
Dipika
34
Manfred
58
```

Object-oriented programming states that member data should be encapsulated within its object and that direct access to this data from the outside should be prevented. Let's see why this is a critical concept in object orientation.

Understanding encapsulation

Encapsulation, also known as information hiding, is a concept where the object's internal implementation is hidden from everything outside the object.

Encapsulation can be described in many ways. The American computer engineers James Rumbaugh and Michael Blaha described it like this:

"One design goal is to treat classes as "black boxes," whose external interface is public but whose internal details are hidden from view. Hiding internal information permits implementation of a class to be changed without requiring any clients of the class to modify code."

The vital key here is the *interface*. An interface is what we use to communicate with an object. Look at the remote controls in *Figure 10.1*. The buttons we can push is the interface. We use them to communicate with the internal logic inside the device.

The remote control object is a *black box* as we can't see the internals of the remote, and there is no need for us to either. The only thing we need to understand to be able to use the object is the interface. If the remote is not working correctly, we can take it to someone who understands the inner workings of it, and they can repair it. If they don't change the interface, the buttons, and what functionality that is associated with them, we won't need to change the way we use the remote before and after the modification.

One thing we should hide from the outside world is the data. No, wait! If the data is hidden inside an object, how could we then use it? Let's look at an example to see what we mean by hiding the data inside an object.

If you walk down the street and you meet another person, you cannot, just by observing that person, see things such as the person's name, what they had for breakfast, their age, and where they live. This data is encapsulated inside the object:

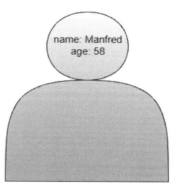

Figure 10.8 – Data encapsulated inside a real-world object

To get this information, we will need to ask the person. We say that objects communicate by passing messages to each other. This looks something like this:

Figure 10.9 – Two objects communicating by sending messages

We will need to modify our class so that the data is hidden and we have a way to communicate with it.

We can hide the data by using the `private` keyword. The class will now look something like this:

```
class Person
    private name
    private age
end_class
```

By declaring `name` and `age` as private, we can no longer access them from outside the class. This means that the lines where we printed the name and age of the two objects will no longer work.

The class, as it looks now, is useless as we can create an object and assign values to its variables, but there is no way for us to do anything with this data after this point as it is hidden from us. We will need to create an interface, such as the buttons on the remote control, that will let us work with the data. We will do that with the help of class methods.

Class methods

A class method is nothing but a function that belongs to a class. The reason we have a different name for these functions is so that we can distinguish between a function that is part of a class and one that is not. As soon as you hear someone mention a method, you know that it is a function that belongs to a class.

Two popular methods that we will find in classes are what are called *getters* and *setters*. A getter is a method that returns the value of a private member variable, while a setter is a method that lets us change its value.

To make a method available outside the class, we can use the `public` keyword. To this, we can add getters and setters for our class, and it will then look like this:

```
class Person
    private name
    private age

    public function get_name()
        return name
    end_function
```

```
    public function set_name(new_name)
        name = new_name
    end_function

    public function get_age()
        return age
    end_function

    public function set_age(new_age)
        age = new_age
    end_function
end_class
```

This will give us access to the member variables. We can now create objects, get the private data stored inside of them, and change their value if needed.

It will look something like this:

```
p1 = Person("Dipika", 34)
p2 = Person("Manfred", 58)

print p1.get_name() + " is " + p1.get_age() + " year old"
p1.set_age(35)
print p1.get_name() + " is " + p1.get_age() + " year old"
```

This will produce the following output:

```
Dipika is 34 years old
Dipika is 35 years old
```

A natural question at this point is why we need to bother having these getters and setters. Why can't we just say that name and age are public and let anyone read and change them as they want? The reason is that keeping the data private and controlling access to it through methods will give us control.

If a stranger walks up to you and asks for your name, you will have some options. You could respond with your actual name, you could tell them that it is none of their business, or you could lie and tell them a different name. You have control over the access to your private data, just as the class will have control over the access to its private data with the help of these methods.

When the `set_age` method is called, we could, for example, check the value that is being passed in to make sure that it is within a valid range. We could, for example, refuse to set the age if it is a negative number or higher than any expected human age. We could make use of exceptions, which we covered in *Chapter 9, When Things Go Wrong – Bugs and Exceptions*, in the *Working with exceptions* section. The `set_age` method would then look something like this:

```
public function set_age(new_age)
    if age < 0 or age > 130 then
        throw ValueError("Error. Age must be between 0 and 130")
    end_if
    age = new_age
end_function
```

We will now get an exception if the value that's being passed to the method is below 0 or greater than 130.

Now, we can add some class methods to the diagram we looked at previously in *Figure 10.2* . In the following image, we can see that we're making use of the lower part of the rectangle for this:

Figure 10.10 – A class with member variables and methods

A class can, of course, have methods other than just getters and setters. It is up to us to decide what methods we want our class to have. Our `Person` class could, for example, have a method called `birthday` where we increase the age of a person by one, as shown in the following code snippet:

```
class Person
    private name
    private age

    public function birthday()
        age = age + 1
    end_function

    // Getters and setters as before are defined here
end_class
```

We could now use it like this:

```
p1 = Person("Dipika", 34)

print p1.get_name() + " is " + p1.get_age() + " year old"
p1.birthday()
print p1.get_name() + " is " + p1.get_age() + " year old"
```

The output of this program will be the same as it was previously:

```
Dipika is 34 years old
Dipika is 35 years old
```

As we can see, the power of object-oriented programming is that objects are self-contained entities that control their data. But object-oriented programming has another powerful feature that will let us reuse code, and that is the concept of inheritance.

Inheritance

If I asked you if I could borrow your phone to make a call, it would not matter if you gave me your smartphone, an old mobile phone from 2005, or even access to a landline telephone. They all share some of the same features, with one of them being the ability to make phone calls. We could define this with a chain of statements, as follows:

- A smartphone is a mobile phone
- A mobile phone is a telephone
- A telephone can make phone calls
- A smartphone can, therefore, make phone calls

We could say that we have several levels of abstractions where we have a relationship between the levels. This is what we call an *is-a* relation. We can illustrate this with the following diagram:

Figure 10.11 – Is-a relations between telephones

We can say that because a smartphone is a mobile phone, it can do anything a mobile phone can. We also know that a smartphone can do things that an old-style mobile phone can't, such as allowing us to use the GPS together with a map app to help us navigate.

A mobile phone, on the other hand, can do everything the landline telephone can; that is, make and receive calls. But it can also do other things, such as allow us to send text messages.

We can also view this relationship as a parent-child relationship. The smartphone is a child of the mobile phone, and the mobile phone is its parent. This also means that a child will inherit from its parent. This is how inheritance works in object-oriented programming.

A class can inherit another class, and by that, get everything that is defined in the parent class and just add the things that make this class unique. To see what this might look like, we will need two classes. We can have a `Person` class that is defined like the one we saw in *figure 10.10*. It might look something like this:

```
class Person
    private name
    private date_of_birth
    private gender
    private address
    private nationality
    private phone_number
    private email_address

    public function get_name()
        return name
    end_function

    public function set_name(new_name)
        name = new_name
    end_function

    // Getters and setters for all the other
    // variables are implemented here
end_class
```

In this class, we define all the member variables as private members of the class, and all the getters and setters are defined as public.

The information used here applies to all people, but we might have some people that we need to store additional information for. This could, for example, be employees. They are people, and by that, all the information we store about a person will apply to them as well, but we have additional data that we want to store about employees. This could be things such as salary and department. We don't want to define them, however, as shown in the following image:

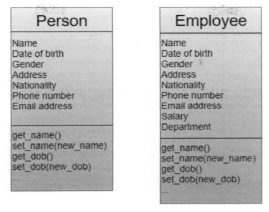

Figure 10.12 – Two classes not using inheritance

Here, we can see that everything we have in the Person class is repeated in the Employee class. The only difference is that we have added **Salary** and **Department**. What we can do instead is we can say that the Employee class will inherit from the Person class and, by that, they automatically get everything that is defined in Person. This will look something like this:

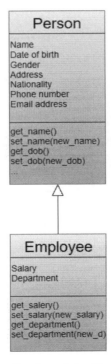

Figure 10.13 – Employee inheriting from Person

Here, the Employee c;ass will inherit everything from Person. The only thing we will need to define in the Employee class is the things that make this class unique. Just as we usually represent classes with the rectangle with three sections, inheritance is visualized with a hollow, arrow-like symbol, as shown in the preceding image.

When implementing this inheritance in code, we don't need to make any changes to the Person class. So, the Employee class will look like this:

```
class Employee inherit Person
    private salary
    private department

    public function get_salary()
        return salary
    end_function

    public function set_salary(new_salary)
        salary = new_salary
    end_function

    public function get_department()
        return department
    end_function

    public function set_department(new_department)
        department = new_department
    end_function
end_class
```

Even though we only have code for the salary and department in this class, from the first line we can say that we inherit the Person class.

Exactly how object-oriented programming is implemented differs from language to language. Languages that support object-orientation will also sometimes have slightly different rules for how object-orientation is used. As always, we will need to learn how the language we are using has defined the object-oriented principles.

The following is a list of some popular languages that support object orientation, either entirely or as an option:

- C++
- C#
- Java
- JavaScript
- Object-C
- PHP
- Python
- Ruby
- Scala
- Swift

Object orientation is one of the major paradigms. It has many fans who like it and think it is a good way to structure code. The next paradigm we will look at has been around for a long time but has gained in popularity in the last few years: functional programming. It is now considered one of the more interesting paradigms by many programmers.

Understanding functional programming

Functional programming is a paradigm that has gained popularity. It is not new; we can trace its roots back to Lambda calculus, which was introduced in the 1930s. In the 1950s, the programming language Lisp was developed and implemented this paradigm.

As we will see, this paradigm has a very different approach to how programs are structured and implemented. You will need to rethink the way you look at programming and code structure to be able to understand the strength of this paradigm.

We will begin by looking at a definition of functional programming. The definition will, itself, be hard to understand, so we will also need to look at some parts of it to understand what this is all about.

One definition is as follows:

"Functional programming is a way of structuring a computer program that treats computation as the evaluation of mathematical functions and avoids changing the state of the program and the use of mutable data."

Let's start by deciphering this definition. The *treats computation as the evaluation of mathematical functions* part might sound scary. If we look closely at this, we will see that this is rather straightforward. Let's look at two mathematical functions and see how we can use and understand them in order to understand what the definition of functional programming is talking about.

Pure functions

We will start simple with the following function:

$$y = x$$

Here, x is the input we provide to the function and y is the result. This simple function just states that whatever we pass a value to it, it will also be returned. A diagram for this function looks as follows:

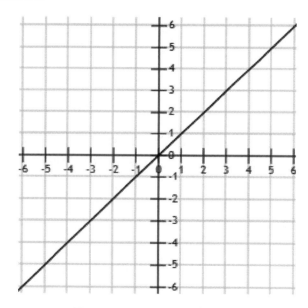

Figure 10.14 – Diagram for y = x

Here, we can see that if **x** is **1**, **y** is also **1** and that if **x** is **-3**, **y** is also **-3**. What's even more essential for us to understand regarding what the definition talks about is the fact that the same input to **x** will always yield the same value as a result in **y**. If we input **5** for **x**, we will always get **5** for **y**.

Let's look at another function to see if the same thing is true:

$$y = mx + c$$

This is a function for a straight line. The value of **m** will define the slope of the line, while **c** will be the value of **y** when $x = 0$. If we set **m** to 2 and **c** to 3, we will get the following diagram:

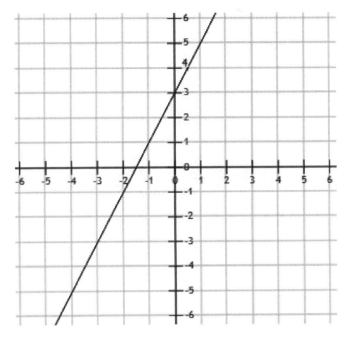

Figure 10.15 – Diagram for y = mx + c when m = 2 and c = 3

Again, the most important thing to learn from this is that the result, the value of **y** will always be the same if we provide the same value for **x**. The value we get for **y** will always be 3 if **x** is 0, and always be 1 if **x** is -1.

When talking about mathematical functions in terms of functional programming, it is this fact that is the crucial thing: a function with the same input will always return the same answer. In functional programming, this is known as a *pure function*.

But isn't this always true for any function? Look at the following function:

```
function add(a, b)
    return a + b
end_function
```

Let's call this function:

```
print add(2, 3)
```

On calling the function, we will always get the following response:

```
5
```

We can say that this is a pure function. But what happens when we call this function from the math module?

```
print Math.random()
print Math.random()
```

Now, the output might look like this:

```
0.34
0.75
```

Calling the random function with the same arguments (none in our case) will not give us the same answer. This is not a pure function. This is the meaning of evaluating mathematical functions in the preceding definition.

Next up is the second part of the definition, *avoids changing the state of the program and the use of mutable data*. Changing the state is something we recognize from when we talked about structured programming. There, we said that *structured programming uses statements to change the program's state*. It seems like functional programming is talking about the absolute opposite of what structured programming did. We said that the state the program is in is defined by the combination of the data stored in all its variables at any given time. Changing the value of one variable will change the state of the program.

What would it mean if a program avoids changing its state? Would we not be able to change any variables? The answer to this is yes, and that is what is part of the final part of the definition: that it also avoids the use of mutable data. What does mutable data mean? We'll see what this is about in the next section.

Mutable and immutable data

Mutable means liable to change, while immutable means unable to be changed. The term *mutable data* means that we have data that we can change. We know that we store data in variables and that we can change it as we please, as shown in the following code block:

```
x = 10
y = 20
x = y
```

Here, we first assign the value 10 to the x variable and then assign the value 20 to the y variable. On the last line, we change the value of x so that it's the same as y, which is 20. We could say that x is mutable as we can change it. But is this proof that x is mutable? In some languages, it is, but in others, this is not true at all, even if the final value in x will always be 20. How is it possible that x changes its value from 10 to 20 if we cannot change it? This sounds impossible.

The answer is in the way a language treats its variables. If we just think of a variable like a box where we can store a value and, at any time, replace it with another value, it is changeable, but if instead we treat a variable like something that is pointing out a value somewhere in the computer's memory, things will be slightly different.

Let's perform a little thought experiment. We can start with the two variables, x and y, and again assign the values 10 and 20 to them, as we did previously:

```
x = 10
y = 20
```

The following diagram illustrates what it may look like if x and y reference a memory location:

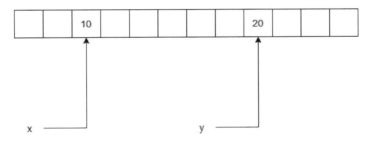

Figure 10.16 – Two variables referencing two memory locations

As we can see, the values 10 and 20 are not stored inside the variables. Instead, the variables are pointing out where these values are located in memory. What will happen if we change the value x references from 10 to 20?

It will look something like this:

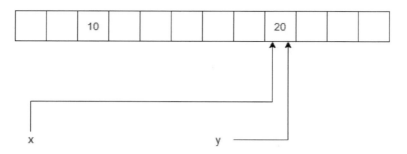

Figure 10.17 – Two variables that reference the same memory location

Now, let's consider what would happen if the value at the memory location can be changed if we change one of the variables if we, for example, run this line of code:

```
y = 22
```

We would then have a situation similar to the following:

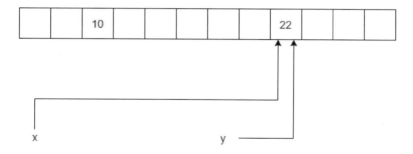

Figure 10.18 – Changing the value of one variable reference

Now, let's print the value of the x reference, as follows:

```
print x
```

We would get the following result:

```
22
```

Even if we never assigned 22 to x, it would have that value as we allowed y to change the content of the memory location of both references.

If we instead make the memory location immutable, what would happen when we assign 22 to y? We would get something like the following:

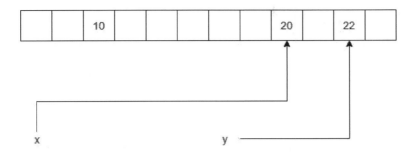

Figure 10.19 – Assigning a new value to an immutable variable

As we can see, the value did not change at all. Instead, y is now referencing a new memory location. If y was redeclared, we would get a new fresh variable with the same name as the old y variable.

This is how immutability works. The variables are not changed. Instead, a new value is created in another location in memory. As we cannot change any variables, we can't change the state of the program either.

But why is it important that our variables are immutable and that we can't change the state of the program? The answer is called side effects.

Avoiding side effects

A side effect in computer programming is when an expression modifies some values in the variables that are outside its local environment. To understand this, let's look at an example:

```
x = 0
function some_func(value)
    x = x + value
    return x + 3
end_function
```

First, this program is very naïve, but it illustrates the point we need to make. Here, we have a variable, x, and a function called some_func. The variable is declared outside of the function but is modified inside it. We can now use the following expression:

```
x = x + value
```

This is modifying a value outside its environment, and the body of the function is the environment that expression lives in.

This is true if the language we are using has defined x as mutable so that we can change it. But in a language where x is immutable, there would be no change. Instead, we would get a new x variable that only exists inside of the function.

What would the disadvantage be if we did this in a language where x was mutable? To see this, we can call the function twice and print its result, as follows:

```
print some_func(10)
print some_func(10)
```

The output will look as follows:

```
13
23
```

This is not a good behavior as calling the function with the same arguments should always return the same value. Here, it does not, and the reason this happens is because the program has side effects. This is because the result the function returns is dependent on what happened in previous calls to the function.

If we have a program that has no side effects, it will be very predictable what will happen when the program runs. If we think about the previous small program, we saw that it will be almost impossible for us to predict what a call to the function will result in as the result will depend on previous calls, as well as what data we provided as arguments in these calls.

The next principle of functional programming is called declarative programming. Let's see what it's all about.

Declarative programming

To understand what declarative programming is, we can compare it to something we know, and that is imperative programming. In imperative programming, we focus on describing how something will be done. In declarative programming, on the other hand, the focus is on what we want to achieve.

To understand this, we will look at some real-world examples. If you go to a restaurant, you can either be an imperative or declarative guest.

The imperative guest would make an order like this:

"I would like the cod, please. First, bake it in the oven for 10 to 12 minutes. In the end, check it regularly so it won't overcook. While the cod is in the oven, please boil the potatoes. To prepare the cream sauce, first, melt some butter in a medium-sized pan over medium heat. Slowly add corn starch and stir for about a minute. While constantly whisking, slowly add whipping cream and milk. Finally, add some parmesan cheese. Let the sauce reduce on a low heat while you whisk occasionally."

If, on the other hand, you are a declarative restaurant guest, you would say something like this:

"I would like the cod, please."

The first guest answers the question of how, while the second one focuses on what.

An excellent example of something declarative in computer science is **SQL**. It is an abbreviation of **Structured Query Language** and is used to store and retrieve data from databases. If we want to get the first and last name of all the customers stored in the customer's table, we could write the following:

```
SELECT firstName, lastName FROM customers;
```

This is declarative as we say what we want – the first and last names of the customers – but we say nothing about how the data will be retrieved. Somewhere in the underlying database system, some parts must know how this will be done, but if we are using SQL, we don't need to understand how this is done.

Python is a programming language where we can write both imperative and declarative programs. Let's look at two programs that perform the same thing, one in an imperative way and one in a declarative way.

First is a short program that has been written in an imperative style:

```
strings = ['06', '68', '00', '30']
numbers = []
for value in strings:
    if int(value) != 0:
        numbers.append(int(value))
print(numbers)
```

From the preceding code, we can observe the following:

1. On the first line, we define a list of strings. Each string contains a two-digit number. Values below 10 will be prefixed with a 0.

2. On the second line, we declare an empty list. We will convert the numbers in the first list from strings into integer values and store them in this array.

3. We will then enter a `for` loop. In each iteration of this loop, a value from the first list will be assigned to the `value` variable. The first time it will be 06, the second time it will be 68, and so on.

4. We then have an `if` statement. It will convert the value into an integer and compare it to zero. If that is false – that is, it is anything but zero – we will enter the `if` block.

5. Inside this block, we will append the value we converted into an integer to the list numbers.

6. When we have gone through all the values in the first list, we print the contents of the second list and get the following output:

```
[6, 68, 30]
```

As you can see, the zero prefixes we had for the first value are now gone as these are integers, and 06 is just 6. Also, the value that had a double zero is not in the list at all as it made the `if` statement false, and the line where we appended the value was skipped in that iteration.

The second version of this program is written in a declarative style and looks as follows:

```
strings = ['06', '68', '00', '30']
numbers = [int(value) for value in strings if int(value) != 0]
print(numbers)
```

This program does the same thing as the previous one, but the way it is written is very different. It uses something called a *list comprehension*. It is the part after `numbers =`. If you look closely, you can see a `for` loop in the middle of this expression. It looks just like the `for` loop in the other example. Following this loop, we can see an `if`, and it looks just like the `if` statement in the first program. An `if` at this location in a comprehension serves as a filter. If this is evaluated as true, the current value will be passed to the front of this expression. Here, we convert the value into an integer. This converted value will be part of a list called `numbers`.

This is declarative because we don't say how this value will get into the new list, we just say what will go into the list.

The final principle used by functional programming that we will cover is called first-class functions.

First-class functions

Functional programming uses the principle of first-class functions. A function is said to be first-class if it is treated as a first-class citizen of the programming language in question. A first-class citizen is something that we can modify, pass as an argument to a function, return from a function, and so on.

In a programming language that supports first-class functions, we can do things such as the following:

```
function formal_greeter(name)
    return "Dear, " + name
end_function

function informal_greeter(name)
    return "Yo, " + name
end_function

function greeter(greeter_func, name)
    greeter_func(name)
end_function

greeter(formal_greeter, "Bob")
greeter(informal_greeter, "Bob")
```

This program declares two functions, `formal_greeter` and `informal_greeter`. Both accept a `name` as its argument and will return a greeting with the name appended.

We then have a function called `greeter`. This function accepts a reference to a function as its first argument and a name as its second. The two last lines in the program are calling the `greeter` function. The first one is passing a reference to the formal greeter function, while the second is passing one to the informal greeter.

The `greeter` function will use the function passed to it, so the two calls will result in the following output:

```
Dear, Bob
Yo, Bob
```

Being able to work with functions like this has several benefits. Let's look at an example. Earlier in this chapter, we talked about object-oriented programming, and we defined a class called Person. We saw that we could create several objects from this class, each one representing one person.

Later in this chapter, we will see that programming languages can use more than one paradigm, and if we use one that lets us define classes and use functions as first-class citizens, we can do something very useful.

If we create a couple of person objects with name and age and insert them into a list structure, this might look something like the following:

```
p1 = Person("Dipika", 34)
p2 = Person("Manfred", 58)
p3 = Person("Ahmed", 38)
p4 = Person("Rita", 39)
persons = [p1, p2, p3, p4]
```

We now have four person objects stored in a list called persons. If we want to sort the list, we can use a sorting function provided by the language. But there is a problem. The sorting function will not know what we want to sort on; that is, name or age. It does not even know anything about Person objects as they are defined by a class that we have written. What it knows is how to sort a list, but it needs the help of a function that can receive two objects from the Person class, and which returns true if the first object is larger than the second and false if it is not. We will need to write that function and, in it, define what makes one object larger than the other one. We can decide if it should be name or age.

If we want to sort the objects by their age, we could do the following:

```
function compare(person1, person2)
    return person1.get_age() > person2.get_age()
end_function


sorted_persons = sort(compare, persons)
```

Here, we have a function called compare. It will accept two person objects as its arguments. If the age of the first person is greater than the age of the second person, this function will return true. Otherwise, it returns false.

The sort function accepts as its first argument a reference to this function. When it is performing the sort, it will need to compare two different objects to determine in what order it should place them in the sorted list.

In our example, it will first pass Dipika, who is 34, and Manfred, who is 58, to the function. The compare function will return false since the age of Manfred is greater than the age of Dipika.

The sort function will now take the winner from the last round, Manfred, and pass this object along with Ahmed's object. This time, Manfred will be passed first, so he will be the person1 object in the function, while Ahmed will be person2.

This time, the first object has an age that is greater than the second one, so the function returns true.

This is how the sort function can use a function that we provide to fulfill its task to sort the list. If we want to sort on the names instead, we will only need to change the compare function so that it compares the names instead of the ages.

If we print the sorted_persons list, which contains the sorted list, we will get this result if we sort on age:

```
Dipika, 34
Ahmed, 38
Rita, 39
Manfred, 58
```

If, instead, we sort on the names, we will get the following result:

```
Ahmed, 38
Dipika, 34
Manfred, 58
Rita, 39
```

First-class functions are a compelling feature that let us write functions that are more general-purpose as we can pass another function that will do parts of its job, just as the sort function works.

Functional programming has several concepts that are both powerful and let us write higher quality code. That is the reason why functional programming is constantly gaining popularity and why many non-functional programming languages are borrowing functional concepts.

The following is a list of some popular languages that support functional programming, either as its primary paradigm or are using many concepts from functional programming:

- C++ (since C++ 11)
- C#
- Clojure
- Common Lisp
- Erlang
- F#
- Haskell
- JavaScript
- Python
- Ruby

Functional programming is not only a very interesting paradigm, but it is also influencing many established languages to incorporate functional concepts. The next paradigm is not as widely used as the ones we have looked at so far, but it has some interesting concepts.

Understanding logic programming

This paradigm is based on formal logic. A program written in a language that implements this paradigm is constructed of a set of sentences in a logical form that will express facts and rules about a specific problem domain.

This might sound complicated and strange, but as we will see, the basic concepts of this paradigm are rather simple. Consider the following diagram:

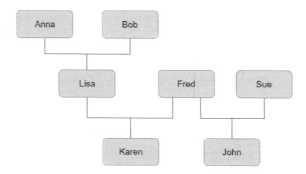

Figure 10.20 – A family tree

In the preceding diagram, we can see a family tree. Looking at it, we can see the following:

- Anna and Bob have a child, Lisa.
- Lisa and Fred have a child, Karen.
- Fred and Sue have a child, John.
- Karen's grandparents are Anna and Bob.

In a programming language that uses logic programming, we can define this family tree using something called *predicates*. This will look something like this:

```
mother(anna,lisa).
mother(lisa,karen).
mother(sue,john).
father(bob,lisa).
father(fred,karen).
father(fred,john).
```

They might seem to come in an odd order, but most logic languages want us to group all predicates of the same kind together so, in this case, we first define all the mothers and, after that, all the fathers.

On the first line, we can see that Anna is the mother of Lisa, while on the fourth line, we can see that Bob is the father of Lisa. The names are called *atoms* because they represent a single value, and atoms need to be defined by lowercase letters only.

We can now define some rules that dictate what makes someone a parent and grandparent. It might look like this:

```
grandparent(X,Z) :- parent(X,Y), parent(Y,Z).
parent(X,Y) :- father(X,Y).
parent(X,Y) :- mother(X,Y).
```

Here, X, Y, and Z are variables. Variables are defined with an initial capital letter. We can read this as

For any X, Y, Z,

> If X is a parent of Y, and Y is a parent of Z

> Then X is the grandparent of Z

The two last rows define what a parent is. It is either if X is the father of Y or if X is the mother of Y.

We can now use this to ask questions like this:

```
grandparent(anna, karen).
```

This question will produce the following answer:

```
yes
```

This is true as Anna is the grandmother of Karen.

We can also ask who Karen's grandparents are, as follows:

```
grandparent(Q, karen).
```

Here, Q is a variable, and we will get the following response:

```
bob
```
```
anna
```

We could also ask who the grandchild of Anna is:

```
grandparent(anna, Q).
```

This will tell us that it is Karen:

```
karen
```

There are, of course, more things that you can do in a logic programming language, but this was a little taste of what logic programming can look like.

The following is a list of some languages that support logic programming:

- ALF
- Curry
- Fril
- Janus
- Prolog

The way we structure the code in logic programming is very different from all other paradigms, making it an interesting *outsider*.

We have now looked at the leading players in the paradigm field. But before we leave these paradigms behind, let's just mention a few more to get a more complete picture.

Other paradigms

The paradigms we have covered so far in this chapter are the most commonly used, but there are several others. Let's have a quick look at some of them.

Function-level

In function-level programming, we have no variables at all. Instead, programs are built from elementary functions, combined with function-to-function operations, sometimes referred to as *functionals* or *functional forms*.

Languages that implement this paradigm are built around the following hierarchy:

- Atoms are the data that the functions operate on. They will only appear as input or output to the programs and will never be found inside the actual program.
- Functions will convert atoms into other atoms. The programming language will define a set of functions, and the programmer can create new ones using functional forms. The program itself is also a function.
- Functional forms are used to convert functions into other functions. They can be used by the programmer to create new forms.

Array programming

In array programming, operations will be performed on an entire set of values at once. These solutions are commonly used for scientific and engineering applications.

Operations are generalized to apply to both scalars and arrays. In this book, we have encountered scalars in the form of variables that can only hold one single value at a time. We have also looked at arrays. If you need a refresh your memory on variables and arrays, you can read more about them in *Chapter 6, Working with Data – Variables*.

The $a + b$ operation will act differently if a and b are scalars and if they are arrays. If they are scalars, the result will be the sum of adding the two values. If they are arrays, the result will be the sum of all values stored in the two arrays.

Array programming can simplify programming at the cost of efficiency. This means that it can be easier to use these kinds of languages when we write the code but running them might take a longer time than if the program is written in a language that uses another paradigm.

Quantum programming

This is the paradigm of the future. To be able to use this paradigm, we will need quantum computers. A quantum computer uses the quantum-mechanical properties particles defined in quantum physics. These particles have a superposition, meaning that before we observe them, they will be in any possible position. A quantum computer will use this by defining something known as a *qubit*. A normal computer has bits that can either be 0 or 1. A qubit will be both, and using this property, a quantum computer will be able to calculate all possible results of any given input in a fraction of the time it takes to perform the same calculations with the kind of computers we are using today.

Quantum programming is not a paradigm per se, but to be able to write programs for quantum computers, we will need languages that will support other kinds of operations than the ones we are using today:

Figure 10.21 – Part of a quantum computer built at IBM Research in Zurich.
Photo by IBM Zurich Lab, cc-by-2.0.

Even though we are just seeing the first quantum computers slowly take form, several languages that we can use for them are already defined. They are built upon already existing paradigms, such as imperative and functional programming. When we have fully functional and accessible quantum computers, we will see an explosion of new languages that will utilize the powers of these computers.

Multi-paradigm languages

Most programming languages will not stick to just one paradigm but instead use several. This is why they are called *multi-paradigm languages*. We can make a table of some of the most popular languages to see what paradigms they support:

Language	Structured	Object-oriented	Functional	Logic
Ada	Yes	Yes	No	No
C++	Yes	Yes	Yes	Some
C#	Yes	Yes	Some	No
Clojure	No	No	Yes	Some
Erlang	No	No	Yes	No
F#	Yes	Yes	Yes	No
Go	Yes	No	No	No
Haskell	Some	Some	Yes	Some
Java	Yes	Yes	Yes	No
JavaScript	Yes	Some	Yes	No
PHP	Yes	Yes	Yes	No
Prolog	No	No	No	Yes
Python	Yes	Yes	Some	Some
Ruby	Yes	Yes	Yes	No
Swift	Yes	Yes	Yes	No

Table 10.1

It can always be argued how much a paradigm influences a programming language. Here, I have looked at the main paradigms we have looked at in this chapter and how the documentation of the languages describes themselves.

A language that is marked with *Some* has implemented some concepts of this paradigm. A language that has a *Yes* in the column for a paradigm might not have this paradigm as its main one but has implemented many of its features.

Summary

In this chapter, we looked at some of the most popular programming paradigms.

The first two that we looked at, structured and object-oriented programming, are the two paradigms that have dominated programming over the last 35-40 years.

In structured programming, the program state is modified using statements, and the flow of the program is controlled using loops and selections, such as if statements.

Object-oriented programming builds upon the ideas of structured programming, but the code is organized using concepts known to us humans, such as classifying things that have similar data and behavior. This is described in classes that act as blueprints for objects that represent real-world things, such as people or bank accounts.

Functional programming is the oldest of the paradigms we covered in this book but has gained popularity in the last decade. In functional programming, we don't want to modify the state of the program and are using the concept of pure functions to achieve this. Writing programs using this paradigm can reduce errors in the code and make our applications more stable.

In logical programming, we define predicates that will define rules that we can use to answer logical questions. Compared to the other three paradigms, local programming is far less popular.

There are many other paradigms available, and they are often rather specialized or used by a few obscure languages.

Most programming languages are multi-paradigm in that they use concepts from more than one paradigm.

In the next chapter, we will see that our work, as programmers, is not done when the code is written.

11
Programming Tools and Methodologies

Now, it's time for us to take a closer look at the development cycle. Producing software is more than just writing code. We must plan what will be coded, write the code, integrate the code we write with already existing code, share our code with other developers, test the code, deploy the code so that the application can be accessed by the users, add new features to the application, and fix bugs and errors that will show up in the code that has been released.

To accomplish this, a development team will typically use different tools and methodologies for how things will be done and in what order.

In this chapter, we will look at all the components that are part of the development process that is not the actual coding.

In this chapter, we will cover the following topics:

- Understanding what a version control system is and what it can be used for
- Understanding unit tests
- Understanding integration tests
- Understanding the concept of a release
- Understanding software deployment
- Understanding code maintenance
- Understanding software development process methodologies

We have lots to cover, so let's start with an essential tool in software development: version control systems.

Understanding version control systems

A **version control system** (**VCS**) is used to manage changes in documents, computer programs, or other collections of files. They are used by programmers to manage different revisions of their code.

It is possible to restore earlier reversions if needed. This makes it safer to edit files, as we always have a way for us to restore what we had if we decide that the changes we made need to be reset.

VCSs are also used so that developers can work together on the same project and, in a safe manner, work in the same source code files. Version control systems also keep track of who changed what in a document, and when the change was made.

Files that are version controlled are stored in what is called a **repository**. When changes are made to a file, the user of the VCS can commit these changes to the repository, and by extension of that, create a reversion point. It is at these points where the version control system takes a snapshot of all the changes made.

To illustrate how this works, we can use one of the most popular version control systems available: Git. Git was created by Linus Torvalds, the creator of Linux, in 2005. It was initially created to be used by the programmers who were working on the Linux kernel code, but soon gained popularity outside the Linux project. Today, it is by far the most popular version control system.

Let's start by writing some code. Let's say we have this code in a file called `calc.code`:

```
function add(a, b)
    return a + b
```

Save this file in an empty folder. We can now use the GIT software to create a repository. This means that we can start to version control the files within this folder. From the command line, we can do this by writing the following code:

```
git init
```

At this point, nothing is version controlled yet. We will need to tell GIT what files we want to add to version control. We can do that with the following command:

```
git add calc.code
```

Our file is now staged. This means that its changes will be tracked, but we will need to do one more thing to record the changes that have been made to our file. What we'll do is called a **commit**. A commit will record our changes and store them in our repository. Let's do that with the following command:

```
git commit -m "Initial Commit"
```

`-m` tells `git` that we will provide a commit message, and the message is what comes within the quotes. The messages will help us see what is changed in a commit, so we should take some time to come up with descriptive messages.

The changes we have made are now stored on what is called the *master branch*. The following diagram illustrates what this looks like:

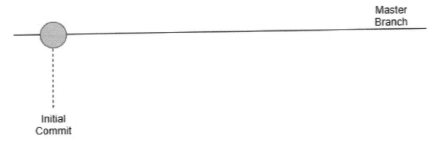

Figure 11.1 – The master branch after our initial commit

We would now like to continue to work on our program and add more code to this file. To make life a little bit safer, we can create a new branch and make our changes in this branch. We will soon see why this might be a good idea.

To create a new branch called `subtract`, we can use the following command:

```
git branch subtract
```

Creating a new branch will give us an exact copy of the branch we created it from, which in this case is the master branch. This can be illustrated as follows:

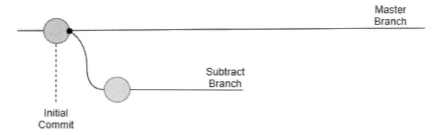

Figure 11.2 – Creating a new branch called subtract from the master branch

We are still on the master branch, so any changes we make will be on this branch. So, before we do anything else, we should switch branches. We can do that with the `checkout` command:

```
git checkout subtract
```

We are now on the `subtract` branch. Now, we can update our source code file, so let's add another function, making the file look like this:

```
function add(a, b)
    return a + b

function subtract(a, b)
    return a - b
```

If we save these changes, we can add the file to the staging area and commit the changes with the following commands:

```
git add calc.code
git commit -m "Added the subtract function."
```

We can illustrate this commit with another circle on the submit branch, as shown in the following diagram:

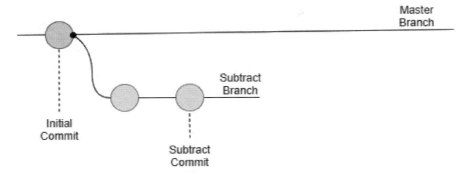

Figure 11.3 – Committing to our new branch

Now that we have committed our changes to GIT, we can switch branches. Let's do that with the following command:

```
git checkout master
```

If we open our file now, we will see the following content:

```
function add(a, b)
    return a + b
```

The changes we made are not here. This is because these changes are not in the master branch. Keeping the file open in our editor, we can now switch back to the subtract branch by using the following command:

```
git checkout subtract
```

Like magic, the changes we made to the file are back, and the subtract function is as we left it:

```
function add(a, b)
    return a + b

function subtract(a, b)
    return a - b
```

This illustrates that if we, for some reason, decide that the changes we made were no good, we can always go back to our master branch, and everything will be like it was before we started. However, if we, on the other hand, are happy with the changes, we can now bring the two branches together. In GIT, this is called a **merge**. The first thing we should do before merging the two branches is make sure that the branch we want to merge is active. In this case, it is the master branch, so we write the following:

```
git checkout master
```

Now, we are ready to merge the changes we made back into the master branch. We can do this with the following command:

```
git merge subtract
```

This means we take the changes made in the branch called subtract and merge it with the content of the current branch, master. We can illustrate this with the following diagram:

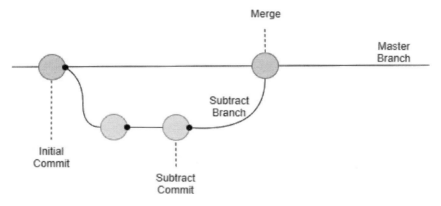

Figure 11.4 – Merging the subtract branch with the master branch

This is how we can use version control with GIT on our local machine. Now, let's see how we can use it to collaborate with other programmers who work on the same project as us. For that, we will need not only our local repository but also a central repository that we can use to update the other on the changes we make.

Let's assume that Alice and Bob are both working on the same project and want to use GIT to update each other on the changes they make to any files in the project. They will not only have their local GIT repositories, as we saw in the preceding example, but they will also connect to a centralized repository. Any changes they make can now be pushed to this repository, and they can also pull down any changes the other person made from that repository.

This will look something like the following:

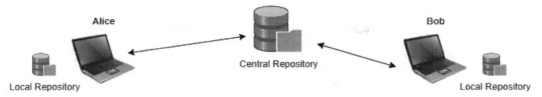

Figure 11.5 – Two programmers connected to a central repository

We can now assume that they will both work on the same file we saw previously, `calc.code`, and that it has the same content as we left it with, like this:

```
function add(a, b)
    return a + b


function subtract(a, b)
    return a - b
```

The central repository is often referred to as the **origin**. Let's say that Alice now wants to create a `multiply` function:

1. The first thing she should do is pull down the latest version from the central repository (origin) with the following command:

    ```
    git pull origin master
    ```

    Here, `origin` points out the central repository, and `master` is the branch she wants to pull down.

2. She now has the latest version, and she can begin implementing her function. She decides to do this in a new branch, so she executes the following command:

    ```
    git branch multiply
    ```

3. She will then switch to this branch with the following command:

    ```
    git checkout multiply
    ```

4. Now, she can make the necessary changes, so she adds the following code to the file:

    ```
    function add(a, b)
        return a + b
    ```

```
function subtract(a, b)
    return a - b


function multiply(a, b)
    return a * b
```

Let's leave Alice here and check what Bob is doing.

While Alice has started her work, Bob decides he wants to create a `divide` function:

1. Just like Alice, he will pull down the latest version of the `master` branch and create a new branch called `divide`, switch to it, and then change the `calc.code` file, so that it looks as follows:

```
function add(a, b)
    return a + b


function subtract(a, b)
    return a - b


function divide(a, b)
    return a / b
```

At this point, Alice is happy with her changes, so she commits them to her branch and merges her branch with the master.

2. Now, she wants to push these changes to the central repository. Before she does that, though, she wants to make sure that changes have been made to the central repository. So, first, she tries to pull down any changes to her repository with the same command she ran previously:

```
git pull origin master
```

3. Since nothing has happened to the central repository since her last pull, nothing will happen. She can now push her changes with the following command:

```
git push origin master
```

Now, her changes are stored in the central repository. At this point, her local version of the `master` branch and the version stored in the central repository are identical.

Let's go back to Bob, who has finished his function. He commits his changes to his local repository in his branch and merges it into the master branch. Now, he is ready to commit his changes to the central repository:

1. Just like Alice, first, he wants to make sure that he has the latest changes from the central repository, so he issues a `pull` command:

```
git pull origin master
```

2. This time, things will not go so well. He gets a message that there has been a merge conflict. What's that? He opens the code file, and he now sees this:

```
function add(a, b)
    return a + b

function subtract(a, b)
    return a - b

<<<<<<< HEAD
function multiply(a, b)
    return a * b
=======
function divide(a, b)
    return a / b
>>>>>>> div
```

What happened was that he and Alice made changes to the same file on the same line, which is at the end of the file in this case.

GIT became confused due to this and needs help to decide what will be in the file.

Bob looks at this and understands that Alice has added a function to the same location in the file that he did, and he understands that both functions should be there.

The `<<<<<<< HEAD` marker indicates the beginning of the conflict. What is between that line and the `=======` line is the changes he pulled down. The code between `=======` and `>>>>>>> div` are his changes.

3. Since he decides that both functions should be in this file, he removes the three marker lines from the file, so it now looks like this:

```
function add(a, b)
   return a + b

function subtract(a, b)
   return a - b

function multiply(a, b)
   return a * b

function divide(a, b)
   return a / b
```

He can now commit his changes to his local repository and then push the changes so that Alice can get the changes later.

This illustrates how a version control system can be used to share work between multiple programmers in a project. There are, of course, many other aspects of version control systems that we did not cover here, but now, you at least have an idea about what a version control system can do for you and how it can be used to share work with others.

This tool is used throughout the development process. Now, let's look at what we do when the code is written, as well as how we can make sure that it is working before we push it to the central repository.

It's now time for unit testing!

Unit testing

Testing our code is essential so that we can verify that it does what it should. We will also use tests to make sure that any changes we make to the code have not made things that previously worked stop working or behave in an undesired way.

Several kinds of testing can be done on our code, and the first type of test we will look at is called a **unit test**. The unit part indicates that the test will be done on a separate unit of our code. This is typically at a function level. This means that we will try to isolate one single function (or another small unit of code) and run our tests on just that unit.

These tests are typically written by the developer of the code unit to be tested and are often automated. This means that as soon as a block of code is ready to be committed to the version control system, it must first pass the unit test written for it.

Since the unit test only tests a single code unit, they are typically rather trivial. To test our `calc` functions, we must first decide what we want to test. First, we can set up some test cases for valid input and match these inputs to some expected results.

We could do this in a table like this one:

Function	Value for a	Value for b	Expected result
add	2	3	5
add	0	10	10
subtract	2	3	-1
subtract	7	4	3
multiply	10	2	20
multiply	15	2	30
divide	10	2	5
divide	21	3	7

Table 11.1

We can use this to write our tests.

Unit tests are typically written in a separate file that will call the code to be tested. They might look something like this:

```
function test_add_one()
    result = add(2, 3)
    assert.equal(5, result)
```

The first argument, `assert.equal`, is what we expect as a result, and it is compared to the content of the `result` variable. If they match, this test will pass; if not, the test will fail. We can now go ahead and create tests in the same manner for the rest of our test cases:

```
function test_add_two()
    result = add(0, 10)
    assert.equal(10, result)
```

```
function test_subtract_one()
    result = subtract(2, 3)
    assert.equal(-1, result)

function test_subtract_two()
    result = subtract(7, 4)
    assert.equal(3, result)
```

Here, we are just listing the first ones, but we continue like that with the rest.

For simple tests like these, the structure will be the same—call the function we want to test, store the returned value in a variable, and compare the returned value with the expected one. We should also think of odd cases and what kind of result we expect to get. For example, what will happen if we make this call to divide? Here is how the code appears:

```
result = divide(10, 0)
```

As we discussed in *Chapter 9, When Things Go Wrong – Bugs and Exceptions*, we can't divide a number by zero. This will result in an exception. If we expect to get an exception when this is done, the function works, but if we expect the function to handle this case, it will need to be modified. This is done so that it returns whatever we decide it should return. This may happen if we decide that we should get another exception that indicates that we can't pass a 0 as the second argument. So, no matter what we expect, it should be tested.

This is one type of test that we should run on our code, but these tests will just test a single unit; that is, an isolated part of the application. We will also need to perform another type of test, called an integration test. We'll see what this is in the next section.

Integration testing

Integration testing is about putting several units together and testing them so that they work correctly when they are no longer isolated, but work together.

Units that work together will need to communicate, and they will communicate by passing data between them. This means that integration testing is about checking that the data transfer and data representation aspects work.

Imagine that we are working on a project that is divided into several modules. To speed up development time, we let several programmers work on the separate modules. This might look something like this:

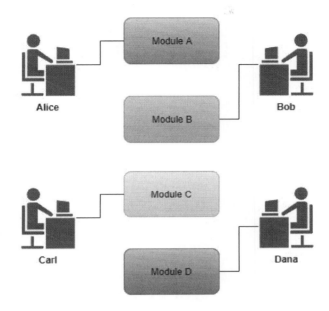

Figure 11.6 – Four developers working on four different modules

These four developers will now start to write their modules, and they will make sure that their modules meet the requirements by running unit tests on them. But the only thing these tests will show is that this module works in isolation.

But in the final application, these modules will need to interact with each other, and when they do, they will need to send data back and forth. The problem here is that all four programmers are human, and humans tend to interpret even the most detailed description differently. So, if Carl needs to pass a value for a year to the module Alice is writing, he might pass it as a two-digit value, such as 23. But Alice, who is writing the code receiving this data, might expect that the year comes in a four-digit format, so she expects 2023.

If we trace the communication between the modules when they are put together, this might look something like this:

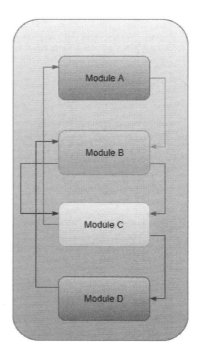

Figure 11.7 – Modules communicating

This is just a small example. In real applications, there will be many more modules and many more lines of communication. But the point is that we will need to verify that all the data that's passed back and forth is valid and works in all situations.

In this case, we will need to do what's called an **integration test**. This is when we test that different parts of the application are working when they're put together.

This can be done in several ways. There is a big-bang approach we can take, which means that we wait for all the modules to be completed, and then we put them together and test them. The disadvantage of this is that the modules will not be ready at the same time. If Alice, who writes Module A, is done with her work, she will need Bob to finish his work before she can integration test her module, as her work is making a call to Bob's work. The same goes for Bob: he needs Carl to finish his work before he can integrate his module into the application.

There are other approaches where we don't wait for all the parts to be finished before we begin testing. Instead, we create *fake* modules, called **stubs** and **drivers**. A stub is a module that gets called by another module, while a driver is a module calling another module. We can create these to pass and accept data so that we can begin testing. They are not fully functional modules, but they act as the real modules for the sake of testing. As modules get completed, they can replace these stubs and drivers, and tests can then be performed on the real modules.

Having these tests in place is essential, partly because it verifies that the modules can interact with each other, but also for the future. When we add new functionality later, either by changing existing modules or adding new ones, we want to make sure that everything that worked previously still does. Inserting new code into an existing application can have unwanted side effects, and we must make sure that this has not happened.

Other types of tests

Unit and integration testing are not the only types of tests we have. Depending on what kind of application we are creating and what requirements our software has when it comes to things such as data integrity, handling large workloads, compatibility with other applications, and so on, we can choose to expose the code for several different test types.

Let's briefly look at some of these tests.

System testing

System testing tests a system when it is completely integrated into its execution environment. Here, we will test things such as whether the login works, whether we can create and edit data in the application, whether the user interface presents data correctly, and whether we can delete entries.

These things are typically tested earlier in the development process too, but they need to be verified when the source code is in its live production environment.

Acceptance testing

Acceptance testing is often divided into four different types:

- User acceptance testing
- Operational acceptance testing

- Constructional and regulatory acceptance testing
- Alpha and beta testing

Let's understand these in detail:

- **User acceptance testing**: This is a way to verify that the solution created works for the end users of our application. The questions we are trying to answer with these tests are if the users can use the software, if it is what they asked for, whether they have any trouble using it, and if the application behaves as anticipated.

- **Operational acceptance testing**: This is done to verify the operational readiness of an application before it is released to end users.

- **Constructional and regulatory acceptance testing**: This is done to verify that the developed software fulfills the conditions specified in the agreement that was entered into with the organization that ordered the software. Regulatory testing verifies that the software conforms to the current regulations.

- **Alpha and beta testing**: These are two tests that are performed to verify and identify all possible issues and bugs. Alpha testing is performed early in the development process, while beta testing is done near the end of the development process. They are both conducted by potential users of the finished product or by a group of people with a similar skill level as the end users of the application.

Regression testing

Regression testing focuses on finding defects after a significant code change and seeks to uncover software regressions. A software regression is a bug that will make some features in an application stop functioning after the update. There is also software performance regression, where the software still operates correctly, but where an update harmed the system's performance.

These were some other tests we can perform on our software. There are many more, but the ones we have covered here are among the most typical tests you will get exposed to as a software developer.

When we have code that is tested, we can make it available to the end users of our application. Before we talk about how to make the code we have written available to our users, we should stop and talk about what a release is.

Software releases

When creating software, we don't want to start with an idea for the finished project and then get to work on everything that this application needs to do and, several years later, finally publish the finished software. The reason we don't want to do this is that during development time, several things will happen; for example, the requirements for this application might change, new laws can make us need to do things differently, and competing software solutions might be released, to name a few.

Instead, we want to implement some core features, release them to our users, and then immediately begin the development of the next release, which will contain some more features. This can be illustrated as follows:

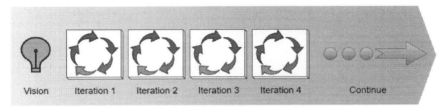

Figure 11.8 – Development process through continuous iterations

We start with a vision or an idea. Then, we take some fundamental parts of this idea and implement them in what is called an **iteration**. During this iteration phase, we perform several steps, all of which we will look at in more detail soon. At the end of the iteration, we have code that works that we can release to our users. We then begin the next iteration, implementing more features that are released as soon as this iteration is complete.

The steps that are taken during an iteration will vary, depending on the development methodology, but commonly, it will be something similar to the following:

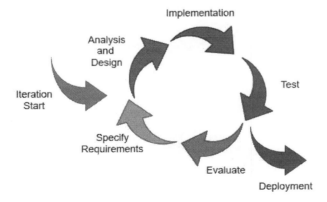

Figure 11.9 – Typical steps during one iteration

Here, we can see that we take our ideas and requirements into the development cycle. First, we will perform an analysis and design the steps. Here, we are trying to answer two questions:

- What is it that we will do (analysis)?
- How can we do it (design)?

When we know what we should do and how to do it, we can start to implement the different parts that go into this iteration.

As we finish a section of code, it gets unit tested, and then all the code undergoes integration tests. Other tests might also be performed before the code is released to end users. Releasing the code is called a **deployment**, a step we will look closer at soon.

What we have accomplished now is a release, and this means that our software now has some new features or bug fixes.

We can now begin the next iteration. This is completed by evaluating the iteration we just ended. This is done so that we can fine-tune our workflow, see whether we have discovered some problems during the last cycle, or any other issues that we need to consider in the next iteration.

We can then specify what will go into the next iteration, and by using that repeat the whole process.

Now, let's take a closer look at the deployment phase to learn what it is and how it can be done.

Understanding software deployment

When we have some code to release, we will need to deploy it. Deployment is the process of making sure the software is installed in the right location, that it is secured to prevent any hacker attacks, and making sure that privileges are given to the software so that it can read and write files as needed.

When the code is deployed, we usually want to test it again to make sure that everything is still working the way it is intended.

Deploying the code is usually done in several steps. Developers will typically have a server that's used during the development process. This is called the **development server**, and during development, the code can be executed and tested on this server. It will often come with a development database that, if the application we develop uses a database, is used to simulate the real data the application handles. Still, it can be modified any way the developer wants as it is detached from the real data the users see and work with.

Before the code is moved to the production server, that is, the server the application users will use to run the application, the code is usually moved to an intermediate server, often referred to as a **staging server**. The role of this server is to be as much like the production server as possible so that the new code can be tested alongside the code that was already released. The idea is to make sure that everything runs smoothly and that no bugs appear when the new code hits the live production server.

The staging server also has a database. The data in this database is often copied from the production database to make sure that everything is a mirror of the real server.

Finally, when the team is confident that everything works correctly, the code is moved to the production server. Apart from moving the code, other adjustments might be needed, such as adding things to the production database that the new software version will need, adding other applications and code libraries that are used by the new code, and so on. This is depicted here:

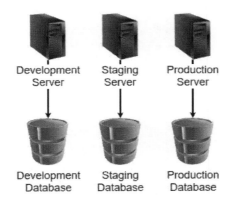

Figure 11.10 – Example of servers and their databases

We must also have a strategy for how we can undo this deployment if needed. No matter how thorough our test has been, when the code hits production and users start to use it, things that we never imagined begin surfacing. Users might behave in unpredicted ways, and there might be differences in the production environment compared to the staging environment that we overlooked.

We always hope for the best, but we will need a plan for what we will do if things backfire. What we want is a way to undo all the changes and go back to what we had before the deployment as quickly as possible. This is called a **rollback strategy**.

We can accomplish such a rollback in several ways. One of them would be to take a backup of the production database before the deployment occurs. This way, we can ensure that we have a snapshot of how all the data in the application was, before the release of the new code.

The actual code is usually deployed to the server with the help of a VCS, so rolling back the actual code to a previous version is rather simple.

The steps involved in deploying code to the production environment are often automated, meaning that different tools and applications take care of all the steps. Let's see how this automation works.

Deployment automation

It is often a good idea to automate as many of the deployment steps as possible. The reason is that there are usually many steps involved that need to be done in the correct order, a job ideally suited for automation. At the same time, it's something where humans often make mistakes by forgetting to do something or do something in the wrong order.

Depending on the complexity of the system, we can use several tools that will help us accomplish automated deployment.

Automating deployment will ensure that we have high-quality code since the automation process typically runs tests and lets the code through to the production server that passes the tests.

It will also save time as the deployment steps will be performed much faster by the deployment tools than they would be if humans performed them.

When the code is deployed, the work with it is not over. Deployed code must be maintained.

Code maintenance

A typical software developer will spend more time maintaining existing code than writing new exciting features.

This is not very strange if we think about it. First, the lifespan of an application is typically much longer than the time it took to develop it. This means that there are more and more softwares out there that are running and performing their tasks.

Programs that are used will always need maintenance as users will find bugs that we must fix, new features will be added to the application as demands from users change, and old features must be updated and improved.

This means that developers spend most of their time in old code, fixing and updating it. This can be code written decades ago by someone who has left the company a long time ago, or it can be written by you just the other week.

If you think ahead to what your life as a programmer will look like, you will most likely imagine yourself writing new, exciting software that uses the latest tools and features that are out there. Still, the fact is that it is much more likely that you will be poking around in code written a long time ago, in a version of the language that was released when you were in preschool.

At times, you will have the chance to write that brand-new, cool, and shiny piece of software, but remember, if you do a good job, that code will live on and will need to be maintained by others (or yourself) in the future.

That is the life of a software developer. This means that we need to ensure that the code we write is as maintainable as possible. A skilled software developer is someone who writes highly maintainable code. This means that the code is clear, easy to understand, and easy to change, without the risk of people introducing some unwanted side effects in the application.

There is a simple rule we can follow to help us create maintainable code: the boy scout rule.

The legend of the boy scout rule says:

> *Leave the campground cleaner than you found it.*

I have no evidence that this rule was ever used by actual scouts. It is more likely a variant of a message the founder of the scout movement, Robert Baden-Powell, left to the movement before his death. In that message, he said, *Try to leave this world a little better than you found it.*

In the book *Clean Code,* the author, Robert C. Martin, also known as Uncle Bob, transformed this rule so that it could be applied to code. He states that if we apply this rule when we maintain our code, we should always leave our code a little cleaner and better each time we maintain it so that its quality will increase over time. We can rephrase the boy scout rule in relation to software development so that it says, *Always leave the code you're editing a little better than you found it.*

The changes do not have to be huge. You will not have to rewrite large sections of code. If you change a variable name to something that better describes the value it is holding, or adding documentation to a piece of code where it was missing previously will increase the code's quality slightly.

> **Note**
>
> In *Chapter 12, Code Quality,* and *Appendix A, How To Translate the Pseudocode into Real Code,* we will dive deeper into how we can write high-quality code, among other things, while keeping maintainability in mind.

Now that we have an idea of how to get the software to our users, when we are done writing and testing it, we should take a closer look at the actual development process.

Software development process methodologies

Since the 1960s, different methodologies have been developed to help system developers be more productive, on target, and create higher quality code. Here, we will look at some of the more essential methodologies – some that are in use today and some that have been superseded by newer and more flexible ones.

Waterfall development

The waterfall development model is one that almost everyone loves to hate. We will look at it anyway, as many newer methodologies have been developed as a reaction to it.

The reason it is hated, is that it will not take changing requirements into account.

In the waterfall model, several defined steps are completed, one preceding the next. An example of these steps can be seen in the following diagram:

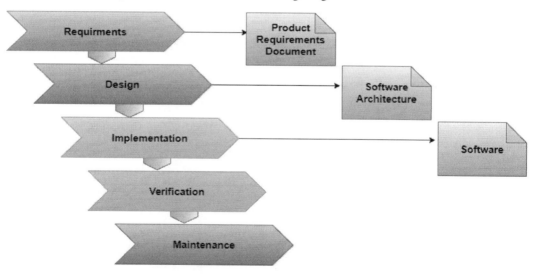

Figure 11.11 – The steps in the waterfall model

This is how the model works:

1. First, we gather all the requirements needed for this application.

2. After that, we make a system design, where we describe how different responsibilities will be divided between different parts of the application.

3. Then, we write the code.

4. During the verification phase, the code is tested.

5. Finally, when the software is released, it goes into the maintenance phase, where it is maintained.

The main criticism of this model is that it will not capture new requirements that might (and often will) arise during the development phase. The process of going from an initial idea to a finalized product can be rather long, and during this time, a lot of things will happen that will have an impact on this application. New laws can come into place, competing applications might be released, new versions of operating systems and other software that this application relies on might be released, and so on.

If we have a development model that cannot capture these changes, we will most likely have developed a product that is outdated before it has even been released.

Now that we have looked at a methodology that is not in use anymore, or at least, no one will say that they are using it, we can look at some that are in use and that are created as a reaction to the waterfall model.

Spiral model

In 1986, the American software engineer Barry Boehm described and depicted a model that, instead of going from one phase to the next, was shaped as a spiral.

This idea has since been developed and modified into several new methodologies. Still, the basic idea of driving the development process by a spiral has been prevalent since then.

One key concept in the spiral model is that risk is taken into consideration as a critical concept when developing software.

In the following diagram, we can see a simplified version of the spiral model:

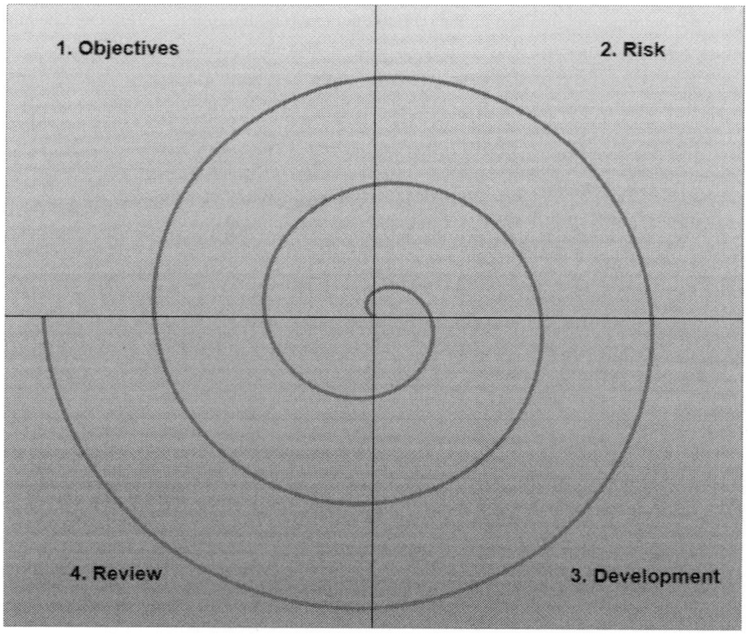

Figure 11.12 – A simplified version of the spiral model

Here, we have four distinct phases. Instead of going through them once in order, we will iterate through them over and over as many times as necessary until the application is developed. Let's take a look:

1. In the first phase, we look at the objectives, as we see them at this point in the development process.

2. We then look at the risks. What can hinder us from succeeding in implementing the objectives we just determined? By identifying the risks, we have a higher chance of avoiding them or at least minimizing the impact they will have on our software.

3. When that is done, we will go ahead and develop and test the software.

4. The last phase is a review phase. Here, we look back at what we have done in the other three phases during this iteration, including what went well and what problems we had. We can learn from this so that the next iteration is better.

We will then start over with the objectives for the next iteration by determining the risks and developing and reviewing them repeatedly.

The growing spiral illustrates that, for each iteration, more of the software has been created.

Even if the spiral model was created as a reaction to the shortcomings of the waterfall model, this claim shows that the problem is not the Waterfall model in itself, but that the development process becomes very prolonged and therefore can't react to rapid changes in requirements.

The spiral model gave inspiration to several new methodologies, where the development process is divided into smaller iterations. The next one is one such example and the one that is currently the foundation of how most software projects are run.

Barry Boehm also said that this model is just a series of small waterfall models.

Agile development

Agile software development refers to a group of software methodologies, all based on iterative development.

The term *agile* comes from a group of 17 software developers who met at a resort in Snowbird, Utah, in 2001. After the meeting, they published *Manifesto for Agile Software Development*.

The manifesto is a short description of what should be prioritized during the software development process.

It can be found at `https://agilemanifesto.org/`.

This manifesto is then outlined in more detail by twelve principles, called *Principles behind the Agile Manifesto*, and they can be found here at `https://agilemanifesto.org/principles.html`.

These ideas had a significant impact on the software industry, and several new software development methodologies were developed in response to the manifesto.

Let's look at some of the more popular of these.

Agile Scrum methodology

This methodology, better known as Scrum, is a lightweight project management framework that uses an iterative and incremental approach.

In Scrum, the product owner – a person with the power to decide what items will go into the application – plays a central role. This person needs to play an active role throughout the development process.

The product owner works closely with the development team to create a prioritized list of system functionality, called the **product backlog**. The product backlog consists of whatever needs to be done to deliver a working software system successfully. The items in the backlog can be things such as the features of the application, bugs that need to be fixed, and non-functional requirements such as certification, accessibility, and data integrity.

When the properties in the backlog have been prioritized, a team of developers (and potentially other roles, if needed) will start to develop in what can be called *potentially shippable increments*.

This means that the team will take some of the highest prioritized items from the backlog and start to implement them during a short time frame, known as a **sprint**. A sprint will typically last for somewhere between 14 and 30 days.

The outcome of the sprint is preferably fully functional so that it can immediately be put into production, and users can start using this functionality.

The team will then start over with a new sprint. This will be repeated as many times as necessary.

Lean software development

This Agile methodology is iterative, just like Scrum, and focuses on delivering fully functional batches. The methodology is highly flexible and does not have any rigid rules or guidelines.

Its main idea is to eliminate what is called *waste*. This is done by letting users of the system select only the precious features for the system. These features are then prioritized and delivered in small batches.

It relies on rapid and reliable feedback from the users of the software. In Lean development, the work is *pulled* by customer requests.

Extreme Programming (XP)

This methodology was first described by Kent Beck, an American software engineer who took software best practices to an extreme level. One example of this is code review. Standard practice is that another developer should review all the code before it can be merged with the code that goes into a release. In XP, this is done by using the concept of *pair programming*. Pair programming is when two developers are using one computer to develop code. One is called the *driver* and is the one that will write the code. The other developer is called the *observer* or the *navigator* and will observe and review what the driver is doing. The two will frequently switch roles.

Compared to the traditional code review process, this will speed things up as the review is done during the development phase. Other benefits of pair programming include the fact that the driver will consistently get input from the observer regarding how to solve the current task.

The goal of XP is to reduce the cost of changes in the requirements. To do this, XP uses short development cycles.

In XP, changes in requirements are a natural, inescapable, and desirable aspect of software development.

Summary

In this chapter, we looked at some of the more essential concepts that go into software development that have nothing to do with the actual coding. Even if we are not working on large-scale, professional projects, we should still version control our code, write tests to verify that the code does what it is supposed to, and work iteratively.

We began by learning that version control systems are a great tool that will help us not only be able to go back in time to an earlier version of the code, but also help us share our code with other developers in our team.

Then, we saw that to verify that the code we have written is doing what it is supposed to, we need to test it. In this case, we have something called unit tests and integration tests that we should perform to make sure that the application produces the correct result and that the new code does not produce any side effects, which would produce an undesirable result for a code that worked successfully in a previous version.

After this, we saw that the software release life cycle defines what steps are to be performed to make a piece of code mature enough to be released to end users. When code is ready to be released, we need to deploy it to the environment (for example, as an application server) so that the end users of this application can access it. When the code is used, we need to maintain it. Bugs will be discovered, features will need to be added or changed, and so on.

Lastly, we learned that to handle the development process, a software development team will typically use a development methodology. The methodology will describe in what order things should be done, how the team will cooperate to achieve a good result, and how to decide what will go into a software release.

In the next chapter, we will take a look at how we can write high-quality code, and what we mean by code quality.

Section 3: Best Practices for Writing High-Quality Code

In this section, we will talk about code quality, what it is, and some best practices to help us write high-quality code.

This section has the following chapter:

12
Code Quality

There are many aspects of code quality. We can talk about efficient code, which is code that runs fast or doesn't waste resources such as memory. It can also be source code that is easy to read and understand for us humans and therefore is easy to read and maintain. In this chapter, we'll talk about this and look at some best practices for writing high-quality code.

We will also look at some examples of things we should try to avoid if we want to write high-quality code.

In this chapter, we will learn about the following topics:

- Understanding what code quality is
- Writing readable code
- Writing efficient code
- Understanding that smart code is not always smart
- Understanding some of the best practices for writing quality code

Before we learn how to write quality code, we should define what code quality is.

Defining code quality

It is tough to define the meaning of quality when it comes to program code. The reason is that all developers will have their own opinion of what it means. One developer can argue that we should focus on writing readable code as it will be easier to understand and maintain and, by that, reduce the chance of us inserting any bugs into the code. Another developer could argue that we shall focus on writing compact code; that is, as few code lines as possible. Even if the code is harder to read, less code will give us fewer chances to introduce bugs in the code.

Here, the two developers would argue for the same thing – fewer bugs in the code – with two contradictory positions.

Let's look at a small example using Python as our language. We want to create a list that holds all possible combinations we can get by rolling two dice.

The first one will use more code, but it will be easier to understand:

```
two_dice = []
for d1 in range(1, 7):
    for d2 in range(1, 7):
        two_dice.append((d1, d2))
```

On the first line, we create an empty list.

Then, we have a `for` loop for the first dice. The d1 variable will get the value 1 the first iteration, 2 the second, and so on. Remember that the end value, 7, is when it will stop, so this is 7, not 6, as it will stop when it reaches this, giving us the values 1 to 6.

We will then do the same kind of loop for the second dice.

On the last line, we will insert the values of d1 and d2 into the list. Having an extra pair of parentheses on appending the values will put them in what is called a **tuple**. A tuple is like a list, but it cannot be changed once we have inserted values into it. We do this to indicate that d1 and d2 belong together as one combination.

We can accomplish the same things with a single line of code. It will look like this:

```
two_dice = [(d1, d2) for d1 in range(1, 7) for d2 in range(1,
    7)]
```

As we can see, the second example has less code but at the cost of readability.

But who is right – the developer arguing for readability or the one arguing for less code? We can't say, as they both are right.

What we need is a better definition of what code quality is, and more importantly, it should be measurable.

Many efforts to define a model for measuring code quality have been made, and one of the better known is CISQ's quality model. We'll see what that is next.

CISQ's quality model

The **Consortium for Information Software Quality (CISQ)** has defined five rules that can be used to measure the quality of code. It was first defined with business software in mind but was later extended to also include embedded systems, used mainly in **Internet of Things (IoT)** applications. These rules are as follows:

- **Reliability**: Reliability measures the level of risk and the likelihood of failures. It will also measure the defects that are injected into existing code when it is updated or modified. The goal of measuring reliability is to prevent the time an application can't run because of severe bugs.

- **Performance efficiency**: When an application is running, the speed with which it performs its operations depends on how the code is written and structured. Measuring the efficiency at a code level will help to improve both the overall response time of an application and how we identify the potential risk of applications that need to process data at a high speed that fail as they fail to process data fast enough.

- **Security**: The security rule will measure the likelihood of potential security breaches due to poor coding practices.

- **Maintainability**: When we are talking about the maintainability of code, we usually refer to three things. We say that the code should be, namely, *adaptable*, which is code that we can adapt to changes as per the requirements; *portable*, which is code that can be used on different platforms, such as different operating systems; and *transferable*, which is code that can be transferred from one development team to another.

This can be applied to, more or less, all code, but we want to be able to do all three of these with as little effort as possible.

- **Size**: Size is not a quality attribute per se, but the size of the code can have an impact on its maintainability. The more code we have, the harder it will be to navigate, understand, and follow its logic.

We have now talked about the quality aspects regarding code. But what about quality from the user's perspective?

Understanding user quality

What the CISQ model focuses very little on is quality from the user's perspective. An application can match all the CISQ rules, but a user of this application may still consider it being of poor quality.

Dr. Tom DeMarco, an American software engineer, has proposed that *a product's quality is a function of how much it changes the world for the better.*

This statement can be interpreted as meaning that an application's functional quality and user satisfaction are more important than the structural quality of the code.

The American computer scientist Gerald Weinberg has said that *Quality is value to some person.* This implies that quality is subjective – what one person would define as quality in an application might be the opposite for another person. This view will focus on asking the questions *Who are the people that want to value our software?* and *What will be valuable to them?*

With these definitions in mind, we will start to realize that crafting software is much more than just writing code. Even if the code has excellent quality, if the users don't like what we have created, they will not use it. It is like if we build a chair using the best craftsmanship, but if it is incredibly uncomfortable, no one will buy it.

We must, therefore, understand our users and their needs. Doing so is not always easy as our potential users might not know about these needs. Before you had your first smartphone, you did not miss it as you did not know what it could offer you. Now, on the other hand, you would miss it just after a few hours if it was taken away from you.

To get to the point where we understand our user's needs before they understand it, we need to use our imagination. We can start by asking some simple questions. They could be, what problem will this application solve? Who will benefit from it? Is there a pattern that the people who will benefit from using this application have in common? What kind of applications does this group already use? Are there features, patterns, or ideas used in those applications that we can reuse in our application to make this group more familiar with how our application works from the start?

When we have an idea about who our future users might be, we will need to focus on the flow within the application. We all know how frustrating it is when we use a program, or any other product for that matter, and we can't figure out what to do. We try one thing after the other, and rather soon, we lose all interest in using it.

If you invest time and money in developing something, you should at least give that great idea of yours every chance to succeed.

Great! We now have an idea of what code quality is and we also understand the quality aspects from a user perspective. I am sure you want both in your software, so let's put them together.

Putting them together

If we think about it, the art of creating quality software is, of course, neither writing code with high quality nor writing an application that the users find valuable; it is both.

As we have seen in earlier chapters, applications that are used will be updated, modified, and extended. This means that the code needs to be read by other programmers (or by us) if we want to find where changes need to be made.

It will all boil down to a question about money. We want to create software that gives our users added value and we can sell our application. But maybe even more important is that the programmers that maintain the code of the application can work efficiently. If they can find a bug quickly, they will spend less time fixing it.

If the code is easy to read and understand, the programmers will also have a higher chance of avoiding inserting new bugs into the code, thus reducing the cost of fixing them.

One problem many programmers will face is that they are not given the time needed to create the quality code they want and that can be understood. Tight time schedules, managers who don't fully understand the importance of well-crafted code, and impatient customers can all be aspects that will force programmers to produce code quickly, resulting in a loss of quality. This is, of course, a very short-term approach.

You might ship the software faster, but with lower quality, both for the users and for the programmers who will need to maintain the code in the future. This will most likely be less cost-efficient than crafting high-quality code to begin with.

It should also be noted that if we start a project with poorly written code, this project will most likely always contain low-quality code as the cost of going back and improving all the code will be too high.

We have everything to win if we do a good job and write quality code and deliver software that is considered high quality by our users.

The rest of this chapter will not focus on user quality. That does not mean that it's not essential, but this is a book about writing code, so let's see how we can do that with quality and style.

Writing code with readability in mind

Code that you write will not only be executed by the computer. It will also be read both by yourself and by others. Therefore, is it essential that you write code that is as easy to read and understand as possible.

There are some simple rules we can follow that will assist in achieving readable code.

Using comments and documentation wisely

When creating code, you need an understanding what you do and why you do it. But when coming back to your code a couple of months later, it is not always as clear what these thoughts were and why you wrote things the way you did. Commenting on tricky lines of code is a great way to document your thoughts for both your future self and others that will read your code.

But comments can also make the code less readable. Never comment on things that are obvious – things that any programmer, including yourself, will understand.

You should use comments when you look at a line of code and understand that a reader who sees this line will need to stop and think before understanding what it does.

Commenting on functions and methods is often a good idea. These comments will usually come right before the function or method or as the first thing inside it. What you should use depends on what language you are using, as well as the conventions used by programmers of that language.

In the following screenshot, we can see an example of this for a JavaScript function:

```javascript
/**
 * Insert table headings
 * @param {HTMLTableElement} table - The target HTML table
 * @param {Array} headers - Array of cell header names
 */
function insertTableHeadadings(table, headers) {
    const thead = table.createTHead();
    const row = thead.insertRow();
    for (const header of headers) {
        const th = document.createElement("th");
        const text = document.createTextNode(header);
        th.appendChild(text);
        row.appendChild(th);
    }
}
```

Figure 12.1 – Documenting a JavaScript function

The following is what we can infer from the preceding code:

- The first text line in this comment describes the overall responsibility of this function. Then, using the predefined @param name, the meaning of the two parameters are documented.

- Within the curly braces, the data type that is expected is defined. This is especially important if the language we are using is dynamically typed. A dynamically typed language will accept any type we assign to a variable, rather than using only the type we specify. JavaScript is dynamically typed, so this will assist any programmers using this function.

- After that comes the name of the parameter (table and headers).

- Then, after a dash, we will document what this parameter is used for.

Many editors used by programmers can use this documentation if formatted correctly. The format we can see here is called JSDoc.

In the following screenshot, we can see that when we write the code that will call this function, the editor can show us the information that was found in this comment:

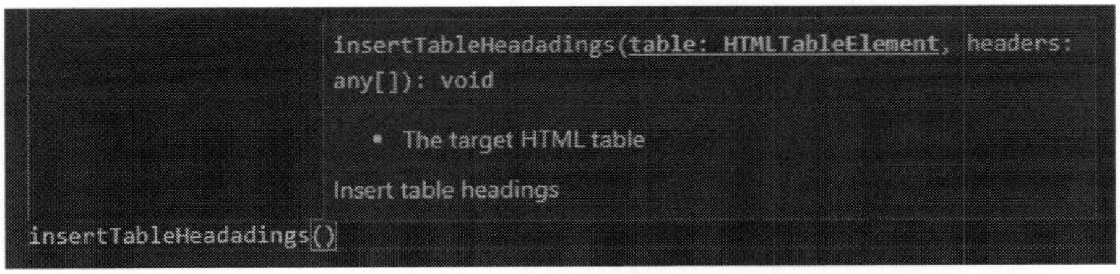

Figure 12.2 – Programming editor showing data from the function documentation

Comments are not the only way we can document our code. We can also let the code be partly self-documenting by naming things nicely.

Using names as documentation

By naming variables and functions wisely, the names by themselves will act as documentation. Look at the following function:

```
function download_and_extract_links(url)
    page = download_page(url)
    links = extract_links(page)
    return links
end_function
```

Here, we have a function that will download a web page and extract all the links found on that page. When we call this function, we pass the address to the page we want to extract the links from. That address is stored in the `url` parameter.

Inside, a function called `download_page` is called. As the name describes clearly what that function does, when reading the code, there is no need for us to go to that function to understand what it does. The variable that receives the returned data is called `page`, so we understand what data it holds.

We can see the same thing on the next line. If a function is called `extract_links`, we can assume that is what that function does. We store the data we get back in a variable called `links`, so our assumption seems to be right.

The function names will almost act like a table of content when reading this function. We understand what happens there, and we can go there if we want, but there is no need to do so just to learn what it does. The idea of a table of content in a book is that you will both learn what a chapter is about and learn where to find it. The same thing applies here. If we name our functions well, they will let us know what they do. Most integrated development environments will let us click the name, which means we will be taken to that function if we want to read it.

Later in this chapter, in the *Limiting function/method length* section, we will learn more about how to use this technique.

To be able to understand what good code looks like, we must see both good and bad code. Therefore, to become a good programmer, we must read code.

Reading other people's code

As a beginner programmer, the best thing we can do is read code written by experienced developers.

A good source is open source projects. Experienced programmers develop these projects, and their code is available online for anyone.

Pick any project, preferably in the same language you are using. At first, approaching such a project might be overwhelming as there will be maybe hundreds of files structured in several folders. But take your time and poke around in this file structure. Maybe the most important thing is not to understand the file structure of the project, but just looking at the code and trying to understand parts of it.

This will give you an insight into how experienced programmers structure their code. It should be noted that all senior developers will not always do a perfect job, but most of the time, the code you can see here would be considered to be of relatively high quality.

If you look at code written by a beginner programmer and compare it with the code written by an experienced one, you will see the difference. Now, refer to the following code:

```
1   using System;
2   using System.Linq;
3   namespace Calc
4   {
5   class Program
6   {
7   static void Main(string[] args)
8   {
9   //Values
10  string myScen;
11  string newScen = "";
12  int numbChar = 0;
13  double countedWords = 0;
14  //User entered sentence
15   Console.WriteLine("Enter your sentence");
16   myScen = Convert.ToString(Console.ReadLine());
17  //Calculate number of characters, not counting space
18  for(int i = 0; i < myScen.Length; i++)
19  {
20  if (myScen[i] == ' ')
21  continue;
22  numbChar++;
23  newScen += myScen[i];
24  }
25  Console.WriteLine("There are {0} characters in total.", numbChar);
26  //Calculates averege number of characters
27  countedWords = myScen.Split(' ').Average(n => n.Length);
28  Console.WriteLine("There are {0} characters on average in these words.", countedWords);
29  }
30  }
31  }
```

Figure 12.3 – A program that was written by a beginner programmer

Look at the preceding program. It is written in C# and will ask the user for a sentence. It will then calculate the number of characters, not counting spaces, that the user entered and finally calculate and print the average number of characters of the words in the sentence.

This code has many characteristics of a beginner programmer. I have been teaching programming for 30 years and this is not, by far, the worst example I have seen. Now, refer to the following code:

```
1   using System;
2   using System.Linq;
3
4   namespace Calc
5   {
6       class Program
7       {
8           static void Main(string[] args)
9           {
10              Console.WriteLine("Enter your sentence");
11              var sentence = Console.ReadLine();
12
13              // Count the number of spaces
14              var spaceCount = sentence.Count(f => f == ' ');
15
16              Console.WriteLine("There are {0} characters in total.", sentence.Length - spaceCount);
17
18              var averageCharCount = sentence.Split(' ').Average(word => word.Length);
19              Console.WriteLine("There are {0} characters on average in these words.", averageCharCount);
20          }
21      }
22  }
```

Figure 12.4 – The same program shown previously, written by an experienced programmer

Now, compare the code we provided at the start of this section with the code shown in the preceding screenshot, which is the very same program written by an experienced programmer. A user of these two programs will not be able to tell any difference. Executing both will produce an output like this:

```
Enter your sentence
hi there people
There are 13 characters in total.
There are 4.333333333333333 characters on average in these
words.
```

From the user's perspective, we can say that the quality of the two programs is identical.

But the quality of the code is not identical at all. Let's list some of the differences:

- The first version – written by a beginner programmer – does not use any indentation, making the code very compact and hard to read.

- The first version does not use any blank lines, while in the other version, the blank lines divide the code into sections.

- In the first version, the `newScen` variable is assigned values, but it is never used, so it can be removed from the program.

- In the first version, the variable `names` do not reflect what they are storing. In the second version, the `myScen` variable is renamed to `sentence`, `n` is renamed to `word`, and `countedWords` is renamed to `averageCharCount`.

- The first version is using a `for` loop to count all the characters except spaces. In the second version, a language-specific construct is used to do the same thing on a single line.

- The first version declares all the variables at the beginning of the `main` method. In the second version, they are declared when they are first used.

- The first version uses some other unnecessary code, such as `Convert.ToString` on line 16, and some of the comments do not add any new knowledge to the reader of the code.

Even if you don't understand the code, just looking at it reveals that the second version is much more pleasant to look at.

Also, note that even though the second program introduced blank lines in the code, the number of lines dropped from 31 to 22.

As a beginner programmer, you are very focused on getting things to work, and you should. But when you get there and your program is working, you should go back and look at your code and think about how you can raise the quality. Maybe you won't come up with the same one-line solutions the experienced programmer is using, but at least you can use blank lines, indentation, and sensible variable names.

To be able to learn to write high-quality code, you will need to be exposed to it, which is why reading code written by senior developers will help you write better code. Don't forget that when you do read it, try to understand as much as you can about the code you are reading. It might be a slow process, but it is not like reading a book – you don't have to read all the code there is. Take a function or a method and focus on only the code you find there. A good source to go to is the Stack Overflow website, where programmers can ask questions and other programmers will answer them. Go to `https://stackoverflow.com/` and look around. You can filter the questions so that you will only see questions related to the language you are interested in. Focus on the answers, as the people who answer these questions are often very experienced and their code is often of high quality. You can, of course, also use this site to ask your own programming questions, and who knows – soon, you might be answering some too.

Rewriting your code

As we saw in the previous example, just making the program work is not enough. When it does, we shall go back and look at the code we just wrote to see if we can restructure it to make it more pleasant to look at and read, and maybe come up with a better solution to the problem we are trying to solve.

An excellent way to tackle a programming task is first to come up with a working solution, and then when you have it, work on it and tweak it to make it better. This will not only result in better code quality, but you will also learn from it, and the next time you face a similar problem, you will start with a better first solution.

This is why an experienced programmer will not start with something like what was shown in *Figure 12.3*, but with something closer to what was shown in *Figure 12.4*.

Going back to the code you have written will make you look at it with fresh eyes, and you will see things that you did not see when you first wrote the code.

Letting your code go through several iterations will be beneficial in more than one way. Hopefully, it will give you higher quality code. You also understand the problem your code is trying to solve better because if you process the problem in your head and work on a solution, you will gain a broader and more in-depth understanding of the problem itself and how it could be solved.

You will also improve your language and programming skills as you will need to learn more about the language you are using, in order to use the right features the language has to offer for this problem.

Even programmers who have used a language for years will discover things they had no idea existed.

With more experience, you will also recognize patterns in the problems you are solving and the code you are writing. As you do, the process of rewriting your code will be faster. Not only will you come up with improved ideas quicker, but your code will also start at a higher level to begin with.

Always have readability as your primary focus when rewriting your code. Sometimes, you need to sacrifice readability to make the code more efficient or faster, but if it is your primary goal, this will be reflected in your code.

When you look at your code, you should always ask yourself the most fundamental question: Is this code I would like to read if someone else wrote it?

If the answer is no, change it so you can answer yes.

Readable code is excellent, but the code should be efficient too.

Writing code with efficiency in mind

When we talk about efficient code, we can mean several different things. Let's look at some of the things people might mean when they talk about efficient code.

Removing redundant or unnecessary code

You should always make sure that you remove redundant code. Redundant code is code that does not affect the output of the application, but will be executed.

Look at the following code:

```
number = 10
for i  = 1 to 1000
   number = number + i
end_for
number = 20
print number
```

Here, we created a variable, number, and set it to 10.

Then, we have a for loop. This loop will iterate 999 times. The first time this happens, the i variable will have a value of 1; the second time, it will be 2, and so on until it reaches 1000. Then, we will exit the loop.

Each time we're inside the loop, we will take whatever value the variable number currently has, add the current value of i to it, and store the result in the number variable.

After we exit the loop, we assign the value 20 to the variable number, and by doing that, we will overwrite the value we just calculated.

This means that everything we did before the line where we assigned 20 to number is unnecessary. Deleting those lines will not have any effect on the output of the program, but when we run the application, this unnecessary loop will run, and by that, consume some resources and waste time.

Having code like this will also make the code harder to read as we will spend some time trying to figure out what the loop does and why it is there.

With the unnecessary code removed, we can now see how we can use the computer's hardware more efficiently.

Optimizing the use of memory and processors

It is easy to waste memory without even knowing it. Depending on what language you use, memory will be handled differently.

There might also be features in your programming language that will use the computer hardware in a more efficient way than the first solution you come up with. Let's look at one example from Python.

In this example, we will concatenate strings together using two different techniques. In the first version, we will use the + operator to concatenate them. We will repeat this 2 million times and measure how long it takes. Refer to the following code:

```python
s1 = "aaaabbbb"
s2 = "ccccdddd"
result = ""
for _ in range(2000000):
    result += s1 + s2
```

Let's see how this code works:

- On the two first lines, we create two variables, s1 and s2, that hold the two strings we want to concatenate.

- On the third line, we create a variable called result, which, initially, is an empty string.

- We then enter our loop, which will iterate 2 million times. The underscore after for is there because we won't need a variable to hold the current iteration value (which is 0 the first iteration, 1 for the second, and so on).

- Each time we're inside the loop, we take what is currently in the result variable and add it together with the content of the s1 and s2 variables.

After the first iteration, result will contain the following:

```
aaaabbbbccccdddd
```

After the second iteration, it will contain the following:

```
aaaabbbbccccddddaaaabbbbccccdddd
```

The result, after 2 million iterations, will be a string that is 32 million characters long!

Now, let's create the same application but use another technique for concatenating the strings. This is not as easy to understand, and don't worry if you don't get how the code works.

Python has something called the **string join** method. It is designed to join strings together in a very efficient way. The code for the program looks like this:

```
s1 = "aaaabbbb"
s2 = "ccccdddd"
result = "".join(s1 + s2 for _ in range(2000000))
```

This program will also iterate 2 million times, concatenate the two strings together, and produce a string that is 32 million characters long.

The first program we wrote took about 42 seconds to complete on my computer.

The second program will, on the same machine, complete in 0.34 seconds.

Adding two strings together as many times as we did here is, of course, not something we do very often, but these two programs illustrate the impact of choosing one solution instead of another.

It is not only language constructs such as the one we saw here that can also improve the performance of our applications. Choosing the right algorithm can also have a significant impact on speed and memory usage.

Using efficient algorithms

An algorithm is a solution to a problem. The algorithm will describe the logical steps needed to get something done. Let's look at an example. If we have a sequence of numbers and we want this sequence sorted, we can use a sorting algorithm. We have several algorithms to choose from, and all will get the job done; that is, sorting a sequence.

The reason we have more than one algorithm is that they are more or less effective when it comes to speed and usage of memory. How hard it is to write the code that implements the algorithm will also differ.

Let's look at one of the easiest sorting algorithms to implement: bubble sort. It is also one of the least effective algorithms, as we will see:

```
function bubbel_sort(sequence)
    do
        swapped = false
        for i = 1 to length(sequence) - 2
```

```
            if sequence[i] > sequence[i+1] then
                    swap(sequence[i], sequence[i+1])
                    swapped = true
            end_if
        end_for
    while swapped
    return sequence
end_function
```

Look at the code and see if you understand what it does. I will not go through the details of it. Instead, we will go through the bubble sort algorithm step by step. After we have done that, you can come back to the code and try to figure out what is happening here.

The sequence we will work with looks like this:

```
sequence = [5, 3, 1, 8, 2]
```

Let's look at the logic of bubble sort:

1. In the following image, you can see a graphical representation of the sequence we are working on:

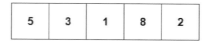

Figure 12.5 – The sequence to be sorted

2. Bubble sort will start by comparing the first two values – in our case, **5** and **3** – as shown in the following image:

Figure 12.6 – Comparing the first two values

If they are not in the right order, they will be swapped. As they are out of order, **3** will be moved to the first position, while **5** will be moved to the second, resulting in the following sequence:

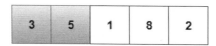

Figure 12.7 – The values 5 and 3 swap places

3. Next, **5** and **1** will be compared, and again get swapped if they're not in order, as shown in the following image:

Figure 12.8 – Comparing 5 and 1

They are not in the correct order, so they get swapped, as shown here:

Figure 12.9 – The values 5 and 1 swap places

4. Now, **5** and **8** are compared, but as they are in the right order, nothing is done, as shown in the following image:

Figure 12.10 – The values 5 and 8 are in the right order

5. Then, **8** and **2** will be compared, as follows:

Figure 12.11 – The values 8 and 2 are compared

They will be swapped as they are out of order, as shown here:

Figure 12.12 – The values 8 and 2 swap places

We have now reached the end of the sequence and, as you can see, it is not sorted. But one item is sorted, and that is the value 8. As this is the largest value in the sequence, it has been pushed to the end, and by that, it has reached its correct location.

This is where the name of the algorithm comes from, since one value has bubbled to the end.

At this point, the algorithm will start over, comparing the first two values and swapping them if necessary. This time, though, the last value – 8, in our case – will not be part of the comparison as it has already found its place.

After the second round, the sequence will look as follows:

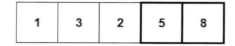

Figure 12.13 – The sequence after two rounds

5 and 8 are now in the correct location (marked with a thicker border), and the algorithm will start over again.

In the third run, the values **1**, **3**, and **2** will be considered, and after that run, the sequence will look as follows:

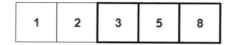

Figure 12.14 – The sequence after three rounds

As we can see, the sequence is now sorted, but the algorithm will pass over the remaining values once more. It will discover that it could go over them without swapping any values, and this means that the sequence is sorted, and we are done.

The reason bubble sort is inefficient is because it will go over the sequence multiple times. In fact, in the worst case, it will need to do as many passes as there are items. For a short sequence such as this one, this isn't a problem, but for a larger sequence, it will be noticeable.

Other sorting algorithms are much more efficient, but they're harder to write code for. Examples of these include Quicksort and Merge sort. We will not cover how they work here as they are somewhat complicated. If you want to know more about these algorithms, you can do a web search – you will find lots of useful resources that will explain how they work and give you readymade code for them in any programming language you want.

If we compare bubble sort and Quicksort, we will see the difference. On my computer, bubble sort sorted a sequence of 10,000 values in 9.8 seconds. Quicksort managed to sort the same sequence in 0.03 seconds.

The reason Quicksort and Merge sort will do better in most cases is that they will need to perform fewer operations. It should also be noted that bubble sort can beat the others if the sequence is sorted or almost sorted to begin with. If we have a sorted sequence, bubble sort will go through it once and discover that it is sorted and stop.

This was just a small example, but it illustrates the impact of choosing an efficient algorithm can have on the performance of your application.

We will sometimes hear people talk about smart code. What is it, and is it always smart to use it? Let's check it out!

Is smart code smart?

When you are a beginner programmer, you are happy that your programs work at all, and you will not pay much attention to what your code looks like or how it performs. The important thing is that you get the result you want on the screen.

But as you get more experienced and learn more, you will start to embrace what you might consider smart solutions. A smart solution, for you, might be that you can rewrite 10 lines of code so that it now is done in three.

The question you always should ask yourself is whether changes that are made to working code improve it in any way. Only if they do will the new code be considered smarter than it was before.

Imagine that you wrote a little game in Python. It has a loop that runs 10 times, and in each iteration, it will ask the user for a number, either 0 or 1. It will also randomly pick either a 0 or a 1. If the user guessed the same number as the computer picked, the user wins; otherwise, the user loses. The code might look as follows:

```
from random import randint

for _ in range(10):
    guess = int(input(f'Enter your guess, 0 or 1: '))
    if guess == randint(0, 1):
        print('You win')
    else:
        print('You loose')
```

Figure 12.15 – A small guessing game in Python

This program does not have an error checker for if the user enters a number other than 0 or 1, but apart from that, it works fine, and you feel happy.

But then you feel it is time to code this game smarter, and you end up with something like the following:

```
from random import randint
[print('You win' if int(input(f'Enter your guess, 0 or 1: ')) == randint(0, 1) else 'You lose') for _ in range(10)]
```

Figure 12.16 – Same program as before, written in one line

When running the two programs, you won't notice any difference. But is the second version smarter in any way? It sure takes up fewer lines, and if we count, also fewer characters. But what have we gained? Will the second program run faster? That is a somewhat irrelevant question for this kind of application as the program will spend most of its time waiting for the user to enter a number.

What about readability? Just because the second program has fewer lines and fewer characters does not make it easier to read and understand – it is the opposite. Even an experienced programmer will need to spend more time understanding the second program compared to the first.

There is only one reason for you to create something like the second example, and that is as an exercise to use language features, but that's it. Go ahead and make your small programs as compact as you can; you will learn a lot from it, but when writing code that will be used for something else, you should have readability in mind.

There are situations when small, smart tricks are in their correct places. Look at the following function:

```
function is_legal_age(age)
    if age >= 21 then
        return true
    else
        return false
    end_if
end_function
```

You can pass an age to this function, and it will return true if this age is equal to or greater than 21; if not, it will return false.

This function works, but we can make it smarter, and this time the change will be an improvement. If we think about what is happening inside the function, we see that the if statement will compare the age passed to this function with 21. If the if statement is true, we return true. If it is false, we return false. This means that we return the same thing as the condition evaluates to, so why not return that? Let's change the function:

```
function is_legal_age(age)
    return age >= 21
end_function
```

That is a smart change as we made the code more compact and easier to read and got rid of any unnecessary code.

Being smart when coding can mean different things to different people. I was once working on a telecom project that was written in C. There was a bug, and I was assigned to fix it. But when reading the code, I was horrified. I have tried to recreate what parts of it looked like:

```
if (a5 < c4 && d3 == a2 || c9 < e5 && d7 > b10 && b5 != d2 && c3 == e2) {
    if (d7 == e9 && d1 > b5 || c3 == b9) {
        if (e1 == d6 || a8 != c9) {
```

Figure 12.17 – Code that is extremely hard to read

As you can see, there are three if statements nested inside each other. In the real example, there were at least 20 levels of nested if statements like this!

Also, the variable names are saying nothing about what data they hold. We need to try to figure out what values these variables will have for us in order to enter the innermost if statement.

I did spend almost 2 weeks understanding and rewriting the code before I could even begin searching for the bug.

Now, you might be wondering why I am showing this example here. This can hardly be considered smart code. The consultant who wrote it probably thought this was smart. Maybe the idea was to be irreplaceable, and that can be smart from a consultant's point of view. But that's not smart from the point of view of the company that owns the code. I can also mention that if that was down to the tactics from the consultant's side, it did not work as he or she was no longer with this company.

Whatever you do, never write code like this. Instead, you should keep some best practices for writing quality code in mind.

Code quality – best practices

As stated earlier in this chapter, what we focus on here is the quality of the code, not the quality of the user experience when using our applications.

When writing code, there are some things we can keep in mind to make our code *better*, quality-wise.

We will look at some best practices and talk about why it is a good idea to use them.

Limiting line length

Long lines are never a good idea. Look at any newspaper and think about why the text hardly ever runs on one line across the full width of the page:

Figure 12.18 – A newspaper uses columns to limit the line length. Photo by Wan Chen on Unsplash

A rule of thumb is that if the line is wider than what can fit on the screen, then it is too wide. Use your common sense and divide the code into several lines if needed, but do so in a way that makes sense.

Take a look at the following screenshot. The code shown here is just one single statement and could have been written on a single line, but that line would have been very long and hard to read. Instead, it has been broken up in separate lines, and the line breaks occur in a natural location so that the code is easier to read:

```
var time = [
    [seconds % 10, document.getElementsByClassName("s-2")],
    [(seconds - seconds % 10) / 10 % 10, document.getElementsByClassName("s-1")],
    [minutes % 10, document.getElementsByClassName("m-2")],
    [(minutes - minutes % 10) / 10 % 10, document.getElementsByClassName("m-1")],
    [hours % 10, document.getElementsByClassName("h-2")],
    [(hours - hours % 10) / 10 % 10, document.getElementsByClassName("h-1")]
];
```

Figure 12.19 – A lengthy statement that has been broken up into several lines

Some programming editors will assist you in determining the maximum length of your code lines by showing a line to indicate when it is time to add a line break.

It is not only the length of the code lines that should be limited. Next, we will see that this also applies to the length of functions and methods.

Limiting function/method length

A function or method should do one thing only, and they should be small. If your functions are hundreds of lines long, you need to make them smaller. When they are 50 lines long, you should probably make them even smaller.

Long functions are hard to read, and it is hard to follow the logic as it goes in and out of `if` statements and loops.

There is no fixed rule for how long a function should be, but I try to keep my functions below 20 lines if I can.

The important thing is not the actual line count. Instead, you should focus on writing code that is easy to read. To help you write your functions and methods, you should let logic guide you.

If you have a long function, just by looking at it, there might be clues that it is made up of multiple logical blocks. The things that can be an indication of this is blanks lines in the code as they are often used to indicate a logical transition of sorts. These decided segments of code can be good candidates to be lifted out of the original function and instead go into a function of their own. We can then just call that function from the place where the code was previously.

Another hint can be code that is indented by more than one level. Each level of indentation marks a block of code. Look at the logic that goes on there and ask yourself if you can't make the code cleaner by turning these blocks into functions.

Writing high-quality small functions is an art that takes practice to master, but if you don't practice, you will never master it. Get into the habit of always reviewing code you've written and ask yourself if the function or method you just wrote only does one thing.

But what is one thing? Is the game Mario Kart one thing? Is asking the user for their credit card number one thing? Is incrementing a number one thing?

If a function has a single task, then we might be able to break this task into several subtasks. We could then let the main task be a function and let this function call a function for each subtask.

Look at the following screenshot. Here, we can see a function written in C++. Its task is to search a file for a specified string pattern and replace it with a new pattern. Instead of doing all the steps needed, it is broken up into sub-tasks, each located in a separate function:

```cpp
void update_file(string file_name, string old_pattern, string new_pattern)
{
    auto file_content = read_file_content(file_name);
    auto updated_content = update_content(file_content, old_pattern, new_pattern);
    save_file_content(file_name, updated_content);
}
```

Figure 12.20 – An example of a C++ function that uses other functions to fulfill its task

From the preceding code, we can observe that the following:

1. First, we will call a function that reads all the contents of the file specified and returns it to us as a string.

2. Next, we will call a function that will call a function called `update_content`. To this, we are passing the original content of the file, the string we want to be replaced, and the string we want to replace the old string with.

    This function will return an updated version of the file content. This updated content is then saved to a file with the same name as the original file, and by that, the old file will be overwritten.

As the function names describe what the function is doing and the variable names describe what gets returned from those functions, reading this code is now very easy.

Reading this function will almost be like reading an index of a book. We can see that, first, we read the content of a file. Good – and if we trust that the only thing that function does is performing exactly the same thing, there is no need for us to go and look at that code. The same thing goes for `update_content` and `save_file_content`.

This is much more readable than what it would have looked like if we had everything in one function. Look at the preceding screenshot once more and compare it to the following one:

```cpp
void update_file(string file_name, string old_pattern, string new_pattern)
{
    string file_content;
    string line;
    ifstream in_file (file_name);
    if (in_file.is_open())
    {
        while ( getline (in_file, line) )
        {
            file_content += line + "\n";
        }
        in_file.close();
    }
    else
    {
        cout << "Unable to open file" << endl;
        return;
    }

    string::size_type n = 0;
    while ( ( n = file_content.find( old_pattern, n ) ) != string::npos )
    {
        file_content.replace( n, old_pattern.size(), new_pattern );
        n += new_pattern.size();
    }

    ofstream out_file (file_name);
    if (out_file.is_open())
    {
        out_file << file_content;
        out_file.close();
    }
    else
    {
        cout << "Unable to open file" << endl;
    }
}
```

Figure 12.21 – The original update_file function

When we see these two versions of the function, it is easy to understand why we want to reduce the function's length and let the function and variable names do the documentation.

If we look at the structure of the code in the preceding screenshot, we can see two blank lines. They divide the code into three sections, and these sections are what we have moved into the three functions. The first section is what became the `read_file_content` function. The second section became `update_content`, while the last section became `save_file_content`.

When we move the code sections into separate functions, we will need to modify the code slightly, but that is usually not hard and is done rather quickly. The main logic is already there.

The final version of all four functions will look something like the following:

```cpp
string read_file_content(string file_name)
{
    string file_content;
    string line;
    ifstream in_file (file_name);
    if (in_file.is_open())
    {
        while ( getline (in_file, line) )
        {
            file_content += line + "\n";
        }
        in_file.close();
    }
    else
    {
        cout << "Unable to open file" << endl;
    }
    return file_content;
}

string update_content(string file_content, string old_pattern, string new_pattern)
{
    string::size_type n = 0;
    while ( ( n = file_content.find( old_pattern, n ) ) != string::npos )
    {
        file_content.replace( n, old_pattern.size(), new_pattern );
        n += new_pattern.size();
    }
    return file_content;
}

void save_file_content(string file_name, string file_content)
{
    ofstream out_file (file_name);
    if (out_file.is_open())
    {
        out_file << file_content;
        out_file.close();
    }
    else
    {
        cout << "Unable to open file" << endl;
    }
}

void update_file(string file_name, string old_pattern, string new_pattern)
{
    auto file_content = read_file_content(file_name);
    auto updated_content = update_content(file_content, old_pattern, new_pattern);
    save_file_content(file_name, updated_content);
}
```

Figure 12.22 – The primary function and its three helper functions

If we want to, we can ignore the first three functions and just read the last one to get an idea of what is going on here.

Another thing we should consider is avoiding deep nesting when it comes to control structures, such as conditional and loop statements.

Avoiding deep nesting

It is sometimes tempting to put several `if` statements or `for` loops inside each other. But many levels of nested `if` statements or `for` loops can make them hard to read and understand.

Look at the following code:

```
function calculate_pay(age)
    if age > 65 then
        result = 25000
    else
        if age > 20 then
            result = 20000
        else
            result = 15000
        end_if
    end_if
    return result
end_function
```

Here, we have an `if` statement and in its `else` part, we have a new `if` statement with an `else` part. This is unnecessarily complex and hard to follow. We can rewrite it like this:

```
function calculate_pay(age)
    if age > 65 then
        return 25000
    if age > 20 then
        return 20000
    return 15000
end_function
```

The two functions will give us the same result, but the second one will return as soon as it knows the correct amount. By doing that, it reduces the number of lines, avoids the nested `if` statement, and overall makes the code cleaner and easier to read.

When you have nested structures that go beyond one level, you should ask yourself if there is a better way to do this. The first thing you can do is what we did here and place the control structures after each other, rather than within each other.

Another option is to move the logic into separate functions and call them instead. In some situations, this will simplify the code and make it easier to read.

Another thing we want to avoid is repeating ourselves. To help us avoid that, we can use the DRY principle.

Using the DRY principle

DRY stands for **Don't Repeat Yourself** and was formulated by Andy Hunt and Dave Thomas. It states the following:

"Every piece of knowledge must have a single, unambiguous, authoritative representation within a system."

This states that we should not repeat the same or similar code more than once. A clear indication that you are about to contradict this principle is when you copy and paste code to a new location in your program, maybe with only some slight changes. This should always be avoided.

The idea of DRY boils down to dividing the code into small reusable parts. Let's look at an example.

Let's assume you have some data and that this data is stored in a dictionary type (you can read more about the dictionary type in *Chapter 6, Working with Data – Variables*, in the *Dictionary type* section).

Sometimes, you want to print this data to the screen, while other times, you want to save it to a file. You might end up with two functions that look as follows:

```
function show(data)
    print data["name"]
    print data["price"]
    print data["weight"]
    print data["height"]
    print data["width"]
end_function

function save(data)
    data_to_save = data["name"] + "\n" +
```

```
                    data["price"] + "\n" +
                    data["weight"] + "\n" +
                    data["height"] + "\n" +
                    data["width"] + "\n"
    save_file("data.txt", data)
end_function
```

The first function, show, will print the items in the dictionary on the screen.

The second function, save, will build a string containing all the items in the dictionary. It adds a line break between each item. \n means newline and is used to indicate that a linefeed should occur at this location.

Both functions deal with the same data, but it might not be obvious that we are repeating ourselves here – at least not until we need to update the dictionary. Let's say that we need to add an item to the dictionary, maybe the manufacturer. We would need to make changes to both functions. The new code would look like this:

```
function show(data)
    print data["name"]
    print data["manufacturer"]
    print data["price"]
    print data["weight"]
    print data["height"]
    print data["width"]
end_function

function save(data)
    data_to_save = data["name"] + "\n" +
                    data["manufacturer"] + "\n" +
                    data["price"] + "\n" +
                    data["weight"] + "\n" +
                    data["height"] + "\n" +
                    data["width"] + "\n"
    save_file("data.txt", data)
end_function
```

As you can see, the line for the manufacturer was added to both functions. What would happen if we forgot to add it to one of them? At some point, we will discover the difference, but when we do, we can't be sure if the `manufacturer` line was added to one function or removed from the other.

Let's apply the DRY principle to the code. If we think about what is happening, we will discover that the `show` function has multiple lines within `print`. We also know that `print` will print something on one line and then insert a line feed so that the next `print` will start on a new line.

But what would happen if we had one `print` that printed a string like the one in the `save` function? It contains the new line indicator, `\n`, in all the locations where we want a new line, so printing that string will give the same result as our current `show` function.

We can make use of this and add a function that creates and returns that string, and then both functions can call that function, as shown in the following code:

```
function create_string(data)
    return data["name"] + "\n" +
          data["manufacturer"] + "\n" +
          data["price"] + "\n" +
          data["weight"] + "\n" +
          data["height"] + "\n" +
          data["width"] + "\n"
end_function

function show(data)
    print create_string(data)
end_function

function save(data)
    save_file("data.txt", create_string(data))
end_function
```

Here, we have the `create_data` function, which creates the string and returns it to the caller. It is called from both the `show` and the `save` functions. In `show`, the `create_string` function is called first of all, and the string that gets returned will be printed.

In the `save` function, we call the `create_string` function from within the call to a function called `save_file`. The returned string will be passed as the second argument to the `save_file` function, just as it was in our first version.

This also makes the code more readable and shorter.

Many languages or software companies have *scandalized* the way we format the code we write. This is called *code conventions*, and this is what we will look at next.

Using code conventions

Most programming languages have code conventions. These are recommendations for how we shall organize our files, indent our code, format comments, and use naming conventions, just to mention a few.

These are not rules but a recommended code style and the idea is that if all programmers using a language use the same code convention, their code will look more or less the same. This means that if you know the convention, it is easier for you to navigate the code and read it. It is, therefore, essential to learn the convention for every programming language you are using.

We will look at some typical conventions and see how they differ among a couple of languages.

Naming conventions

A naming convention is a set of rules for formatting the names of variables, types, functions, and other entities in the source code.

Sometimes, programming languages come with official naming conventions. Other times, they are not official but commonly used by the community using a language. Some companies have developed their own naming conventions for the code written within that company.

A naming convention is not about how you name things, but how you format the names. A naming convention dictates how uppercase and lowercase characters should be used and how names consisting of multiple words should be formatted. Some different styles are frequently used. Let's look at some of them.

Camel case

In camel case, each word in a multi-word name has an initial capital letter, except for the initial letter. For example, if we want to store a value for the outside temperature, the name used for that variable would be `outsideTemperature` in camel case.

Camel case is also known as camel caps. The name refers to the apparent humps that the capital letters form. One early use of this style was by the Swedish chemist Jöns Jacob Berzelius, who suggested, in an 1813 essay in Annals of Philosophy 2, that chemical elements should be written as one-letter or two-letter symbols with the first letter capitalized. That would allow formulae such as *NaCl* to be written without any spaces.

Pascal case

Pascal case is like camel case, with the only difference being that the first letter is also written using a capital case. So, the pascal case, the outside temperature variable would be named `OutsideTemperature`.

Pascal case gets its name from the programming language Pascal. Even though Pascal is case-insensitive, the practice was popularized by the Pascal convention to use this style.

Snake case

In snake case, all letters are written in lowercase, and an underscore separates words. The outside temperature variable, when written in snake case, would be `outside_temperature`.

Snake case has been in use for a long time but did not have any established name. An early reference to the name *snake_case* comes from Gavin Kistner, who, in 2004, wrote a post named *Appropriate use of CamelCase* in the group *comp.lang.ruby on Usenet*. In it, he said the following:

"BTW...what *do* you call that naming style? snake_case? That's what I'll call it until someone corrects me."

Indentation conventions

There are several different styles that are used when it comes to indentation and how compound statements are indicated.

For languages that use braces, how the braces are placed is a never-ending debate. Let's look at some variants.

K&R style

The K&R style originates from the Kernighan and Ritchie book *The C Programming Language* from 1978.

When following this style, each function has its opening brace on a new line and the same indentation level as the function header.

Blocks inside the function will have their opening brace at the same line as the statement they are opening.

The following screenshot shows an example of the K&R style:

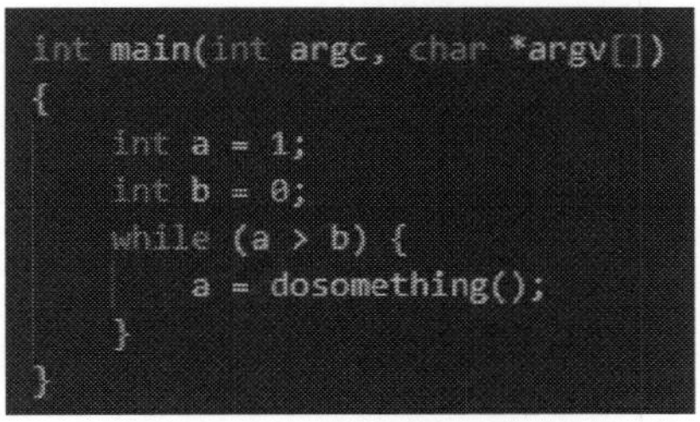

```
int main(int argc, char *argv[])
{
    int a = 1;
    int b = 0;
    while (a > b) {
        a = dosomething();
    }
}
```

Figure 12.23 – The K&R bracing style

1TBS

1TBS is an abbreviation for **one true brace style** and is a variant on the K&R style. The only difference is that the opening brace for functions is located on the same line as the function header. Also, in 1TBS, control structures only containing one line will always have braces, a habit not always used in the K&R style. See the following screenshot for an example of this style:

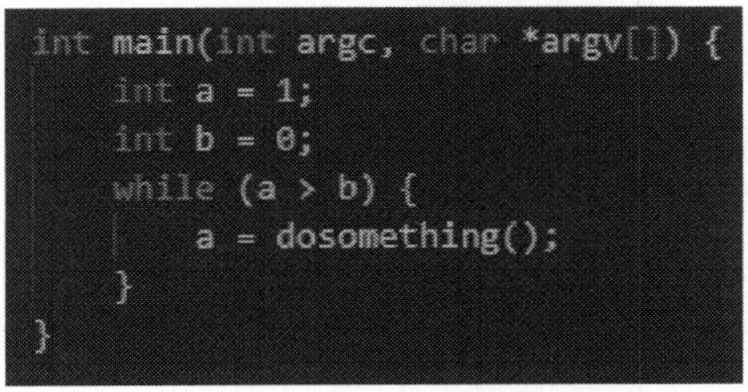

```
int main(int argc, char *argv[]) {
    int a = 1;
    int b = 0;
    while (a > b) {
        a = dosomething();
    }
}
```

Figure 12.24 – The 1TBS bracing style

Java

In Java, a commonly accepted practice is to use the K&R style, extended so that all opening braces are on the same line as the statement it opens. This applies to control structures, classes, and methods.

See the following screenshot for an example of this style:

```
public class TheClass {
    public static void main(String[] args) {
        int i = 0;
        while (i < 5) {
            System.out.println(i);
            i++;
        }
    }
}
```

Figure 12.25 – The Java bracing style

Allman style

The Allman style, named after the American programmer Eric Allman, puts all opening braces on a new line.

People arguing for this style means that it becomes easier to see where a block begins and ends, when the opening and closing braces are on the same indentation level.

See the following screenshot for an example of this style:

```
int main(int argc, char *argv[])
{
    int a = 1;
    int b = 0;
    while (a > b)
    {
        a = dosomething();
    }
}
```

Figure 12.26 – The Allman bracing style

Lisp or Python style

This style can be used in any language that uses braces, but is mostly used by languages that don't use braces and use an indentation level to identify blocks of code instead, such as Lisp and Python. In the following screenshot, we can see a Lisp program that uses this style:

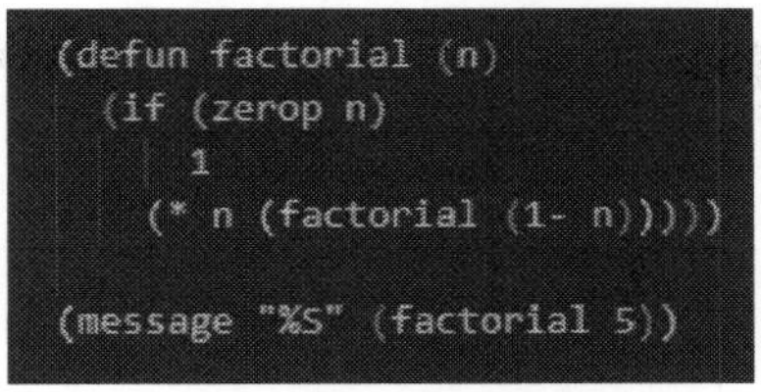

```
(defun factorial (n)
  (if (zerop n)
      1
    (* n (factorial (1- n)))))

(message "%S" (factorial 5))
```

Figure 12.27 – The Lisp block indentation style

In the following screenshot, we can see the same program written in Python, using the same type of indentation to mark blocks:

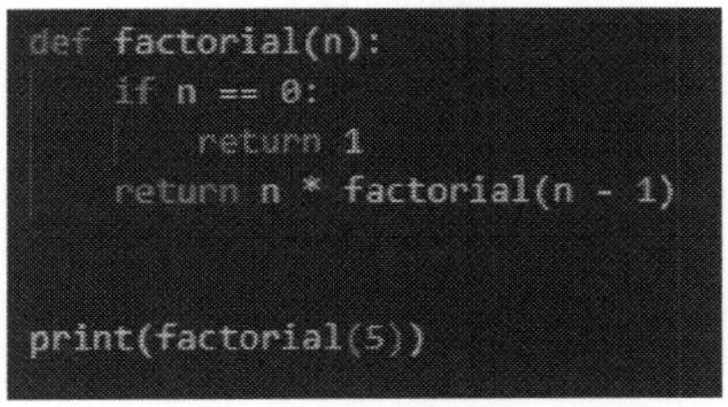

```
def factorial(n):
    if n == 0:
        return 1
    return n * factorial(n - 1)


print(factorial(5))
```

Figure 12.28 – The Python block indentation style

In Python, the indentation levels are part of the language. This is sometimes called the **offside rule**, a name coined by the British computer scientist Peter J. Landin, most likely as a pun on the offside rule in football, compared to languages that use braces, meaning indentation levels are not decided on by the language.

These are not the only conventions you will find described in a convention document. Next, we will look at some other things you most likely will find when reading them.

Other conventions

Other conventions might be described for a language. One thing that is often described in a convention document is how comments should be formatted.

Some languages have tools that can generate documentation from the comments found in the code. For this to work, the comments must follow a strict format. Some examples of these are Java's Javadoc and Doxygen for C and C++.

Some languages also support special kind of comments known as **docstrings**. They are comments, but when regular comments are stripped away from the executable code by the compiler, they are retained so that the programmer can inspect them when the program is running.

There can also be conventions for how the source code files should be organized in folders and packages (to learn more about packages, see *Chapter 4, Software Projects and How We Organize Our Code*, in the *Working with packages to share code* section). There can also be conventions in place for how to name files.

A code convention can also dictate the use of tabs versus spaces when we indent our code. Here, most conventions prefer the use of spaces over tabs, but there are exceptions to this.

You might also find things that are not directly related to coding and coding style in a coding convention document. For example, one thing that you might find is recommendations for source file encoding. The file encoding dictates how the characters in the file will be interpreted. The two most frequent encodings are ASCII and UTF-8. Sometimes, there are recommendations about part of a file. The convention document might state that comments or string literals must use a particular encoding, not the whole file.

Another thing often found in code convention documents is how blanks lines and spaces should be used. For example, in the official Python style guide, called Pep 8, it is stated that two blank lines should separate functions and methods within a class by one blank line, and that there should never be more than one blank line between code lines within a function or method.

There can also be recommendations regarding how to write expressions. Again, the Python style guide says that these lines use a recommended style:

```
i = i + 1
submitted += 1
x = x*2 - 1
hypot2 = x*x + y*y
c = (a+b) * (a-b)
```

Compare those to the following lines, which do not follow the recommended style:

```
i=i+1
submitted +=1
x = x * 2 - 1
hypot2 = x * x + y * y
c = (a + b) * (a - b)
```

The last convention we will cover here, which can also be found in code conventions, is how long lines should be break up long lines into several lines.

For example, when working with a long line that contains binary operators (such as +, -. *, and /), we can break up these operators, but what would happen if the operator appears as the last character on a line or as the first on the next one?

Look at this example:

```
full_name = title +
            first_name +
            middle_name +
            last_name
```

Now, compare it to this variant, where the operators are moved to the next line:

```
full_name = title
            + first_name
            + middle_name
            + last_name
```

The American computer scientist Donald Knuth states, in his book *The TeXbook* from 1984, the following:

"Although formulas within a paragraph always break after binary operations and relations, displayed formulas always break before binary operations and relations."

This would suggest that when a formula is printed, it is always printed in the form shown in the second example. This is not a universal truth, though. If you read mathematical texts, you will find both forms represented, and sometimes even a third form where the operator is both at the end of the line and the beginning of the next.

But sometimes, this argument by Knuth is used to recommend the form where the operator begins a line over the one where it comes at the end.

Different conventions are a topic most programmers have an opinion about. Still, if there is one in place, either for the language you are using or the project you are working on, you should stick to it, even if it contradicts what you think is a good way of writing code.

Summary

In this chapter, you have reached the end of this journey into programming, and you now know what it takes to write quality code that is efficient and easy to read and maintain.

We talked about the fact that we have two aspects of quality when it comes to software – one being the quality of the code and the other being quality from the user's perspective.

We then turned our attention to how to achieve code quality. First, we talked about how we can create readable code and how this will improve the code's overall quality.

After that, we looked at how efficient code, which is code that efficiently uses the computer's resources, will improve the quality of our code.

Smart coding tricks are not always the smart way to write code if code quality is something we value. We saw some examples of things we should avoid.

Finally, we looked at some best practices that we can use to increase the quality of the code we write.

With this, we have come to the end of the main chapters of the book. I hope you have enjoyed this journey as much as I have. I have tried to put together everything that is relevant and important from a beginner's point of view, and I am sure many of you will benefit from it.

Appendix A
How to Translate the Pseudocode into Real Code

The code examples in this book have, for the most part, been written using pseudocode, as the aim of the book is to give you an understanding of what programming is, rather than focusing on any particular language.

To be able to write code, you will need to use a real language, and here we will look at some of the more popular ones and see how the code used in this book would translate into these languages.

The languages we will look at are as follows:

- C++
- C#
- Java
- JavaScript
- PHP
- Python

For each language, we will start with a short introduction.

You will not be able to start to write your very own programs just from these short examples, but you will get a feel for these languages, and maybe seeing them like this will help you decide what language you want to learn first.

Before we look at the different languages, we will have a couple of pseudocode examples. These examples will then be translated into the preceding six languages. So, let's begin!

The pseudocode examples

In this section, we will look into a few code examples for pseudocode.

Hello world in pseudocode

The first example will be a short program that just prints **Hello, World!** to the screen.

In our pseudocode, it will look like this:

```
print "Hello, World!"
```

Variables declaration in pseudocode

In this example, we will create a couple of variables. The first one will store an integer. The second one will store the value from the first one but converted into a string:

```
my_int_value = 10
my_string_value = string(my_int_value)
```

The for loop in pseudocode

In this example, we will have a `for` loop that iterates 10 times and prints the values 0 to 9:

```
for i = 0 to 10
    print i
end_for
```

Functions in pseudocode

In this example, we will create a small function that will accept three integers as arguments. The function should then return the largest of them. We will also call the function and display the result.

In the function, we first check whether the first argument is larger than the two others. If it is, we have found the largest value, and we return it.

As we do a return as soon as we find the largest value, we will not need to use any `else` statements in this program as a return will exit the function immediately.

We will, therefore, only need to compare the second argument with the third. If the second is larger than the third, we return it; otherwise, we will return the third argument as it must be the largest value. This is shown with the following code:

```
function max_of_three(first, second, third)
    if first > second and first > third then
        return first
    end_if
    if second > third then
        return second
    end_if
    return third
end_function


maximum = max_of_three(34, 56, 14)
print maximum
```

while loops, user input, if, and for loops in pseudocode

In this example, we will illustrate several concepts at the same time.

This program will ask the user to enter numbers, as many as they want. They can stop entering new values by entering a negative number. All values, except the final negative one, will be stored in a dynamic array.

Before the program exists, we will print all the values that we have stored with the following code block:

```
values = []
inputValue = 0
while inputValue >= 0
    print "Enter a number: "
    input inputValue
    if inputValue >= 0
```

```
          values.add(inputValue)
     end_if
end_while
```

From the preceding code, we see that:

1. First, we create a dynamic array. Remember that this is a list in which we can add and remove values during the program execution; that is, it is not a fixed-size array for which we will need to define how many items we want to store in it:

2. We will then enter a `while` loop, and inside it, ask the user for a number.

3. We will add the entered number to the dynamic array and will keep doing that until the user enters a negative number. This negative number should not be added to the array, but instead, it will act as an indication that the user is done entering numbers so we can exit the loop.

C++

C++ was developed by Bjarne Stroustrup, a Danish computer scientist, and he initially called it C with Classes. The work began in 1979, and he wanted to create a language that had the power of the C programming language and the object-oriented features he had been exposed to when programming for his Ph.D. thesis.

In 1982, he renamed the language C++, where the two addition operators are a reference to the ++ operator in C, which increments a variable by one. The idea is that C++ is C with one thing added, and that thing is object-orientation.

The first commercial release of the language was in 1985.

C++ is a general-purpose compiled programming language that is often used in situations requiring high execution speed, where the programmer is in control over how data is stored and managed in the computer's memory.

Here are some quick facts about it:

- **Name**: C++
- **Designed by**: Bjarne Stroustrup
- **First public release**: 1985
- **Paradigm**: Multi-paradigm, procedural, functional, object-oriented, generic
- **Typing**: Static
- **Most frequently used file extension(s)**: `.cpp`, `.h`

Hello world in C++

All applications that are written in C++ need to have a function called `main` that will act as the starting point for program execution.

The output is shown to the console window by using what is known as an output stream. The language provides a ready-made object from the `ostream` class for this purpose, called `cout`. The language also provides a function (this type of function is known as a manipulator function in C++) called `endl`, which will add a newline character to the output stream. Data is sent to the output stream using the `<<` operator.

The `std::` part in front of `cout` and `endl` indicates that these two are defined in the standard namespace of the language.

As the `main` function in C++ should return an integer value that indicates the result of the execution, we return `0`, which is the value representing success.

Note that all non-compound statements in C++ end with a semicolon, as follows:

```cpp
#include <iostream>

int main()
{
    std::cout << "Hello, World!" << std::endl;
    return 0;
}
```

Variable declaration in C++

As C++ is a statically typed language, we must specify what data type a variable can use. After that, this will be the only data type this variable can handle.

Strings in C++ are defined in a class, and to be able to use that class, we must include `string`, as we do in the first line.

Inside the main function, we first declare our integer variable. We specify that the type is an integer with `int`.

Then, we want to convert our integer into a string. We can do that with the help of a function called `to_string`. It is defined in the standard namespace and must be preceded by `std::`.

When declaring the type for the `string` variable, we must also state that the `string` class is located in the standard namespace:

```cpp
#include <string>

int main()
{
    int my_int_value = 10;
    std::string my_string_value = std::to_string(my_int_value);
    return 0;
}
```

We can, if we want to, simplify this program and let the compiler figure out what type the variables will have. The `auto` keyword will help us with this. As we are assigning a value to the variables as we create them, they will be of the same type as the data we assign to them. Refer to the following code:

```cpp
#include <string>

int main()
{
    auto my_int_value = 10;
    auto my_string_value = std::to_string(my_int_value);
    return 0;
}
```

The for loop in C++

C++ uses the C style of `for` loops. It has three sections, separated by a semicolon, as shown here:

```cpp
#include <iostream>

int main()
{
    for(int i = 0; i < 10; i++) {
        std::cout << i << std::endl;
    }
}
```

From the preceding code, we see the following:

- The first section will initialize the loop variable to its starting value; in our case, that will be 0.
- The next section is the condition that will tell us for how long the for loop will run; in our case, that is as long as the variable is less than 10.
- The final section is how the variable will change in each iteration. We are using the ++ operator here so that the variable will increase by one each iteration.

Inside the loop, we will print the value of the loop variable.

Functions in C++

A function in C++ must first state its return type – that is, what data type the function returns. We must also specify the type each argument has. In our case, we will pass in three integers, and as the function will return one of them, the return type will also be an integer.

Note that in C++, the && symbols means and:

```cpp
#include <iostream>

int max_of_three(int first, int second, int third)
{
    if (first > second && first > third) {
        return first;
    }
    if (second > third) {
        return second;
    }
    return third;
}

int main()
{
    int maximum = max_of_three(34, 56, 14);
    std::cout << maximum << std::endl;
}
```

while loops, user input, if statements, and foreach loops in C++

We need to use a dynamic data structure so we can add as many values as we like while the program is running. One such option we have in C++ is to use a class called `vector`. This class is created such that it can hold data of any type, and that is why we have `int` between < and > in the declaration. Let's see how this works:

1. As with so many other things, the `vector` class needs to be specified as belonging to the standard namespace with `std::`.

2. Next, we declare the integer variable that will accept the input. We will set it to 0 for now. We need that value on the next line when we enter our `while` loop. As the loop iterates, as long as `input_value` is equal to or greater than 0, we must set it to a value within that range.

3. Inside the loop, we print a message to the user that we require a value. To get input from the user, we use `cin`, which works a bit like `cout` but in reverse. Instead of sending things to the screen, it accepts things from the keyboard. Usually, when we talk about `cout` and `cin`, we don't say that the output goes to the screen and the input comes from the keyboard, as these can be remapped to be other things such as files. Instead, we say that `cout` goes to the standard output, which is usually the screen, and `cin` reads from the standard input, which is usually the keyboard.

4. When we have the input, we check whether it is 0 or a positive value. These are the only ones that we want to store in our vector. If it is, we use a method called `push_back` on our vector, which will insert the current value into the vector at the end.

5. This will continue until the user enters a negative value. Then, we exit the `while` loop and enter something that is called a **range-based** `for` loop in C++. It is like a `foreach` loop in that it will iterate through all the items we have in the vector. The current item will be stored in the variable value, and inside the loop, we print it. The code for it is here:

```cpp
#include <iostream>
#include <vector>

int main()
{
    std::vector<int> values;
    int input_value = 0;
```

```
while (input_value >= 0) {
    std::cout << "Enter a number: ";
    std::cin >> input_value;
    if (input_value >= 0) {
        values.push_back(input_value);
    }
}

for (auto value : values) {
    std::cout << value << std::endl;
}
}
```

C#

C#, pronounced like the musical note with the same name, is a language developed by Microsoft and was first released in 2000 as a part of the company's .NET initiative. The language was designed by Anders Hejlsberg, a Danish software engineer, who first called it **Cool** (for **C-like Object-Oriented Language**). Microsoft renamed it before its first official release for copyright reasons.

The language is designed to be a simple, modern, and object-oriented programming language. The language is primarily used within Microsoft's .NET Framework.

Note that all non-compound statements in C# end with a semicolon.

Here are some quick facts:

- **Name**: C#
- **Designed by**: Anders Hejlsberg, Microsoft
- **First public release**: 2000
- **Paradigm**: Object-oriented, generic, imperative, structured, functional
- **Typing**: Static
- **Most frequently used file extension(s)**: .cs

Hello world in C#

All programs written in C# must exist within a class, and one class in our project must have a method called `Main` that will be the starting point for the program execution. It should also be noted that all C# applications should exist within a project.

The first thing we should note is that the first thing we see on the line containing the `Main` method header is the `static` keyword. Declaring a method as `static` means that it can execute without the need to create an object of the class it is defined in. Simply put, this means that the `Main` method can be executed as a function; that is all we need to know at this point.

`Console` is a class that handles all the input and output for console applications in C#. A console application is a program that does not have a graphical user interface. All input and output is done through a console or terminal window, using just text.

Inside the `Console` class, there is another static method called `WriteLine`. Here we can see that a `static` method can be called using the class name. This method, `WriteLine`, will output whatever we send to the console window. Refer to the following code:

```
using System;

class Program
{
    static void Main(string[] args)
    {
        Console.WriteLine("Hello World!");
    }
}
```

Variable declaration in C#

As C# is a statically typed language, we must specify what data type a variable can use. After that, this will be the only data type this variable can handle.

We declare the `myIntValue` variable as an integer using `int`.

In C#, `int` is not just a primitive data type, as in many other languages. It is something called a `struct`. A `struct` is, in a way, the same thing as a class. This `struct` will inherit things from a class called `Object`, and this class defines a method called `ToString` that we can use to convert the integer into a string:

```
using System;

class Program
{
    static void Main(string[] args)
    {
        int myIntValue = 10;
        string myStringValue = myIntValue.ToString();
    }
}
```

We can simplify this program by letting the compiler figure out what data type the variables will have. As we are assigning a value to them as we declare them, the compiler will create them as that data type. We do this with the help of the `var` keyword:

```
using System;

class Program
{
    static void Main(string[] args)
    {
        var myIntValue = 10;
        var myStringValue = myIntValue.ToString();
    }
}
```

The for loop in C#

C# uses the C-style of `for` loop. It has three sections, separated by a semicolon:

- The first section will initialize the loop variable to its starting value; in our case, that will be 0.

- The next section is the condition that will tell us for how long the `for` loop will run; in our case, that is as long as the variable is less than 10.

- The final section is how the variable will change in each iteration. We are using the ++ operator here so that the variable will increase by one each iteration.

Inside the loop, we will print the value of the loop variable:

```
using System;

class Program
{
    static void Main(string[] args)
    {
        for(int i = 0; i < 10; i++)
        {
            System.Console.WriteLine(i);
        }
    }
}
```

Functions in C#

The first thing we should note is that in C#, there are no functions as all code must be defined within a class, and functions that are declared inside a class are called **methods**. They do behave like normal functions, though.

As we saw in earlier examples, if we want to call a method without having an object of this class, the method must be declared `static`, and that is the first thing we see on the line where we declare the function.

In C#, we must also specify what data type a method will return. That is why it says `int` in front of the method name. It will return an integer as we pass in three integers, and it will return the largest of the three. As we can see, we must also state the data type for each of the arguments.

Note that in C#, the `&&` symbols means and. Refer to the following code:

```
using System;

class Program
{

    static int MaxOfThree(int first, int second, int third)
    {
        if (first > second && first > third) {
            return first;
        }
        if (second > third) {
            return second;
        }
        return third;
    }

    static void Main(string[] args)
    {
        int maximum = MaxOfThree(34, 56, 14);
        System.Console.WriteLine(maximum);
    }
}
```

while loops, user input, if statements, and foreach loops in C#

We need to use a dynamic data structure so we can add as many values as we like while the program is running. One such option we have in C# is to use a class called `List`:

- This class is created so a list can hold data of any type, and that is why we have `int` between < and > in the declaration.

- Next, we declare the integer variable that will accept the input. We set it to 0 for now. We need that value on the next line when we enter our `while` loop. As the loop iterates as long as `inputValue` is equal to or greater than 0, we must set it to a value within that range.

- Inside the loop, we print a message to the user that we want a value. To get input from the user, we use the ReadLine method that is located in the Console class. The value we get from ReadLine is a string. That is why we use the Int32.Parse method. It will convert whatever the user enters into an integer.

- When we have the input, we check whether it is 0 or a positive value. It is only 0 values that we want to store in our list. If it is, we use a method call Add on our list, which will insert the current value into the list at the end.

- This will continue until the user enters a negative value. Then, we exit the while loop and enter a foreach loop, which will iterate through all the items in the list.

The current item will be stored in the variable value, and inside the loop, we print it:

```
using System;
using System.Collections.Generic;

class Program
{
    static void Main(string[] args)
    {
        List<int> values = new List<int>();
        int inputValue = 0;
        while (inputValue >= 0) {
            System.Console.Write("Enter a number: ");
            inputValue = Int32.Parse(System.Console.ReadLine());
            if (inputValue >= 0) {
                values.Add(inputValue);
            }
        }

        foreach(var value in values) {
            System.Console.WriteLine(value);
        }
    }
}
```

Java

Work on the Java programming language started in 1991, and the design goals were to create a simple, object-oriented language with a syntax that was familiar to existing programmers.

James Gosling was the leading designer behind the language, and he initially named it Oak, as an oak tree was growing outside his window. For copyright reasons, it was later renamed Java after the Java coffee.

An essential concept in the design of the language was to let programmers write once and run anywhere, abbreviated to *WORA*. The idea is that an application written in Java can run on most platforms without any modification or recompilation.

The portability was achieved by letting the Java source code compile into an intermediate representation, called *Java byte code*, instead of platform-specific machine code. The byte code is then executed by a virtual machine that is written for the hardware hosting the application.

Here are some quick facts about it:

- **Name**: Java
- **Designed by**: James Gosling, Sun Microsystems
- **First public release**: 1995
- **Paradigm**: Multi-paradigm, object-oriented, generic, imperative
- **Typing**: Static
- **Most frequently used file extension(s)**: `.java`, `.jar`

Hello world in Java

Java requires all code to be written within a class, and all applications need one class that has a method called `main`.

One peculiarity of Java is that every class must be written in a source code file that has the same name as the class. As the class in this example is named `Hello`, it must be saved in a file called `Hello.java`.

To print something to a console window, we will be using `System.out.println`. Now, `System` is a class that, among other things, handles input and output. Inside the `System` class, an output stream is defined, called `out`, and this stream has a method named `println`, which prints the data passed to it and terminates by inserting a newline character at the end of the stream.

Note that all non-compound statements in Java end with a semicolon:

```java
class Hello {
    public static void main(String[] args) {
        System.out.println("Hello, World!");
    }
}
```

Variable declaration in Java

As Java is a statically typed language, we must specify what data type a variable can use. After that, this will be the only data type this variable can handle.

We first declare our integer variable using `int`.

All primitive data types have a class representation in Java. We can use the `Integer` class to convert our integer to a string. We do that by calling a static method in the `Integer` class and passing the integer value we want to be converted to it:

```java
class Variable {
    public static void main(String[] args) {
        int myIntValue = 10;
        String myStringValue = Integer.toString(myIntValue);
    }
}
```

Java does not have a feature for automatic type deduction, like the `auto` and `var` keywords we find in C++ and C#.

The for loop in Java

Java uses the C-style of `for` loops. It has three sections, separated by semicolons. The first section will initialize the loop variable to its starting value; in our case, that will be 0. The next section is the condition that will tell us for how long the `for` loop will run; in our case, that is as long as the variable is less than 10. The final section is how the variable will change in each iteration. We are using the ++ operator here, so that the variable will increase by one each iteration.

Inside the loop, we will print the value of the loop variable:

```java
class For {
    public static void main(String[] args) {
        for(int i = 0; i < 10; i++) {
            System.out.println(i);
        }
    }
}
```

Functions in Java

The first thing we should note is that in Java, there are no functions as all code must be defined within a class, and functions that are declared inside a class are called methods. They do behave like normal functions, though.

As we saw in earlier examples, if we want to call a method without having an object of this class, the method must be declared as static, and that is the first thing we see on the line where we declare the function.

In Java, we must also specify what data type a method will return. That is why it says int in front of the method name. It will return an integer as we pass in three integers, and it will return the largest of the three. As we can see, we must also state the data type for each of the arguments.

Note that in Java, the && symbols means and:

```java
class Function {
    static int maxOfThree(int first, int second, int third) {
        if (first > second && first > third) {
            return first;
        }
        if (second > third) {
            return second;
        }
        return third;
    }

    public static void main(String[] args) {
        int maximum = maxOfThree(34, 56, 14);
```

```
        System.out.println(maximum);
    }
}
```

while loops, user input, if statements, and foreach loops in Java

We need to use a dynamic data structure so that we can add as many values as we like while the program is running. One such option we have in Java is to use a class called `ArrayList`:

1. This class is created so a list can hold data of any type, and that is why we have `Integer` between < and > in the declaration. In Java, we cannot use a primitive data type as the type to store in the list. Instead, we use the class representation of `int`, which is `Integer`.

2. Next, we declare the integer variable that will accept the input. We set it to 0 for now. We need that value on the next line when we enter our `while` loop. As the loop iterates as long as `inputValue` is equal to or greater than 0, we must set it to a value within that range.

3. Java does not have a built-in method for user input, so we need to create an object from a class called `BufferedReader` that can handle the input. We call this object `reader`.

4. Inside the loop, we print a message to the user that we want a value. To get input from the user, we use our `reader` object and its `readLine` method. The value we get from `readLine` is a string. That is why we use the `Integer.parseInt` method. It will convert whatever the user enters into an integer.

5. When we have the input, we check whether it is 0 or a positive value. It is only 0 values that we want to store in our list. If it is, we use a method called `add` on our list that will insert the current value into the list at the end.

6. Java will force us to handle the event of the user entering something other than a number. If they do, we will get an exception when we try to convert the string to a number. That is why we need the `try` block with a `catch` statement. If the user enters anything other than numbers, we will enter the `catch` statement.

7. This will continue until the user enters a negative value. Then, we exit the
    `while` loop and enter a `for` loop that will iterate through all the items in the
    list. The current item will be stored in the `value` variable, and inside the loop,
    we print it:

```java
import java.io.BufferedReader;
import java.io.IOException;
import java.io.InputStreamReader;
import java.util.ArrayList;

class For {
    public static void main(String[] args) {
        ArrayList<Integer> values = new
            ArrayList<Integer>();
        int inputValue = 0;
        BufferedReader reader = new BufferedReader(new
                            InputStreamReader(System.in));
        while(inputValue >= 0) {
            System.out.print("Enter a value: ");
            try {
                inputValue = Integer.parseInt(reader.readLine());
                if (inputValue >= 0) {
                    values.add(inputValue);
                }
            } catch (NumberFormatException | IOException e) {
                e.printStackTrace();
            }
        }
        for (int value : values) {
            System.out.println(value);
        }
    }
}
```

JavaScript

In the early years of the World Wide Web, there was only one web browser with support for a graphical user interface, namely Mosaic, released in 1993. The lead developers of Mosaic soon started the Netscape corporation and released a more polished browser called Netscape Navigator in 1994.

The web was a very different place in these early years, and web pages could only display static content. Netscape wanted to change this and decided to add a scripting language to its Navigator. At first, they looked at two options for how to achieve this. One was to collaborate with Sun Microsystems and use the Java programming language. The other option was to let the newly hired Brendan Eich embed the Scheme programming language into the browser.

The decision was a compromise between the two. Brendan Eich was tasked with creating a new language, but its syntax should be closely related to Java and less like Scheme. The language was first named LiveScript, and that was the name it was released under in 1995.

As Java was the brand new language at the time, the name was changed to JavaScript so it could get more attention. The similarity in names between the two languages has led to much confusion over the years, especially among people not so familiar with programming.

Here are some quick facts about JavaScript:

- **Name**: JavaScript
- **Designed by**: Brendan Eich
- **First public release**: 1995
- **Paradigm**: Event-driven, functional, imperative
- **Typing**: Dynamic
- **Most frequently used file extension(s)**: .js

Hello world in JavaScript

The first thing we should note about JavaScript is that it is designed to have its programs executed within a web browser. You can run JavaScript applications in a console window, but to be able to do that, we will need a JavaScript engine that can execute the code for us. One such engine is Node.js, which can be downloaded for free from https://nodejs.org.

JavaScript is a scripting language, so we will not need to put our code within any particular function or class.

In JavaScript, we can use the `console` object to output data. It is usually used to print data to a web browser's debugging console, but if we use Node.js to execute that application, the output will be printed to the console window. The `console` object has a method called `log` that will output anything we pass to it.

Note that all non-compound statements in JavaScript end with a semicolon:

```
console.log("Hello, World!");
```

Variable declaration in JavaScript

JavaScript does not have a specific data type for integers. Instead, it has a data type called `Number` that handles both integer and floating-point numbers.

We declare variables either by using the older `var` keyword or the newer `let`.

As JavaScript is dynamically typed, we will not need to specify what type a variable will use. This will be inferred automatically when we assign a value to it.

Converting a number into a string can be done with a method in the `Number` class called `toString`. As our variable, `myIntValue`, is an object from the `Number` class, it has such a method. Note that we are passing the value `10` to the `toString` method. This is the base we want the number to be in. We want a decimal number, so we pass `10`. This is done as follows:

```
let myIntValue = 10;
let myStringValue = myIntValue.toString(10);
```

The for loop in JavaScript

JavaScript uses the C style of `for` loops. It has three sections, separated by semicolons:

- The first section will initialize the loop variable to its starting value; in our case, that will be `0`.
- The next section is the condition that will tell us for how long the `for` loop will run; in our case, that is as long as the variable is less than `10`.
- The final section is how the variable will change in each iteration. We are using the `++` operator here, so that the variable will increase by one each iteration.

Inside the loop, we will print the value of the loop variable:

```javascript
for (let i = 0; i < 10; i++) {
    console.log(i);
}
```

Functions in JavaScript

As JavaScript is dynamically typed, we will not need to specify any data type for the return value of the function or for the arguments as we need to do in C++, C#, and Java.

We use the `function` keyword to define that this is a function.

Note that in JavaScript, the `&&` symbols mean `and`:

```javascript
function maxOfThree(first, second, third) {
    if (first > second && first > third) {
        return first;
    }
    if (second > third) {
        return second;
    }
    return third;
}

let maximum = maxOfThree(34, 56, 14);
console.log(maximum);
```

while loops, user input, if statements, and foreach loops in Java

First of all, we must note that this example will not do JavaScript justice, as JavaScript is not created to write applications like this one. This has to do with JavaScript being designed to run within a web browser and not as console applications.

In JavaScript, things are often done asynchronously. That is, the program code will not run in sequence as we are used to in most other languages and situations. If we try to implement this program in the same way as the pseudocode version and the version written for all other languages, we will see that it goes into an endless loop just asking us to enter a value, over and over again.

This program is somewhat complicated, so let's not go into too much detail. The first lines are there to create something that will handle the input. At the heart of it is a function called `question` that will return a `promise` object. A `promise` object is something that promises to give us a value at some point in the future. To be able to use this `promise`, it must be called from a function, and that function must be declared as `async`. This means that this function can use the `promise` (to simplify things somewhat).

This function does not have a name, but as you can see, it is surrounded by parentheses and has two empty parentheses at the very end. This construct will make this function execute immediately:

1. Inside this function, we create a dynamic array called `values`. We will initialize it to be empty, as we don't have any values to store in it yet.

2. Next, we find the variable we will use for our input. We set this to `0` so that when we come to the `while` loop on the next line, we will enter the loop.

3. On the next line, we will use all the code we see at the top of the program, which handles the user input. We say that we `await` the `question` function. The `await` keyword will let the application go and do some other things if it needs to, but when we get a value entered by the user, we will come back here and resume execution. That is a short description of how asynchronous calls work. This is an advanced topic, so if this code confuses you, no problem.

4. If the value entered is greater than or equal to `0`, we push this value to the back of our array.

5. When the user enters a negative number, we exit the `while` loop and enter a `for` loop that will iterate as many times as there are items in the array. The `pos` variable will have an index value, `0` the first time, `1` the second time, and so on. When we want to print the values inside the loop, we can use this value as an index into the array, so that we get the first value the first time, the second time, and so on. Refer to the following code:

```
const readline = require("readline");

const rl = readline.createInterface({
```

```
  input: process.stdin,
  output: process.stdout,
});

const question = (q) => {
  return new Promise((res, rej) => {
    rl.question(q, (answer) => {
      res(answer);
    });
  });
};

(async () => {
  let values = [];
  let inputValue = 0;
  while (inputValue >= 0) {
    inputValue = await question("Enter a number: ");
    inputValue = parseInt(inputValue);
    if (inputValue >= 0) {
      values.push(inputValue);
    }
  }

  for (let pos in values) {
    console.log(values[pos]);
  }
})();
```

PHP

In 1994, Rasmus Lerdorf, a Danish-Canadian programmer, wrote several **Common Gate Interface (CGI)** programs in C. CGI is an interface specification that will let web servers execute programs that can generate dynamic web content. Lerdorf created this for his private web page and extended and added functionality to handle web forms and database communication. He named the project **Personal Home Page/Forms Interpreter**, abbreviated to **PHP/FI**.

Lerdorf has later admitted that he never intended to create a new programming language, but the project got a life of its own, and a development team was formed, and in 1997 PHP/FI 2 was released.

The language is primarily used on web servers to create dynamic web content.

Here are some quick facts on it:

- **Name**: PHP
- **Designed by**: Rasmus Lerdorf
- **First public release**: 1995
- **Paradigm**: Imperative, functional, object-oriented, procedural
- **Typing**: Dynamic
- **Most frequently used file extension(s)**: .php

Hello world in PHP

The primary use of PHP is to run alongside a web server, and applications written in PHP will most often be used to produce dynamic web content. But we can run PHP applications as standalone console applications if we download the PHP executable from https://php.net:

- As PHP code can be written in the same document as HTML code, all PHP source code that we write must be within php tags. The opening tag is <?php and the closing tag is ?>.

- We use echo to display our message in the console window. You will not need to use any parentheses with echo, as it is not a function but a language construct.

  Note that all non-compound statements in PHP end with a semicolon:

```php
<?php
  echo "Hello, World!";
?>
```

Variable declaration in PHP

As PHP is a dynamically typed language, we will not need to provide any implicit information on what data type to use when we declare variables. The variable type will be deducted automatically for us, and the type we end up with depends on what we assign to the variable.

An oddity that PHP has inherited from the language Perl is that all variable names must start with a dollar sign. In Perl, this had a meaning as different signs identified different types, but PHP only has the dollar sign for all types.

Let's try this. We first assign the value 10 to our $myIintValue variable.

To convert this integer into a string, we will use a strval function and pass the integer to it. This will convert this value into a string, as shown here:

```php
<?php
  $myIntValue = 10;
  $myStringValue = strval($myIntValue);
?>
```

The for loop in PHP

PHP uses the C style of for loops. It has three sections, separated by semicolons. The first section will initialize the loop variable to its starting value; in our case, that will be 0. The next section is the condition that will tell us for how long the for loop will run; in our case, that is as long as the variable is less than 10. The final section is how the variable will change in each iteration. We are using the ++ operator here so that the variable will increase by one each iteration.

Inside the loop, we will print the value of the loop variable.

As echo in PHP will not provide any newline character, we will need to append it after our loop variable in each iteration. We can concatenate the value of the loop variable and the newline character (\n) by inserting a period between the two:

```php
<?php
  for($i = 0; $i < 10; $i++) {
      echo $i . "\n";
  }
?>
```

Functions in PHP

As PHP is dynamically typed, we will not need to specify any data type for the return value of the function or for the arguments as we need to do in C++, C#, and Java.

We use the `function` keyword to define that this is a function.

Note that in PHP, the `&&` symbols mean and:

```php
<?php
function maxOfThree($first, $second, $third) {
    if ($first > $second && $first > $third) {
        return $first;
    }
    if ($second > $third) {
        return $second;
    }
    return $third;
}

$maximum = maxOfThree(34, 56, 14);
echo $maximum;

?>
```

while loops, user input, if statements, and foreach loops in PHP

In PHP, we can create a dynamic array by using `array()`. An array in PHP is not an array but an ordered map, in other languages known as a dictionary or an associative array. But for this application, this does not matter:

1. After the array is created, we declare the input variable that will hold the values the user enters. We set it to `0`, so when we come to the `while` loop on the next line, we will enter the loop.

2. Next, we will use `readline` to get a value from the user. We can pass a string to `readline`, and that string will be printed to the screen as a prompt to the user. This way, we will not have a separate line that prints this message.

3. The value we get from `readline` will be a string, so we use `intval` to convert it to an integer.

4. Next, we check whether the value is greater than or equal to 0. If it is, we will use the `array_push` function. This function takes two arguments. The first one is the array into which we want to push a value, and the second argument is the value we want to be pushed.

5. When the user enters a negative number, we will exit the `while` loop and enter a `foreach` loop that will print all the values the user entered. If you compare this program with the ones written for the other languages, you will see that the array and the variable have switched placed in PHP compared to the others.

Inside the `foreach` loop, we print the values to the console:

```php
<?php
  $values = array();
  $inputValue = 0;
  while($inputValue >= 0) {
      $inputValue = intval(readline("Enter a value: "));
      if($inputValue >= 0) {
          array_push($values, $inputValue);
      }
  }

  foreach($values as $value) {
      echo $value . "\n";
  }
?>
```

Python

Python was designed and created in the late 1980s by the Dutch programmer Guido van Rossum as a successor to the ABC language. The main design philosophy behind the language is code readability.

While developing the language, van Rossum enjoyed the British comedy group Monty Python and decided to name his new language after them.

The popularity of the language has grown exponentially over the last few years, and it is now ranked as one of the most popular languages out there.

It is a general-purpose language that can be used for most types of applications. The common uses for the language include the development of web applications and use in data science. As it is considered one of the easiest programming languages to learn for beginner programmers, it is often used as an introductory language.

Here are some quick facts about it:

- **Name**: Python
- **Designed by**: Guido van Rossum
- **First public release**: 1990
- **Paradigm**: Multi-paradigm, functional, imperative, object-oriented, structured
- **Typing**: Dynamic
- **Most frequently used file extension(s)**: .py

Hello world in Python

As Python is a scripting language, we will not need to put our code within any special function or class. To print a message to the console window, we will just use the print function and pass whatever we want to print to it:

```
print("Hello, World!")
```

Declaring variables in Python

As Python is a dynamically typed language, we will not need to provide any information on what type our variables will use. That will be deducted automatically for us when we assign a value to the variable.

To declare an integer variable, we just assign an integer to it.

To convert this integer to a string, we can use a class called str and pass the integer to it. As everything in Python is an object, this will return a new string object to us:

```
my_int_value = 10
my_string_value = str(my_int_value)
```

The for loop in Python

When it comes to `for` loops, Python will be different from all the other languages we look at here. It does not implement a `for` loop that uses the C-style format. A `for` loop in Python will iterate over a sequence of some sort. As we don't have any sequence, we can use something called `range`. Now, `range` looks like a function, but in reality, it is something that is called a **generator**. A generator will generate one single value in a range of values each time a new value is needed. By providing the value `10`, at the first iteration, it will generate the value `0`. In the next iteration, the generated value will be `1`, and so on up to `9`.

Also, note that Python does not use braces to indicate a compound statement, as we can see in this `for` statement. Instead, the content of the `for` loop is indented with four spaces. Also, note the colon as the last character on the first line. It is an indication that the next line should be indented:

```python
for i in range(10):
    print(i)
```

Functions in Python

As Python is dynamically typed, we will not need to specify any data type for the return value of the function or for the arguments as we need to do in C++, C#, and Java.

We use the `def` keyword to define that this is a function:

```python
def max_of_three(first, second, third):
    if first > second and first > third:
        return first
    if second > third:
        return second
    return third


maximum = max_of_three(34, 56, 14)
print(maximum)
```

while loops, user input, if statements, and foreach loops in Python

In Python, we can use a list to store the values the user enters. A list in Python is dynamic, so it can grow as the user enters new values:

1. We declare the list and make it empty, to start with.

2. Next, we declare the variable we will use for the user input and set it to 0. The reason we use zero is so that when we come to the line with the `while` loop, we want the condition to be true. It will be true if the `input_value` variable is 0 or greater.

3. Inside the `while` loop, we will use the `input` function to let the user enter values. The `input` function lets us pass a string to it, and that string will be displayed to the user. This takes away the need we have in some other languages to actually print this message first and then get the user input.

4. The value we get from the `input` function is a string, so we need to convert it to `int`. We do that by passing the entered string to `int()`. This will create an integer with the value entered.

5. Next, we check whether the entered value is greater than or equal to 0. If it is, we will append it to our list.

   When the user enters a negative number, we will exit the `while` loop and continue to a `for` loop. `for` loops in Python always work like `foreach` loops. A `for` loop wants a sequence, and it will go through all the values of that sequence. Our list is such a sequence, so we will get one item each time we iterate, and we can now print that item value, as shown here:

```python
values = []
input_value = 0

while input_value >= 0:
    input_value = int(input("Enter a number: "))
    if input_value >= 0:
        values.append(input_value)

for value in values:
    print(value)
```

Appendix B
Dictionary

A

ALGOL – A family of programming languages developed in 1958 by a committee of European and American computer scientists.

Algorithm – A set of rules or a description of steps to be followed in problem-solving operations. Examples of algorithms used in computer science are sorting and searching algorithms.

Analog – Using signals or information represented by continuously changing a physical quantity, such as the voltage or spatial position.

Application – A computer program that is designed for a particular purpose.

Arithmetic – A branch of mathematics dealing with the properties and manipulation of numbers.

Arithmetic overflow/underflow – The result of a calculation that exceeds the memory space designated to hold the result.

Array type – A data type that represents a collection of elements that can be selected by the use of indices.

ASCII-table – A character-encoding standard that uses numbers to represent characters.

Assembly language – A name used for any low-level programming language that has a strong correlation between its instructions and the corresponding machine code instructions.

B

Base 10 – See **Decimal**.

Base 16 – See **Hexadecimal**.

Base 2 – See **Binary**.

Binary – A numbering system that works in base 2 – that is, it only uses two digits: zero and one.

Blank line – Used in programming to separate blocks of code that logically belong together.

Block comment – A comment in programming code that spans several lines. See **Comment**.

Boolean algebra – A branch of algebra in which operations are performed only on the true and false values. The name comes from George Boole, who introduced it in 1847.

Boolean type – A data type that stores the Boolean `true` and `false` values. See **Boolean algebra**.

Break – A statement used by many programming languages to exit the current code block. See **Code block**.

Breakpoint – Used when debugging applications to pause the execution at a particular line of code.

Brief code – A precursor of the Short code programming language. See **Short code**.

BUG – A tag used as a comment to indicate code that contains a bug that has not yet been fixed.

Byte – A group of binary digits, usually 8, that is operated on as a single unit.

Byte code – Intermediate code that a programming language can be compiled into. It can then be interpreted more efficiently if the source code was interpreted directly.

C

C – A programming language designed by Dennis Ritchie at Bell Labs in 1972. Its syntax has influenced many other programming languages.

C# – Pronounced C sharp. A programming language developed by Microsoft in 2000.

C++ – A programming language created by Bjarne Stroustrup in 1985. It was developed as an object-oriented extension to the C programming language.

Camel case – A practice for naming multi-word identifiers, such as variables and function names. In camel case, the first word is written in all lowercase, and the first character in any word that follows is written in uppercase. All spaces are removed. Camel case written in camel case is `camelCase`.

Central processing unit – The component of a computer in which operations are controlled and executed.

Class method – In object orientation, a class method is a function that belongs to a class. A class method is called on the class itself, rather than an instance. See **Method**.

Class – In object-orientation, a class is a template used for creating objects. See **Object**.

Client software – An application that plays the client role in a client-server solution.

Client-server – A distributed application structure that partitions the workload between a server and one or more clients. The client initiates the communication, and the server provides a function or a service to the clients.

Clojure – A programming language created by Rich Hickey in 2007. The language is a Lisp dialect. See **LISP**.

Cloud computing – On-demand availability of computer system resources, such as storage or computing power, that is accessed over the internet.

COBOL – This acronym stands for **Common Business-Oriented Language** and is a compiled English-like programming language designed for business use. COBOL was developed in 1959 by a group called CODASYL and is based on the FLOW-MATIC programming language. See FLOW-MATIC.

Code block – A block of code that usually spans several lines and belongs to the same statement. The beginning and end are often marked with { and } or an indentation.

Code module – A section of code that implements a particular functionality. It is usually packaged in a single unit, such as a code file.

Command prompt – See **Terminal window**.

Comment – A programmer-readable explanation or annotation in the source code. Comments give instructions to humans and are ignored by the programming language.

Common Lisp – A programming language developed to consolidate other Lisp dialects. It was released in 1984.

Compiled language – A programming language that will translate all the statements that make up a program. When all the statements are translated, the program can be executed. Programs written in a compiled programming language will typically be faster than programs written in an interpreted language.

Composite type – A data type that is made up of more than one value.

Compound statement – A statement that is the body of other statements. Some examples are `if`, `for`, and `while` statements.

Continue – A statement used in loops. When encountered, the current iteration will be halted, and execution will immediately continue with the next iteration.

CPU – See **Central Processing Unit**.

D

Database – An organized set of data, stored and accessed electronically. Other applications typically use the data.

Debugger – A tool used by programmers to find errors in a program code. It will let the programmer step through the code line by line while executing the code, and the programmer can inspect the values of variables and the execution path that is taken.

Decimal – A numbering system that works in base 10 – that is, it uses 10 digits to represent numbers. It is the numbering system that we usually use.

Dictionary type – A data type that stores data in key-value pairs. The key value must be unique for every item in the dictionary.

Directive comment – A comment in the source code not intended for humans but other programming tools, such as compilers.

Division by zero – An error that occurs in a division where the divisor is zero.

Docstring – A comment that is formatted in a predefined way.

E

Encapsulation – Used in object orientation to restrict direct access to some of an object's components.

Enumeration – A data type, sometimes referred to as `enum`, that has a set of named values.

Expression – An entity in a programming language that can be evaluated for its value, such as `x + 1`.

F

First-class function – If a language supports first-class functions, this means that functions can be passed as arguments to other functions or returned as a result from a function.

FIXME – A tag that is used in comments to indicate that a particular section of code needs to be rewritten or updated.

Floating-point types – A data type that can represent real numbers.

FLOW-MATIC – A programming language designed by Grace Hopper in 1955. It was the first English-like data processing language.

Fortran – A programming language invented in 1954 at IBM by John Backus.

Function – A sequence of program instructions that are packaged as one unit and (usually) given a name.

Function call – A call to a function will pass control to that function. Once the function has executed, control is given back.

Functional programming – A paradigm where programs are constructed by composing and applying functions.

G

Gate – See **Logic gate**.

Go – A programming language designed by Robert Griesemer, Rob Pike, and Ken Thompson that was released in 2009.

H

HACK – A tag that is used in comments to indicate that a particular section of code is a workaround and that this code needs to be rewritten in the future.

Hard drive – An electromechanical data storage device that uses rapidly rotating platters coated with magnetic material. It can be used to store and retrieve digital data.

Hardware – The machine and physical components that make up a computer or other electronic systems.

Hexadecimal – A numbering system that works in base 16 – that is, it uses 16 digits to represent numbers. It uses the digits 0–9, followed by the letters A–F, with A being 10 and F being 15.

I

IaaS – **Infrastructure as a service** is an online service that let users use an instant computing infrastructure that is provisioned and managed over the internet.

IDE – An **integrated development environment** is a program or suite of programs that gives a programmer the tools needed to, among other things, write, edit, debug, and test applications.

Immutable data – Data that cannot be changed once it has got its initial value. See **Mutable data**.

Indentation – A technique for making code more readable where lines of code have initial empty space at the beginning of the line.

Instance – See **Object**.

Integer – A number that can be written without a fractional component, such as 21, 133, -7, and 0.

Integer data type – A data type that can represent integer values.

Interpreted language – A programming language that translates programming instructions from a given programming language into machine code, one statement at a time. Once a statement is translated into machine code, it is sent to the central processing unit for execution.

iOS – A mobile operating system created and developed by Apple Inc.

IP address – A numerical address assigned to each device connected to a computer network that uses the Internet Protocol for communication.

Iteration statement – A statement that causes other statements that are defined within its body to repeat zero an infinite number of times.

J

Java – A programming language developed by James Gosling. It was first released in 1995.

JavaScript – A programming language developed by Brendan Eich. It was first released in 1995.

K

Keyword – In a programming language, a keyword is a reserved word that has a particular meaning in that language.

Kotlin – A programming language designed by the Czech software development company JetBrains. It was first released in 2011.

L

Language syntax – See **Syntax**.

Lisp – A family of programming languages, initially specified by John McCarthy in 1958. Among the modern dialects of Lisp, we can find languages such as Racket, Common Lisp, Scheme, and Clojure.

Logic gate – A physical electronic device that is used to implement logical operations on binary input.

Low-level programming – Creating programs that interact directly with the computer hardware. A benefit of low-level programming is that there is no abstraction level between the hardware and the written code, making the programs execute faster.

M

Machine code – Program instructions written in a numerical format that can be executed directly by the central processing unit.

Member variable – A concept used in object-oriented programming where a variable belongs to one particular object.

Memory – A generic term for all the different technologies a computer may use to store data.

Method – A concept used in object-oriented programming. A method is a function associated with a class and its objects.

Mobile application – An application written to be executed on a mobile device.

Mutable data – Data that can be changed. See **Immutable data**.

N

Namespace – A way to group objects of various kinds and ensure that all objects within the same namespace have unique names.

Napster – A service released in 1999 where users could share music over a peer-to-peer network.

Node – A device in a computer network.

Numeric type – A data type that can represent numeric values. See **Integer data type** and **Floating-point types**.

O

Objective-C – A programming language designed by Tom Love and Brad Cox. It was first released in 1984. It was the primary programming language supported by Apple until the introduction of Swift in 2014. See **Swift**.

Object orientation – A software engineering paradigm in which concepts are represented as objects.

Object-oriented programming – A paradigm based on a concept where programs are constructed using objects.

Object – A representation used in object orientation that is made up of data in the form of fields (often called attributes or properties) and code in the form of functions (referred to as methods to distinguish them from functions defined outside classes).

Ones' complement – The ones' complement of a binary number is accomplished by inverting all the bits in that number (swapping zeros for ones and vice versa).

Opcode – An abbreviation of **operation code**, this is a portion of a machine language instruction that specifies what operation to perform.

Open source – Software for which the source code is made freely available and may be redistributed and modified.

Operand – An input value to an operator. See **Operator**.

Operator – A symbol that performs an operation that behaves like a function but is syntactically different from a function call.

Order of operation – The order in which multiple operations will be executed.

P

P2P – See **Peer-to-peer**.

PaaS – **Platform as a service** is a type of cloud service that provides a platform where customers can develop, run, and manage applications.

Package manager – An application, or collection of applications, that automates the process of downloading, installing, configuring, and removing software.

Peer-to-peer – A distributed network application where the nodes in the network communicate directly with each other.

Perl – A programming language developed by Larry Wall. It was first released in 1987.

PHP – A programming language developed by Rasmus Lerdorf. It was first released in 1995.

Pixel – A physical point in a raster image or the smallest element of a computer screen (or other types of display devices).

Plankalkül – One of the first programming languages, designed by Konrad Zuse. It was first released in 1948.

Processor – See **Central processing unit**.

Punch card – A card with punched holes. The location of the holes can be used to represent data or program code instructions. This was formerly used by computers as the primary storage device.

Pure function – A function that has the property of always returning the same value for the same argument and whose evaluation has no side effects.

Python – A programming language designed by Guido van Rossum. It was first released in 1990.

R

Record type – A data type that is made up of several fields. Each field can be of any other type, including other records.

Register – A component inside a central processing unit used for storing information.

Repository – A storage location for software or code.

Reserved word – A reserved word is a word that is reserved by a programming language and cannot be used by the programmer as a name for things such as functions and variables.

S

SaaS – An online service, **software as a service**, where software is licensed and hosted online.

Scalability – The ability to handle a growing amount of work.

Selection statement – A statement that evaluates a condition to be either `true` or `false` and can execute different blocks of code depending on the result.

Sequence – An enumerated collection of objects.

Server – A computer program or device that provides services and functionality to other devices, called clients.

Set type – A data type that can store a collection of unique values without a particular order.

Scheme – A programming language developed by Guy L. Steele and Gerald Jay Sussman. It was first released in 1975.

Short code – Considered by many as being the first high-level programming language, proposed by John Mauchly in 1949.

Signed magnitude representation – A way to represent negative numbers in binary form.

Simula – A programming language design by Ole-Johan Dahl. It was first released in 1962.

SMR – See **Signed magnitude representation**.

Snake case – A style for formating multi-word names. In snake case, only lowercase characters are used, and an underscore separates words.

Source code – The code written by programmers using the syntax of a programming language.

Standalone application – An application that can work offline.

Statement – A unit of code of an imperative programming language that expresses some action.

String type – A data type that can represent a sequence of characters.

Substring – A continuous sequence of characters within a string.

Swift – A programming language developed by Apple Inc. as the successor of the Objective-C programming language. It was released in 2014. See **Objective-C**.

Syntax – Rules that define what symbols and keywords make up a programming language. It also defines how the keywords and symbols should be combined to form valid source code.

Syntax error – An error that occurs when source code is breaking the syntax rules of a programming language.

T

TCP/IP – A suite of protocols that are used for transmitting data over the internet.

Terminal window – An application that lets the user execute text commands, usually to the operating system.

Text string – See **String type**.

TODO – A tag that is used in comments to indicate that a particular section of code is still not implemented.

Touchscreen – A screen that lets the user control a connected device by touching the screen.

Two's complement – A technique for representing signed numbers in binary form.

U

Unicode – A character-encoding standard that can represent over 140,000 different characters.

Unsigned integer – A data type that can only represent positive integer values.

V

Variable – A named representation of a memory address used in programming to access data.

W

Web browser – An application used to access information on the world wide web.

Other Books You May Enjoy

If you enjoyed this book, you may be interested in these other books by Packt:

Modern Computer Architecture and Organization

Modern Computer Architecture and Organization

ISBN: 978-1-83898-439-7

- Get to grips with transistor technology and digital circuit principles
- Discover the functional elements of computer processors
- Understand pipelining and superscalar execution
- Work with floating-point data formats
- Understand the purpose and operation of the supervisor mode
- Implement a complete RISC-V processor in a low-cost FPGA
- Explore the techniques used in virtual machine implementation
- Write a quantum computing program and run it on a quantum computer

40 Algorithms Every Programmer Should Know

Imran Ahmad

ISBN: 978-1-78980-121-7

- Explore existing data structures and algorithms found in Python libraries

- Implement graph algorithms for fraud detection using network analysis

- Work with machine learning algorithms to cluster similar tweets and process Twitter data in real time

- Predict the weather using supervised learning algorithms

- Use neural networks for object detection

- Create a recommendation engine that suggests relevant movies to subscribers

- Implement foolproof security using symmetric and asymmetric encryption on Google Cloud Platform (GCP)

Leave a review - let other readers know what you think

Please share your thoughts on this book with others by leaving a review on the site that you bought it from. If you purchased the book from Amazon, please leave us an honest review on this book's Amazon page. This is vital so that other potential readers can see and use your unbiased opinion to make purchasing decisions, we can understand what our customers think about our products, and our authors can see your feedback on the title that they have worked with Packt to create. It will only take a few minutes of your time, but is valuable to other potential customers, our authors, and Packt. Thank you!

Index

Printed in Great Britain
by Amazon